Henry James and the Writing of Race and Nation describes a new Henry James – a writer who, rather than fashioning himself as an iconic figure of high culture, tests his commitments in contest with emerging popular forms. Countering trends in cultural studies that have privileged the popular as a unique site of both cultural resistance and identity formation, Sara Blair argues for the importance of literary institutions to those processes in the years spanned by James's career. Beginning with an analysis of the links between racial theory in the 1870s, popular travel narrative, and James's early travel essays and reviews, Blair considers the complexities of his positionings within and against genteel, "Anglo-Saxon," American, and other cultural frames. These gestures become central to James's literary performance, she argues, in his experiments with American realism, as he redirects its nation-building designs. Through detailed analyses of *The Princess Casamassima, The Tragic Muse,* and *The American Scene,* Blair evidences James's growing interest in newly definitive mass forms – including the popular press, photography, and visual culture – through which racial and national identities are being forged. Her book makes a powerful case for reading James and the high culture he shapes with a sense of sustained contradiction, even as she argues for the historical and ongoing importance of literary texts to the study of culture and cultural value.

HENRY JAMES AND THE WRITING OF RACE AND NATION

Henry James and the Writing of Race and Nation

Sara Blair
University of Virginia

CAMBRIDGE
UNIVERSITY PRESS

For my mother and the memory of my father

PS
2127
P6
.B57
1996

Published by the Press Syndicate of the University of Cambridge
The Pitt Building, Trumpington Street, Cambridge CB2 1RP
40 West 20th Street, New York, NY 10011-4211, USA
10 Stamford Road, Oakleigh, Melbourne 3166, Australia

First published 1996

Printed in the United States of America

Library of Congress Cataloging-in-Publication has been applied for.

A catalog record for this book is available from the British Library

ISBN 0-521-49750-7 Hardback

34332921   /2184

CONTENTS

v

LIST OF FIGURES

ABBREVIATIONS

The abbreviations listed below are used throughout the text and notes to refer to these editions. In the case of James's writings, I have chosen either editions that reflect original texts or those prior to his revisions, as appropriate.

James, Henry

Abode	"The Abode of Snow." *Nation* 21 (November 11, 1875):314.
AA	"Across Africa." Review of *Across Africa*, by Verney Lovett Cameron. *Nation* 24 (April 5, 1877):209–10.
American	*The American*. New York: Penguin Books, 1986 [orig. MacMillan, 1879].
AS	*The American Scene*. New York: St. Martin's Press, 1987.
AT	"Anthony Trollope." *Century* 26 (July 1883)3:385–405.
AF	"The Art of Fiction." In *Selected Literary Criticism*, edited by Morris Shapira. New York: Cambridge University Press, 1981.
AN	*The Art of the Novel*. Boston: Northeastern University Press, 1984.
Notebooks	*The Complete Notebooks of Henry James*. Edited by Leon Edel and Lyall H. Powers. New York: Oxford University Press, 1987.
LNT	"Laugel's Notes of Travel." *Nation* 16 (February 27, 1873):152.
Letters	*Henry James: Letters*. Edited by Leon Edel. 4 vols. Cam-

	bridge: Belknap Press of Harvard University Press, 1974–1984.
LC*1*	*Henry James: Literary Criticism.* Vol. 1: *Essays on Literature; American Writers; English Writers.* New York: Library of America, 1984.
LC*2*	*Henry James: Literary Criticism.* Vol. 2: *French Writers; Other European Writers; The Prefaces to the New York Edition.* New York: Library of America, 1984.
IH	*Italian Hours.* New York: Ecco Press, 1987.
NYE	*Novels and Tales of Henry James.* 26 vols. The New York Edition. New York: Charles Scribner's Sons, 1907–9.
PP	*Partial Portraits.* Ann Arbor: University of Michigan Press, 1970.
Places	*Portraits of Places.* London: Macmillan, 1883.
PC	*The Princess Casamassima.* New York: Penguin Books, 1977.
RLE	"Remains of Lost Empires." *Nation* 20 (January 28, 1874):65–6.
RH	*Roderick Hudson.* New York: Harper and Brothers, 1960.
SBO	*A Small Boy and Others, Autobiography.* Edited by Frederick W. Dupee. London: W. H. Allen, 1956.
Tales	*The Tales of Henry James,* edited by Maqbool Aziz. 2 vols. Oxford: Clarendon Press, 1978.
TIC	"Thomson's Indo-China and China." *Nation* 20 (April 22, 1874):279–80.
TM	*The Tragic Muse.* Harmondsworth, England: Penguin, 1988.

Edel, Leon

| Conquest | *Henry James, The Conquest of London, 1870–1881.* Philadelphia: Lippincott, 1962. |
| Middle Years | *Henry James, The Middle Years, 1882–1895.* Philadelphia: Lippincott, 1962. |

Archival Materials

| BSCP | Brotherhood of Sleeping Car Porters Oral History Project, Moving Images & Recorded Sound Division, Schomburg Center for Research in Black Culture. |
| NYPL DC | New York Public Library, Photography Division, Stereographs, Dennis Collection. |

ACKNOWLEDGMENTS

Like most literary scholars, I suspect, in this most genealogical of industries, I have long looked forward to the moment of acknowledgment. I nonetheless feel somewhat overwhelmed by the recollection of the many debts I've accrued beyond those of everyday scholarly activity.

Without the patient, expert help of numerous curators and librarians – who have taught me almost as much about historical scholarship as formal training – this volume could not have been produced. Wayne Furman, of the Special Collections Office of the New York Public Library Research Libraries, James Briggs Murray, Curator of the Moving Images Division of the Schomburg Center for Research in Black Culture, and Susan Tolbert, of the Transportation Division of the Smithsonian Museum of American History, provided invaluable aid and advice. For permission to reproduce images from the British Library Newspaper Library; the Pullman and General Rail Collections of the Smithsonian; the Lewis W. Hine Collection and the Robert Dennis Collection of Stereoscopic Views, Astor, Lenox and Tilden Foundations of the New York Public Library, I am duly grateful.

Among my colleagues in Charlottesville, Rita Felski, J. C. Levenson, David Levin, and Eric Lott read parts of this work carefully, good-humoredly, and with acuity; their questions and challenges have made it appreciably better. Farther afield, I am indebted to Ross Posnock, John Carlos Rowe, and Eric Sundquist for strenuous and exacting readings of the manuscript, to which I hope to have done justice. On more local matters of production, Susan Rosenbaum, Steve Soper, and Morgan Daven provided intelligent and patient proofreading and indexing.

Along with these intellectual debts, I have accumulated others of a more personal kind. In many ways the production of this book has been a family affair. My niece Kitra encouraged me to finish it (even though it didn't have enough pictures); she and her parents, Joe and Karen, have graciously entertained and supported me at every step of the way. My sister Koren has put me up and put up with me; she made the many weeks of time-consuming research in New York far more pleasurable and humane, a great adventure in her company. With my sister Ruth, she assisted me in my research in Venice and Rome, conducted under cover of a Tre Sorelle expedition. Ruth was also an extremely able consultant on matters graphic and practical. And my brother Bill intrepidly let me know when a given argument had "too many words."

For aid and comfort of every kind, in many parts of the globe, my deepest thanks also to Elissa Rosenberg and Karen Shabetai, who have made the life of the alienated intellectual a lot less alienated and a lot more joyful.

Last but most, to Jonathan Freedman, my best reader and friend. To him all the future is dedicated.

Introduction

MAKING A DIFFERENCE: HENRY JAMES, LITERARY CULTURE, AND RACIAL THEATER

In the first volume of his autobiography, *A Small Boy and Others* (1913), Henry James meditates at length on the paths to culture blazed in that most idiosyncratic of academies, the James family itself. Although he details his "exposure" to a host of American cultural resources – vaudeville, circus spectacles, sentimental drama, family reading circles, lamplit slide shows, lyceum lectures – he reserves his most highly wrought prose for a certain version of American theater. Figuring himself in the act of "gaping" at rickety billboards along lower Fifth Avenue that advertise P. T. Barnum's Great American Museum, he passes metonymically from their brisk "blazonry" to the person of "Miss Emily Mestayer," playing the role of Eliza in Barnum's production of *Uncle Tom's Cabin* (*SBO* 90–2). Despite her appearance – "red in the face" and "hoo[k]-nose[d]" – the popular actress in this most spectacularly popular of dramas wears "the very complexion of romance" for the American *littérateur*-in-training; even more importantly, her performance provides a benchmark against which James can measure his own acquisition of the faculty of critical distinction. Viewing another production of Stowe at a lower East side playhouse shunned by "fashion and culture," he can compare renditions of "the tragi-comical Topsy" and "the blonde Eva . . . of pantalettes and pigtails." The ability thus to distinguish constitutes his "great initiation" not only into the culture-building power of the theater but into the precincts of "culture" itself: "I could know we had all intellectually condescended" in having had "the thrill" of such "an aesthetic adventure," he notes, but the adventure itself "was a brave beginning for a consciousness that was to be nothing if not mixed" (*SBO* 94–5).

Of most urgent interest in this passage on American theater is the productive conjunction of signifiers for national identity, cul-

1

tural styles, and race. Even as James's metonymic figures performatively enact a certain, indubitably Jamesian, version of "culture" over and against that of the "Anglo-Saxon millions," they
nonetheless reveal his artful self-representation to be composed of
various sorts of "mixture" and exchange: between the high or "polite" and the low, condescension and adventure, "appetite" and
"appreciation," the aesthetically "rich" and the "vulgar," the "slave
girl" and "her little mistress" (*SBO* 93–5). Far from recoiling in face
of "the shock" of such "opposed forces" (*SBO* 94), James reading
Mestayer reading Barnum reading Stowe makes his "memory" of
the culture of the theater serve his representation of the theatricality of culture itself – or more precisely, of the open-ended dynamic
of contestation and exchange through which "our Anglo-Saxon
taste," the fitfully racialized and nationalized property of an earlier
cultural moment, is acquired and sated (*SBO* 64). The theater, like
James's act of memory and self-memorializing, becomes a "stage of
culture" on which varied gestures of national, racial, and cultural
identification can be distinguished and rehearsed (*SBO* 94).

This book takes as its object of study the range of such gestures
throughout James's renderings of culture and cultural performances alike. At large, I argue two claims: that texts over the range
of his career productively negotiate the race thinking and nation-
building habits and institutions of emergent modern Anglo-America, in varied Victorian, gilded age, fin de siècle, and late capitalist
formations; and that his "mixed" performances of what has recently
come to be studied as whiteness[1] – that is to say, constructions of
American and Anglo-American masculinity, gentility, and a putative
Anglo-Saxon racial identity – not only register but extend the range
of available responses to American racial history in his moment and
in our own. These claims will undoubtedly strike some readers of
James as well as readers generally skeptical about canonical engagements, to borrow a Jamesian locution, as queer or misplaced. But it
is, I contend, precisely because James's *oeuvre* has been so long condemned for a mandarin insularity, relegated to a rarefied realm of
aggressively high cultural striving, that attention to its engagements
with the subject of race thinking in numerous cultural sites proves so
rewarding. With a continuity obscured by the local color line drawn
between his "English" and "American" productions, and by the
boundary laid down between masterfully "proportioned" texts and
those less successfully formalist (*AN* 52), James's intricately self-
conscious declarations of cultural identity negotiate widely disparate
resources, particularly idioms alive in popular culture. Miming and
mining the latter, many of his literary performances energetically

endeavor – sometimes successfully, other times markedly less so – to transform the sites of cultural exchange they occupy, which are always simultaneously sites of James's acts of self-representation.

In the rich range of such attempted transformations, James offers exemplary evidence for the centrality and power with which high literary culture, in dialogue with disciplinary and popular modes of nation-building, conducted race work in Anglo-America during the last decades of the nineteenth century and the first decade of the twentieth. Apparently local and idiomatic skirmishes over literary doctrine, genre formation, and professional authority become, his work attests, sites in which canons of national, class, and broadly racial taste, "type," and "character" take definitively modern shape. These performances, far from insular or merely dismissive of material culture, share, redirect, and revolatilize the broadly racial fantasies and energies of popular texts, ranging from photography, romantic travel narratives, ethnographic studies, minstrelsy, and yellow journalism to the iconography of the industrial city. Borrowing from these arenas of racial production and exchange such figures as the atavistic Italian, the Negro servant, the culturally exhausted European, the Jewish usurer, and even the 100 percent American, James constructs a literary "internationalism" through which definitively national and racial feelings, aspirations, and characterologies are elaborated and transfigured.

To read as such James's contestatory engagements with other kinds of cultural narratives not only evidences the complexity of literature's nation-building or civic habits. It also argues for the evolving value of work on canonical texts, indeed, on master texts and on the institution known as literary mastery, in the critical study of race. My principal project is the reading of James's works – their cultural politics, their representational strategies, their negotiation of emerging distinctions between high and low, nation and literary nationality – relocated in sites of racial production and exchange onto which they open. In this general intention, I participate in a wider revaluation of James's art, and its continuing importance to understandings of the aesthetic, material, and political cultures of modernity.[2] But I also argue that the literary itself, and the widely varied performances comprehending that sphere, is a crucially important site of racial formation, in and through which distinctly American, Anglo-American, and "Anglo-Saxon" racial feelings, entangled with the pursuit of taste and the cultural good, evolve.

My project is consequently in dialogue, and perhaps productive tension, with certain trends in the thinking of race, particularly in the field of cultural studies. That discipline has largely treated race, racism, and racial matters by way of theorizing the production of subordinate groups within contemporary capitalism and its encodings of cultural power, taking popular or mass culture as the most richly imbricated site of race's affective life.[3] This overdetermined move to privilege the popular as a site for the study of cultural habits and transformations has, among other effects, provided a powerful corrective to the conceptual excesses of cultural theory under the banner of the Frankfurt School, in which high culture became hypostatized as a unique site of resistance to a cultural logic of dehumanization instanced by mass entertainment.[4] But it has also left largely unattended the problem of genteel or middle-class institutions – literature being exemplary – as a crucial, volatile resource and site for fluid forms of racial and national filiation. Inverting an over-determined distinction between high and low cultures, focusing on the low as the site of production of authentic or counterhegemonic cultural narratives, the drift of cultural studies has paradoxically been to preserve the high in its own terms as the aestheticized, differently ordinated zone of social meaning-creation it advertises itself, in the late nineteenth and early twentieth centuries, to be.

The cultural force of high culture is further problematized in scholarship in the texts of post-coloniality and imperialist culture, which has tended to reify the literary, and particularly the bookcum-instrumental cultural object, as a primary (and indeed primal) site of ideological reproduction, colonizing, and policing. Tales of romance constitute "adventure . . . indistinguishable from surveillance"; the "rhetorical procedures" of literature, continuous with those of colonialist journalism, constitute a "repertoire" of techniques for the interpellation of colonial subjects; literary practice equates with forms of "existential practice," in which "the space of an Other" of discourse and power – over and against which the self and realm of value of modernity are recuperated – is created.[5] But as Homi Bhabha has influentially argued, the tacit premise of such readings – "the commonplace that the institution of literature works" unremittingly to nationalist or colonialist ends[6] – has obscured the cultural specificity and the performativity of varied, nuanced gestures of literary nationality and filiation, as well as "a particular ambivalence that haunts" postcolonial culture-building, its forms of "address," and "the language of those who write it and the lives of those who live it" (Bhabha 1990, 1, 3). Mindful of such differently situated work, my study seeks locally to recover the complex interaction of high literary culture with its repressed, illegitimate, or disowned resources for the formation of racial feeling.[7] In part, I study James's vexatiously genteel masks and his inversive mimicries so as to consider shifting literary responses to narrative and social challenges from "below" or "elsewhere" as broadly racial performances, embattled in the formation of culture as, in E.P. Thompson's salient phrase, a whole way of conflict.

The notion of performativity that has been so important for Bhabha and other scholars elaborating the condition of postcoloniality is of particular importance to this project, not least because it so aptly registers the complexity of James's racial figures, which tend to hover between metaphor and historical fact.[8] Numerous studies have documented the increasing theatricality of James's self-representations, and his critical uses of a "dramatic analogy" between the theater and fiction as institutions distanced from "social facts" (*AN* 165), capable of fostering, in Victor Turner's well-known argument, a kind of liminoid experience (Turner, 282).[9] Recent work in American material culture has also measured James's fiction against the urgent theatricality and highly spectacular forms of nineteenth-century American social experience, where, the argument goes, highbrow literature increasingly struggles against but unwittingly assists in producing the commodified, theatricalized subject of advertising and conspicuous consumption.[10] In my project, these largely figural versions of social theater buttress a more focused argument to the performative character of racial and national identity and of James's interventions therein. Scholars of racial production and interaction have recently urged flexible attention to the shifting, rather than merely or straightforwardly dominative, force of participation in particular racial cultures or contexts, ranging from turn-of-the-century American burlesque to contemporary Anglo-American film and the antebellum minstrel show (Allen, Hall, Lott). The high literary culture so powerfully aligned with and by James is no less messy and no less multiple in its designs on its readership. Rehearsing culturally specific idioms, James's strategic allegiances to British, American, Anglo-European, and other fluidly constituted cultural communities and icons register the discursive repertoires of whiteness, as well as the anxieties of national identity that attend its very mobility. With recourse to a broad range of symbolic gestures of racial identification, anxiety, fantasy, and restraint, James's texts work contextually both to preserve and to exploit the inherent instability of racial identity in the era of modernity. Their effect is not, I argue, to consolidate a reified literary "power," writ in the habits and values of high gentility, so much as to offer competing tales of the tribe: to dramatize, at least intermittently, the consequences of ritual gestures of broadly racial identification, naming, and exclusion.

At large, I understand the literary culture James is instrumental in transforming as a theater of such operations, a social and psychic space in which performances of race and nation are produced, managed, rehearsed, and variously put on. Indeed, it can be argued that James's canon provides a unique opportunity for rethinking the literary and literary critical production in those formations. Within American Studies, whose precincts James has occupied both centrally and uneasily, his critical reception has been intimately entangled with historically charged terms of race and nation whose shifting meaning the aura of James's mastery has given his readers permission to put under erasure. What does it signify that James's canon has been taxonomized and divided into nationalized canons and periods – the "very American" novels and tales of the 1880s, the distinctly "English" society fiction of the middle years, the "American criticism" of the Victorian *Weltanschauung*, the "very English" genius of the early master texts, no less than the transnational fiction of the master phase – such that, as Richard Brodhead has noted, "we discuss his career as we do national traditions, in terms of periods of artistic style and artistic project"?[11] What particular performances in James's texts have given rise to studies with such suggestive titles as *The American Henry James*, *An American as Modernist*, *The French Side of Henry James*, and *The Cosmopolitan World of Henry James*, or to readings that critically or implicitly engage the activity of nation-building in the making of literary canons and genealogies?[12] (I think particularly here of Philip Rahv's resonant distinction between American "redskins" and "palefaces," the latter exemplified by James, and of R. W. B. Lewis's American Adam, described as "the hero of a new adventure, an individual emancipated from history, happily bereft of ancestry, untouched and undefiled by the usual inheritances of family and race" [Lewis, 5]; I think, too, of Van Wyck Brooks's quite different sense, articulated in the moment of greatest influence for such American nativists as Lothrop Stoddard and Madison Grant, of James as failed American, seeking compensation in a hermetic aestheticism for a failed sense of nation-bound "history.") A matter of equal curiosity is the absence of notable account in the evolving historiography of American Studies of how James's signature production of such cultural objects as the American Girl, the international marriage, and the cosmopolitan imagination has provided terms for the critical elaboration of definitively American structures of feeling, cultural aspirations, and characterologies. Instrumental to the cultural politics of the New Criticism as well as the liberal left, the James canon has underwritten American self-representation throughout the twentieth century, conducted in the negotiation of shifting ideas of nation, literary nationality, transnationality, and (more complexly) race.

Sustained treatment of James's entitling function within the changing precincts and mission of literary studies falls outside the limits of my project. But even this brief survey of the terms of his reception suggests how clearly his performances open a lens onto the instability of race – and particularly of whiteness – as a shifting structure of experience and feeling (and of commodification, violence, and repression). What makes these richly gestural forms of culture-building possible is James's aggressive capitalization on lines of parallel but uneven development in nineteenth- and early twentieth-century Anglo-American race thinking. In both disciplinary and popular contexts James engages, categories of descent – "blood," "stock," "tribe" – are increasingly overlaid with, and radically confused by, general terms of classification – "species" or "kind" – as well as assignments of nation.[13] Ernest Renan, a subject of James's wide-ranging cultural criticism (and a central figure in recent studies of nation and race), would argue in 1882 that such classificatory discourses were premised on a "grav[e] mistake": "race is confused with nation and a sovereignty analogous to that of really existing people is attributed to ethnographic or . . . linguistic groups" (Renan, 8). Renan's monitory argument documents the practices of early anthropology which, in dialogue with the emergent field of linguistics, virtually invented such typological categories as the "Nordic" strain, the Anglo-Saxon "pure stock," and, most infamously, the "Aryan." As a result, by late century highly dissonant terms of descent and origin had become "semantically interchangeable" (S. Anderson, 19). In innumerable theoretical and popular texts charting the progress, nature, and decline of the Anglo-Saxon, "[p]hysical, cultural and socio-economic differences" were "taken up, projected and generalized," "so confused that different kinds of variation" – nation, language, genus, class – were "made to stand for" one another (Williams, 250).

As the passage from A Small Boy evidences, it is James's peculiar genius to exploit this power of social figuration to notably varied ends, including the creation of the cross-cultural marriage plot through which forms of racial and national identity are tested and the seizure of an English novelistic tradition for an Anglo-American cultural province in which distinctly literary mastery will hold sway. Transforming the fraught emptiness of race's signifying terms as a form of modernist capital, James contextually adopts alternative gestures, of ironic gentility, of "queerness," of identification with racial others, so as to reframe the cultural subject's relation to culture-building. These performances evidence the currency of race as a dramatically shifting signifier, whose every instantiation – in high literary notions of an Anglo-Saxon cultural inheritance or a uniquely American cultural purchase, in arguments to citizenship and British immigration law, in popular representations of racial purity and danger – performs a different social meaning. To read James's postures of culture-building as such is thus to begin to reconsider how each such act of figuration extends or redirects the reach of racial terms, reconfigures, in Benedict Anderson's famous phrase, the imagined communities of America and Anglo-America.[14]

While my understanding of James's signature idiom of culture as a form of racial theater represents a departure from previous scholarship, reading his work under the sign of performance is hardly original. In fact, arguments to the performative force of James's formalism – his vauntedly difficult style, his literary "architecture," his epistemological dramaturgy – have been central from the outset to both American and British canonizations of James.[15] But the James of my study is less straightforwardly canonical, a writer in dialogue, in effect, with his own developing, increasingly commodifiable literary and cultural mastery. It would surely be productive to consider the historically salient kinds of race thinking entertained in the very works James names as master texts, as a number of readers have begun to do. Milly Theale's entry into Lancaster Gate in *The Wings of the Dove* is, after all, a scrupulously calibrated drama of nationalized sensibility, in which the very "sound of words," the "denotements" and performances of class identity, enact and challenge "possibilities" of "type" read through the focused lens of Milly's own American "race" (*NYE* 19:148, 153). Likewise, *The Golden Bowl* can be taken as James's meditation on the twentieth-century project of cultural assimilation, conducted within the conventions of the marriage plot; there, the very condition of possibility for cosmopolitan assimilation itself is none other than New World capital, crucially backed by the cultural capital of the pawnbrokering, racially transgressive, problematically assimilated Jew.[16] And in the prefaces to the New York Edition, James works to invent another "state of things" – that is, both a state of mind and a version of the civic or nation-state – in which fiction does the hard labor of transfiguring race and nation as categorical imperatives, mapping a psychic geography of continuously social, universally human "relations." For *this* James, the "very condition" of both literary modernism and American liberal modernity is the supercession of any racialized national identity "whatever" (*AN* 5, 200).

But these master texts achieve their version of culture-building precisely by erasing their tracks; their strenuously subtle performances of Anglo-American "character" and gentility assist in their own detachment from the historical conditions in and through which racial and national identities are historically being forged. Taking up more openly (if not more self-consciously) performative work, I put deliberate emphasis on the continuities of James's writings with popular texts, and on the discontinuities – the shifts and stratagems, the gestural richness – of their identifications with varying racial and national forms. The resulting array of James's "productions," in his own word, ranges from early apprentice criticism and travelogue, canonical declarations of formalist literary doctrine, and problematic engagements with realism, through his novelistic negotiations of distinctively English and American cultural canons, to the differently articulate racial performances of *The American Scene*. My central principle of organization is instrumental rather than generic or literary historical: I mean to forestall a reading of race or nationhood as a thematic "problem," exhausted by or within the developing conventions of James's formalism, as well a reading that refuses any social currency to the literary gestures that comprise that formalism. Consequently, I have posited an other-than-canonical James, one who engages in sometimes tense if fluent exchange with the shifting currency of nation and race, and who variously and contextually works to construct a cultural subject unbound from laws of Anglo-Saxon "nature," liberated into a problematically, peculiarly "internationalist" or "cosmopolitan" state of reception and response.

My study thus begins with a body of James's early writings virtually untreated by his critical readers, but generative of a developing internationalist ethos through which the powers and restraints of Anglo-Saxon and bourgeois mastery are productively contravened. Between 1865 and 1875, James published literally scores of reviews, "notices," and essays, the majority of them in the *Nation*, predominantly concerned with national cultures and characters and texts of leisure or anthropological expedition. Mostly unattributed, they have in effect been dismissed as journeyman pieces of "great charm," produced by a "light, humorous" pen that blithely "race[d] along." Read in the context of emergent forms of Anglo-American racial theater, however, these texts turn out to be far more pur-

posively raced than "carefree" (Edel, *Conquest* 186). Their unifying
concern is none other than the culturally productive effects of racial
contact and exchange, staged in the "first impressions" of genteel
travelers in haunts of difference ranging from urban Paris to Lake
Bangweolo and Kathmandu. More precisely, these texts of James's
own first impressions – whereby he begins to position himself with
respect to variously American, English, continental, genteel, and
urban publics – open out onto a fluid body of scientific and popular
ethnographic texts traversed by strong currents of post-Darwinian
anxiety about racial definition and taxonomy. Mobilizing an ethnographic imaginary of contact and transgression, James hazards alternatively internationalist styles of response, through which the values
of genteel masculinity and racial virility are subjected to the "perpetual friction" of alternative forms of pleasure and power (AA 210;
LC1 822).

In James's terms, this kind of racial theater – what we might
call, with respect to his orientalizing idiom, the unmooring of
racial and national affect from the project of cultural mastery – is
enacted in "the aimless *flânerie* which leaves you free to follow
capriciously every hint of entertainment" (*IH* 149). In more
closely American contexts, the conspicuously Jamesian idiom of
freedom is put in service of quite different projects, to which I
turn in chapter two. In 1883, following on the acclaim awarded
his *Portrait of a Lady* and in anticipation of the appearance of the
first collective edition of his fiction, James undertook a reassess-
ment of the novel as a national institution. The resulting essays of
literary doctrine included "Anthony Trollope," which appeared in
the *Century* of July 1883, and "The Art of Fiction," published in
Longman's in September of 1884. In these venues of cultural
aspiration – the first American, the latter British – James's critical
rhetoric of freedom acquires a certain urgency, becoming newly
central to his performative negotiations of race and nation. Assimilated under the standard of literary realism, both essays entertain
a highly charged idiom of "Anglo-Saxon" racial character and
destiny so as to promote the novel as a vehicle of cultural – rather
than strictly racial – renewal. Redirecting freedom – freedom of
movement, of association, of expression, of feeling – as an Anglo-
Saxon property whose vitality and survival must be ensured,
James franchises the English novel for emergent American traditions and argues for the instrumentality of high culture to modern civic life. Cognate texts, the two essays work to consolidate
James's internationalism, staking his claim as heir to the English
novel within an idiom of American self-determination, negotiating

anxieties of racial and cultural futurity specific to both cultural sites.

My reading of James's local gestures of literary affirmation raises questions about the cultural implications of genre. In chapter three, I conduct a more intensive study of realism as a cultural politics and a structure of racial fantasy. There, I reconsider James's self-representations during the mid-1880s as literary naturalist, and the logic of his naturalist commitments in *The Princess Casamassima*. Rather than dismiss *The Princess* as a failed naturalist text, or celebrate its moral realism, I consider the numerous uses to which it puts the naturalist *Gestalt* of "type." First and foremost, I argue, naturalism provides James an idiom for volatilizing the fictions of identity, class, nation, and community disseminated in the widening arena of journalistic culture, in both high bourgeois and popular forms. At stake, as the novel makes clear, is the power of romances of type: the site of reading and reception through which an ascendant Anglo-American bourgeoisie is produced and unified, determined, through narratives of class fitness and racial character. *The Princess* labors not, however, to widen a tenuous divide between high and low forms of cultural production but to uncover deeper channels of communication across that divide, in which resonant anxieties of whiteness, occasioned by changing demographics, class unrest, and emergent forms of nationalism in Britain and America, become more powerfully entrenched. Yet the idiom of typology and fate has still wider currency in *The Princess*. Professing commitment to naturalist doctrines of racial determination, the novel conspicuously stages self-generative gestures that mimic and enable James's own. At large, I read *The Princess* as an allegory of James's attempts, during the decade of his greatest cultural capital, to alter the terms of social commitment for the high style, itself figured as an arena for producing more richly overdetermined cultural identity and meaning.

In large part, *The Princess Casamassima* stages its own breachings of cultural filiation in the figure of its heroine, whose experimental trials unbind cultural agency from apparently fixed structures of nature and blood, pressing for more open forms of "International" engagement. Her contestatory femininity is broadly representative of the modes in which James enacts an international cultural politics during the years spanned by *The Portrait of a Lady* and *The Tragic Muse*. Implicit in my readings is a redirection of feminist interest in James, which in recent years has reached something of an impasse in responding to the conduct of James's texts and their representations of the culture of conduct and taste. Chapters 3 and 4 address this problem by exploring links between James's novels and notions of gender as a form of typology with which racial and class types are knottily entangled. The kinds of ado James organizes around such heroines as Isabel Archer, Verena Tarrant, and Christina Light increasingly mobilize linked forms of gender and racial panic to probe the cultural logic of purity, freedom, and publicity (and alternatively of contamination, decline, and newspaperism), in plots of the heroine's induction into a higher, cosmopolitan self-culture. While those plots necessarily turn on the figure of woman reified as an object of exchange across national, cultural, and even racial boundaries, they mean primarily to appropriate the threshold experience for more richly imbricated styles of culture-building.

In order to explore the racial and culture-bearing logic of Jamesian engenderment, my fourth chapter turns to *The Tragic Muse*, whose plot and project share certain structural interests with *The Princess*: the contest between high and low modes of producing cultural subjects; the force of racial typologies, exploited as resources for more liberated gestures of cultural filiation; the prominence of women as agents of such gestures throughout the public spheres of Anglo-America. In reading the later novel, however, I give these problems a different configuration, focusing on James's heroine as an agent who enables possibilities for more richly self-conscious forms of cultural agency through which narrowly racialized versions of public culture emerging in fin-de-siècle America and England can be actively contested. Shifting his cultural commitments, James deliberately plays on and against two emerging Anglo-American formations. Most prominently, he mimes and displaces an urgent interest in an "English-speaking brotherhood" pressed by bearers of the white man's burden and white supremacists alike. But he also riskily engages a heightened opposition – largely antisemitic – to the urban and the cosmopolitan. That reaction was evidenced in the furious sensationalizing in 1888–9 of the serial murders of Jack the Ripper, figured as an "alien" Jew whose debased, insatiable appetites and mastery of the metropolis threaten the survival of a unified Anglo-Saxon social body. *The Tragic Muse* exploits these very tropes of Jewish usury and deviance. In his complexly rendered heroine, Miriam Rooth, James mounts a campaign for cosmopolitan culture-building in which Jewishness figures his own performative revision of "Anglo-Saxon" memory, identity, and community. Her convertibility of origins and racial nature underwrites, even as it continues partially to threaten, the very possibility of civic and cultural agency in an increasingly transnational modernity.

The body of James's fin-de-siècle work exemplified by *The Tragic*

Muse has been of relatively lesser interest to readers of and in the American context, but it can be said variously to exploit and expend the symbolic capital of a figuratively American freedom of filiation, reordinating the meaning of whiteness in various sites of contested modernity. With his narratives of American return during the "late" phase, James reconsiders the terms of this investment. Replicating the movement of James's cultural politics, I pass over his master works of fiction to address *The American Scene*. The latter, it can be argued, has become the central place of James criticism and a resonant site for reconceiving the conduct of high cultural performance. I read James's magnificently antimagesterial text, published in serial form in 1905–6 and at full length in 1907, not as an autobiographical record of repatriation or literary ascendancy, but as a fluidly responsive, contextually alert study of emerging idioms and technologies for constructing national and racial subjects. The climax of James's career-long witnessing of and performative intervention in racial theater, *The American Scene* actively probes the turn-of-the-century project of Americanization, rehearsing a dizzying array of racial feelings, habits, and exchanges informing widely divergent sites – from Ellis Island to the Confederate Museum, from the newly erected skyscrapers of Wall Street to the burgeoning pleasure palaces of Palm Beach – for the creation of what Theodore Roosevelt would trenchantly call the American race.

In particular, James's narrative aligns itself with emerging mass cultural modes of documentary, contesting them for the power to name Americanness in its "inveterate bourgeois form" (272). If, as Ross Posnock has argued in a brilliantly revisionary reading, *The American Scene* attempts to create a space of cultural agency and production beyond the reach of bourgeois and progressive expertise, it nonetheless remains vitally alive to the power of those emergent habits of seeing, recording, and constructing preeminently racial feeling. Striking varied postures of response, James vigorously challenges the framing power of what he describes as "phantasmagoric" technologies – photography, stereography, film – to stage and manage American racial theater, and the range of bourgeois America's shifting responses to the project of Americanization. Extending linked idioms of racial panic and progressivism, his narratives of phantasmagoric "excess" and "multiplication" nonetheless contest the forms of mastery and management through which America is being constructed under the sign of entertainment.

James's "documentary" style of response is staged not only in urban America, but in another crucial site of American self-making: the overarching, all-reaching Pullman train. On board, and under its magesterial dome, he occupies a more literal space of racial theater where elaborate rituals of conveyance and uplift, of racial contact and affirmation, are acted out, with the ultimate object of training America's managerial classes for their progressive and republican destiny. Documenting the performative force of these activities, from the schooling in style conducted by "negro porters" and waiters to the anxieties of white bourgeois self-affirmation occasioned by the latter's mastery of genteel codes, James uncovers the racial logic of American forms of speed, efficiency, and luxury. He simultaneously dramatizes the fluidity with which racial narratives invert, obscure, and commodify the conditions of American racial exchange. Remarkably prescient about the way such narratives will hold sway in the modern state in both popular and genteel forms, the restless analyst nonetheless remains aware of the limits of his own documentary project, whose power to explore the material and social conditions of culture-building depends on oppositions – between high and low styles, between the alien and the genteel – that James himself has sought to displace.

Thus scrupuously attentive, the James of my concluding chapter, and indeed of the study as a whole, is purposely dislocated both from his own self-construction and from an ongoing body of critical reception, in which the very range of his cultural performances – American, Anglo-Saxon, genteel, queer, internationalist, cosmopolitan – has assisted in their detachment from the cultural and literary historical conditions of American race- and nation-formation. Throughout, I have engaged uniquely Jamesian topoi and strategies in order to promote or reopen certain critical dialogues: between the richly responsible, finely aware Jamesian imagination and the active labor of culture, or what James calls "the whole conduct of life" (AN 347); between genteel habits and codes and mass cultural projects; between canons of high literary and/or modernist performance, bound over to self-consciously "*representational* values" (AN 246), and conceptions of racial, national, or "civic" subjectivity and agency. I aim thereby to do justice to the enormous range of James's performances of culture – from the consciousness of his own failure to outrun the reach of limiting cultural discourses to the hard-won, relentlessly self-interrogating and unsentimental affirmation of difference. I aim, too, to convey the pleasures and challenges of critical attention to those performances, which urge on their readers committed scrutiny of their own forms of distinction and cultural commitment.

1

FIRST IMPRESSIONS: "QUESTIONS OF ETHNOGRAPHY" AND THE ART OF TRAVEL

In chapter ten of *The American*, James's eponymous protagonist is formally presented to the family of Mme de Cintré. The group includes her "distinguished" brother and *"chef de la famille"* – the Marquis, Urbain, whom Newman has previously mistaken for a butler (*American* 120, 184). That "noble and majestic" personage initiates an exchange of "sustained urbanity" true to his given name and to the deeper interests of the novel:

> 'If I am not mistaken, your occupations are such as to make your time precious. You are in – a – as we say, *dans les affaires.*'
> 'In business, you mean? Oh no, I have thrown business overboard for the present. I am 'loafing,' as *we* say. My time is quite my own.'
> 'Ah, you are taking a holiday,' rejoined M. de Bellegarde.
> ' "Loafing." Yes, I have heard that expression.'
> 'My brother is a great ethnologist,' said Valentin.
> 'An ethnologist?' said Newman. 'Ah, you collect negroes' skulls, and that sort of thing.'
> The marquis looked hard at his brother, and began to caress his other whisker. (*American* 184–5)

Central to this scene of mutual first impressions is an unintended pun: no great etymologist in the English language, Valentin de Bellegarde accidentally identifies the motives of his formidable brother with those of ethnography, the emerging discipline of racial taxonomy.[1] His *faux pas* proves uncannily apt; the "internationalist" logic of the novel turns on ways of "saying" and habits of thought borrowed from the disciplines of ethnography and anthropology, in its dramatic confrontation between the American "national type," comparatively "savage" in its "natural" instincts, and the "strange secrets" of " '[o]ld races' " (*American* 34, 163). James's cautionary tale of the "powerful specimen" of the American takes up the ongoing business of negotiated contact across cultural boundaries, represented in the novel's deep structure as ultimately intractable "difference[s] of race" (*American* 135). At stake in this first meeting, as Urbain "slid[es] his white hands into the white kid" of his gloves and proffers polite wishes "out of the white expanse of his sublime serenity" (*American* 185), is no less than the fate of whiteness itself – the character of the New Man, wresting possibilities for self-knowledge and agency from a dangerously vitiated European civilization.

This brief scene of first impressions opens out in two directions: onto the large and shifting body of James's writing on travel and cultural exchange throughout the 1870s, and onto a fluid extra-Jamesian body of ethnographic texts bound up with what James calls "questions of ethnography" (Abode 314) – scientific and popular anxieties about racial virility, national character, and the fate of the "Anglo-Saxon" type.[2] In the tension between "Manufactures" and "loafing," and in its recourse to an "ethnological" imagination, Newman's self-representation echoes the logic of the American Centennial Exhibition in Philadelphia, with which the initial publication of *The American* in the June 1876 *Atlantic Monthly* coincided. The Exhibition, which attracted nearly one-fifth of the population of the United States (Rydell, 10), conjoined the celebration of industrial technology and "the largest collection in the world of preparations in zoology, entomology" and "ethenology" [sic] with the delights of leisure travel, represented on site by Thomas Cook's American "World Ticket and Inquiry Office." The latter advertised "Tourist tickets to all parts of the U.S.," "the continent of Europe," "Egypt and Palestine" and "around the world travelling East or West . . . no matter how extended and complicated the route" (*Magee's*, 20, 154). Here, as in Newman's encounter with the forces of blood and culture, racial taxonomy mediates confident expansionism as well as nativist anxiety, structuring the pursuit of both leisured and scientific contact with the racial other.

When thus relocated in the embattled arena of race thinking, James's signature international "theme" registers the intentionality with which he forges a putatively literary authority as mediator of distinctive national styles and canons. Engaging ethnographic narratives and their shifting vocabulary for representing race and nationhood, James develops a mode of cultural response that variously negotiates the common currency of typological notions. These negotiations are hardly limited to James's canonical fiction, although critical gestures of such limitation have effectively served to divorce his texts from the cultural politics they complexly engage. An attentive survey of James's publications in the first decade of his career reveals how intricately his works of travelogue and review as well as fiction are entangled with the ethnographic project. During that period, James produced scores of essays and "notices" on the cultural institutions of America, England, Italy, and France, on tales of travel, on ethnographic psychology, and on "racial" histories whose subjects range from "the Hebrew people" and contemporary "Saxons" to "the English mind," produced by such diverse writers on culture as Ernest Renan, Charles Augustin Saint-Beuve, Julian Hawthorne, and most prominently, Hippolyte Taine, whose "famous theory of *la race, la moment, le milieu*" as the grounds of cultural production widely influenced post-Darwinian intellectuals.[3] James also produced a more narrowly ethnographic body of essays on travel and race typology. In reviews of such popular accounts as *Remains of Lost Empires: Sketches of the Ruins of Palmyra, Nineveh, Babylon, and Persepolis* (1874), *The Straits of Malacca, Indo-China and China* (1875), *Observations on a Tour from Chinese Tibet to the Indian Caucasus* (1875), and *Four Thousand Miles of African Travel* (1875) he deliberately traverses the busy intersection of travel literature and anthropology, in which travelers' "first impressions of foreign scenes" give voice and cultural form to anxieties about racial destiny, the progress of American and "Anglo-Saxon" social projects, and the fate of their central institutions and world view (LNT 152; *LC1* 468).

Read in the context of ethnographic thinking, this body of work can be seen as crucial to James's early project, the "creation" of a more "composite" American style of cultural response, put in service to what William Dean Howells would describe as "making us a real American novel" (cited in Gard, 21). Sites of initial trial, James's essays experiment with shifting identities and voices, miming and opposing various models and categories – the Anglo-Saxon "mind," the American "character," the genteel, the European or Continental – of cultural performance.[4] With increasing ingenuity, James mobilizes such unstable models, which inflect and are inflected by ethnographic tenets of race and nation, so as to test and volatilize their limits. Previously canonized as impressionism or epistemological drama, James's stagings of cross-cultural contact in this body of work constitute an ongoing response to the ethnographic imaginary of racial affirmation and transgression. His essays not only demonstrate that James reimagines the work of high or genteel culture in provisional response to contested racial typologies; they also register the complexity and mobility of Anglo-American racial narratives themselves, which recent studies of race and racism have frequently obscured.[5]

More specifically, James's urbane responses to the foreign and the primitive as writ in the genre of travelogue share a certain psychic economy with narratives of disciplinary ethnography. In those texts, as in his own, varied gestures of positioning record both anxieties of cultural or racial supremacy and fantasies of escape from an ongoing crisis of patriarchal and cultural authority, inscribed in theories of racial atavism and decline. James's writings trade in this economy, however, without wholly acceding to what Jackson Lears has identified as its anti-modern nostalgia, or to what Mary Louise Pratt has called the idiom of "anti-conquest," by which the metropole's bourgeois subjects secure their racial innocence even as they assert the cultural hegemony of the Anglo-Saxon (Lears, 225–36; Pratt, 8). Even as James registers fears about the fate of whiteness, of Anglo-Saxon civilization threatened by racial competition and regression, he takes a certain unorthodox pleasure in probing the structure of fantasy through which narratives of "first impressions" construct versions of leisure, cultural acquisition, racial fitness, and the national *mission civilisatrice*.

In the decade of James's developing internationalist mastery, that structure could accommodate, at one extreme, the unassailable confidence in racial quantification of the professional American race theorist John H. Van Evrie, author of *White Supremacy and Negro Subordination* (1868), who asserts of the French paleontologist Georges Cuvier that he "might pick up a bone of any kind, however minute, in the deserts of Arabia, and from this alone determine the species, genus, and class to which it belonged" (Van Evrie, 92). It could with equal ease accommodate the mixed designs during the 1870s of the emergent Anthropological Society of London; members informally called it the Cannibal Club and gavelled themselves to order with a mace in the form of "a Negro head" (Stocking, 247–53). Negotiating the complex psychic range of these cultural performances, James begins to develop a signature ethos of refusal, in which the terms and values of Anglo-American gentility and American masculinity are subjected to "the perpetual friction" of alternative styles of pleasure and power (AA 210; LC2 822). Although his early texts frequently displace the race work and engenderment of the travel idiom into a logic of the picturesque, they nonetheless engage the ethnographic as a theater of liberation and control, through which norms of nationhood, masculinity, and racial hierarchy are both reified and contested.

In order to open James's inaugural self-fashioning onto the ethnographic *Gestalt*, I begin by looking at the climate of racial theory in the 1870s as the context for a number of James's early travel reviews, essays, and occasional texts. The latter's interests, fitful and shifting, nonetheless intersect squarely with the politics and vocabulary of Anglo-America's racial science. Adopting the conflicted forms of gentility and aggression that permeate the ethnographic project, James exploits powerful tensions encoded there between racial purity and danger, bourgeois self-affirmation and fantasized liberation from bourgeois norms, in order to experiment with alternative styles of cultural response. Among these essays, James's 1875 review of David Livingstone's *Last Journals* – a definitive text in the mythology of the "Dark Continent" as testing grounds for the discipline of white manliness[6] – is exemplary in linking the concerns of "sentimental" travel with the cultural politics of ethnography. But his review, along with other texts on Africa and the primitive, does more interesting and varied work than that of replicating a set of received racial pieties or even a "general" scientific "view" of racial hierarchy, supremacy, and decline (LNT 152; *LC1* 468). Rather it reflects, and to a surprising extent productively reflects on, contemporary race thinking so as to suggest the limits of "heroism" as a racial and national mythology (Abode 313).

Although perceptible in James's writings on Africa, this revisionary impulse most fully animates the body of his travel writings on Italy, in particular those on the *ne plus ultra* of Anglo-American orientalism, Venice. Beginning in 1873, James produced a series of essays, to which he returned at several decisive moments in his career, on Venice and the Italian picturesque. In willingly allowing himself to be "directed toward the East" (FTM 361; *LC1* 600), he joins such orientalizing Americans as William Sturgis Bigelow, George Cabot Lodge, Charles Eliot Norton, and his own future chronicler, Van Wyck Brooks, who pursue the lotus of "Nirvana" and "Oriental" passivity as a mode of accommodation to emerging norms of masculine authority (Lears, 234). But James's openness to Venetian "seduction," under the sign of "the Anglo-Saxon abroad" and in "exile" from the forces of gentility, more actively contests those social norms (*IH* 44, 77). On the site of Venice his signature gesture-in-the-making – the refusal of masculine power – ultimately marks not a withdrawal from modernity but a relocation of its cultural energies in a distinctly literary mode. Dramatizing "frictions" and conflicts of cultural filiation, James displaces the definitively genteel style of mastering racial alterity into "an indefatigable and idle curiosity" (LNT 152; *LC2* 469). The resulting style of "observation," which becomes central to his internationalist fiction and his claims for the cultural work it performs, adapts the energies governing ethno-graphic romances; it makes James's own first impressions the grounds of an alternatively Anglo-American style of narrative and civic agency.

Excursion, Ethnography, and the Fate of Whiteness

[The] aim [of M. Taine's work] has been 'to establish the psychology of a people' . . . to discover in the strongest fea-tures of the strongest works the temper of the race and time . . . [He] writes from an avowedly foreign stand-point. The unit of comparison is throughout assumed to be the French mind. The author's undertaking strikes us, therefore, constantly as an *excursion*.

– James, "Taine's English Literature," 1872 (*LC1* 842)

In 1867, after James had begun a regular series of literary reviews and essays for the *Nation*, William Dean Howells privately rated his gifts in a letter to Charles Eliot Norton. "I cannot doubt that James has every element of success in fiction," he wrote. "But I suspect that he must in a great degree create his audience" (cited in Gard, 21). In large part, James undertook that project in his own writings of and on excursion: notes on travel, tales of cross-cultural contact, assessments of the distinctive character of national literatures. In one important respect he would become a victim of his own success in this mode, for the facility with which he performs the work of "*excursion*" has obscured James's engagements with scientific and popular narratives of racial psychology and character. Those en-gagements powerfully underwrite not only what Howells recog-nizes as James's virtual invention of an internationalist aesthetic, but his evolving literary mastery at large (Howells 1882, 25–9).

To take up the art of travel and the subject of national literatures during the 1870s – a moment when leisured travel and disciplinary race thinking had become the Siamese twins of Anglo-American culture – was inevitably to engage evolving narratives of race typol-ogy and character. Popular presses were inundated with memoirs and travelogues by missionaries, colonial bureaucrats, "lady" travel-ers and *belles-lettristes*, which competed with scientific studies of primitivism and racial others for the attention of, and power of legitimating, middle-class readers throughout the Anglo-American metropole.[7] The aspiring American *littérateur* would have shared with ethnographic texts not just an audience for his copious travel essays but several of the institutions and vehicles in which he broke into print. The same journals that nurtured the development of James's Anglo-American *oeuvre* also provided a forum for ongoing debates in ethnography and anthropology, directed toward a genteel audience of "intellectuals" and "educated people" (Stocking, 324). If "Darwin [was] conquering everywhere and rushing in like a flood," some of the most furious waves seethed in "the literary world" of highbrow culture, where arguments over retrogression, monogenism, polygenism and the like were waged in terms notably continuous with the institutional styles of more recognizably literary vehicles.[8]

While the race taxonomies generated by physiognomy and craniometry "flooded" the popular press, such aggressively highbrow journals as the *Fortnightly Review* regularly published the work of leading sociocultural evolutionists, whose substance and style of argument were continuous with those of the professional journals of disciplinary anthropology.[9] E. L. Godkin's *Nation*, where the vast majority of James's early travel writing, reviewing, and cultural critique appeared, published seminal articles on the sociology of race, including work by Herbert Spencer, whose metaphysics of the survival of the fittest enjoyed an unprecedented "vogue" among general readers.[10] Hungry for sensation, alive to the excitements of ethnography's vested interests in the primitive and alien, middle-class American readers actively consumed narratives of whiteness and blackness, of Anglo-Saxon and other, in the conjoined documentation of the ape theory and travelers' tales.

But the traffic between leisured travel and scientific taxonomy is even more highly overdetermined than the facts of print culture or *The American*'s scene of first encounter would suggest, since the emergent professional culture of the sciences of Man was itself rooted in the project of excursion and travelogue. Both Darwin and Alfred Russel Wallace, co-discoverer of the principle of natural selection and a self-confessed primitivist in the romantic mode, began their separate researches with "trave[l] to the earth's farthest reaches" whose representation in both scientific and popular genres relied on "literary counsel" and models (Eisley, 148–9).[11] Throughout the century, the testimonies of professional and leisure travelers provided founding sources for both sociological and "hard" physical scientific theorists of racial nature. American and British ethnographers depended not only on personal experience of the primitive and the alien but even more prominently on material "from the printed pages of books" – that is, of antiquarian and contemporaneous travel accounts in the mode of genteel *belles-lettres* (Stocking, 79). Reprinted, often in revised editions accommodating new "data" harvested from increasing contact with tribal cultures and foreigners, the work of major Anglo-American ethnologists might be characterized as compendia of the travel literature of nineteenth-century Europeans abroad. Travelogues and memoirs penned by gentlemen voyagers, missionaries, and colonial agents flowed from the presses and were prominently placed on the library shelves of geographical societies and other scientific bodies, providing evidence for earlier nonquantitative work on race and for the hard sciences of race that historically succeeded it.[12]

Similarly knotty entanglements between the popular press, literary vehicles, and gentlemanly travel continued to shape the projects of ethnography and anthropology throughout the post-Darwinian era. Francis Galton, a cousin of Darwin, pioneer of modern statistics and coiner of the term eugenics, not only served as Secretary to the Royal Geographic Society but commanded immense respect in the American and British scientific communities. (Lewis Terman, of intelligence quota fame, would assign Galton an IQ of over 200 as compared with only 135 for Darwin, and a mere 100–110 for Copernicus – evolutionary progress indeed [Gould, 77].) Galton began his career as a wanderer of independent means in exotic African and Near Eastern locales, leading an expedition to the Lake Ngami region in the wake of David Livingstone. He led "a very Oriental life" in Syria, returning to England only to learn "the A B C of the life of an English country gentleman," publishing on genetics, racial inheritance, and the work of Robert Browning (Stocking, 92–6).[13] Galton was not initially a quantitative scientist; the most rigorous "hard" anthropology included in his 1853 volume, *The Narrative of an Explorer in Tropical South Africa*, was his attempt, using a surveyor's sextant "from a discrete distance," to obtain measurements of the buttocks of an African woman he advertised as the next Venus Hottentot (Stocking, 94–6). But he labored diligently to develop ever more ingenious ways to measure "the relative worth of peoples." Toward that end, he proposed to assess the comparative value of black, white, and other "primitive civilizations" by studying "the history of encounters between black chiefs and white travelers," as recounted in literary, ethnographic, and historical sources (Gould, 76). Galton's story, as told in the influential volume *Hereditary Genius* (1869), is predictably "familiar": "the white traveller almost invariably holds his own in their presence. It is seldom that we hear of a white traveller meeting with a black chief whom he feels to be the better man" (Galton, 338–9; cited in Gould, 76). The quantitative race analysis for which Galton became celebrated intrinsically depends on the rhetoric and imaginary of gentlemanly travel, whose mythologies of white manliness are legitimized in the language of statistical fact.

In reconstructionist America, armchair speculation and leisure travel played an even more focused role in the discipline of anthropology, since American race theorists tended to promote white supremacy along environmentalist rather than strictly hereditarian lines. Throughout the 1870s, 1880s, and beyond, the American school, heavily influenced by Herbert Spencer's "comparative" method, sought to elaborate general laws of nature operating in social organisms so as to embark on distinctly American projects of racial engineering.[14] A crucial text – almost a *vade mecum* – for that enterprise was Spencer's most widely read and comprehensive work, confidently entitled *Descriptive Sociology: Encyclopedia of Social Facts Representing the Constitution of Every Type and Grade of Human Society, Past and Present, Stationary and Progressive, Classified and Tabulated for Easy Comparison and Convenient Study of the Relations of Social Phenomena* (1873–81). Its eight volumes were much as advertised, "a compendium of attributes and descriptions taken from travelers and catalogued" according to racial "traits" and types. Here and throughout the body of his work, Spencer synthetically adopts travelers' "testimonies" in part or whole to "illustrate the pervasiveness of biological law" in calculated narratives of race character that were both shifting and highly contradictory. Like other scientific texts of race theory on both sides of the Atlantic, Spencer's work shored up notions of racial supremacy and an Anglo-Saxon birthright; that latter notion arguably had particular conceptual power for middle-class readers in America negotiating rapid shifts in cultural and class orientation during the post-War decades (Haller, 128, 133).

These brief forays into the history of disciplinary race theory highlight not the predictable alliance of racism and race theory, but the crucial role of traveler's data and of travelogue as a cultural genre in the emergence of Anglo-American models for race. Such narratives, transported across the porous generic boundaries between science, travelogue, high culture, journalism and popular entertainment, assisted forcefully in the linked transitions to genteel cultural canons and a post-Darwinian racial imaginary, in which, as Henry Adams would retrospectively put it, "Natural selection seemed a dogma to be put in the place of the Athanasian creed" (Adams, 231).

If James's early fictions of racial contact across cultural divides resemble other texts of excursion in sharing a cultural boundary with disciplinary race thinking, they attend increasingly to the demarcation of that boundary and the cultural uses to which it can be put. Unlike the genteel, gentlemanly, and picturesque modes he mimes, his writings on travel adopt and adapt ethnography's shifting vocabularies of race with marked self-consciousness. The best-known among them include the texts collected in *Portraits of Places* (1883), originally published in such American culture-building vehicles as *Atlantic Monthly*, the *Galaxy*, *Lippincott's Magazine*, and the *Nation* and explicitly revised for an English audience. Characteristically Jamesian in their poise, relativism, and interest in the shifting lineaments of culture, the essays in this volume aim to create a broadly internationalist sensibility through the mobilization of ethnographic tropes of nation and race. With disarming fluency, the unhurried observer ranges over the psychic terrain of the Anglo-American urbane: he reads Ruskin while viewing Giotto in Santa Maria Novella, despises the "deadly monotony" of Haussmann's Paris, descends into the crypt of Canterbury Cathedral, wanders the pleasure precincts of Newport and Saratoga, and other American spaces where "the democritisation of elegance" reigns (*Places* 80, 329). Striking "a truce to all rigidities," James enjoys "the profit of comparing one race to another" in a strikingly mobile idiom for the declaration of cultural allegiances (*Places* 69, 75). In alternatively American, English, and "European" postures of response, or "*patriae*," weighing "manners and customs" in the tone of one "living about" among various "national virtues," James exploits the elastic notion of an "Anglo-Saxon" character, civilization, and mind so as to promote a style of performance that forestalls narrower readings of culture, such measurements of "the human race" as are taken by "the desperation of gentility" (*Places* 75–7, 83, 186).

James sustains this urbane posture of response, which tends to offer itself in the guise of cultural fellow-traveling, through the adoption of remarkably mobile forms of cultural allegiance, predicated on apparently secure but instrinsically unstable denominations of nation and race. He observes characteristically English institutions – the pomp of Oxford at Commemoration, the pastoral ritual of lawn tennis, the culture of English country houses – with the "American eyes" of a "shamefully sordid Yankee," but "casual[ly]" positions himself vis-a-vis the "Latin" races as a "Northern observer," an "Anglo-Saxon" who observes "the French genius" through "Anglo-Saxon" lenses (*Places* 134–8, 193, 224, 239, 359, 138). The Yankee in exile magnanimously lauds "the greatness of England," tracing "in English history the sacred source of his own national affection" (*Places* 224), yet for "all the great things" that "the English" have "made a part of the glory of the national character," the nice produc-

tions of this "complicated race" and its "genteel" culture will hardly
do to represent the "swarming vastness – the multifarious possibilities and activities" – of a distinctively American "civilisation" (*Places*
313, 239, 321, 328). Self-consciously "cosmopolite," embracing "that
uncomfortable consequence of seeing many lands and feeling at
home in none" (*Places* 75), James exploits an ethnographic idiom of
filiation so as more variously to position himself within and against
received notions of Anglo-Saxon culture and its "mastered" activities and "invent[ions]" (*Places* 313).

What makes these internationalist performances possible in
their moment (and all but unrecognizable in our own as forms of
race thinking) is precisely the radical instability of the racial idiom
they appropriate. In the post-Darwinian moment, the very terms
of human identity – categories of race, nation, and species – had
become arbitrary, their "proof of existence" in a paleontological
past beyond the reach of scientific recovery (Haller, 4). James's
self-fashioning in the mode of excursion mimes and exploits the
unstable performativity of postevolutionary racial vocabulary. If
the legitimacy of pre-Darwinian scientific models and theories of
racial identity had evaporated, their vocabulary of whiteness and
otherness survived, malleable, contested, empty. Throughout scientific and popular cultures numerous terms with varied biopoli-
tical nuances competed as ways of naming bodies civic, social,
sexual, and politic. Like the ethnographers and travelers whose
work he reviews, James has recourse to a shifting vocabulary that
included evolving if indistinct notions of "races," "branches,"
"stocks," "groups," "tribes," "nations," and "ethnos" or "peoples."[15] Among race theorists of the decade, Galton proposed that
"character" – a composite of traits of race and nation, and not
incidentally a term that resonates powerfully in *Portraits of Places*
as well as James's internationalist fiction – is "heritable like every
other faculty" (Galton, cited in Gould, 77). Louis Agassiz, founder
and director of the Museum of Comparative Zoology at Harvard,
director of William James's anthropological field work, and an
extremely influential proponent of the theory of separate origin
for distinct human races, asserted that "men were created in *nations*, and not in a single pair" (Agassiz, cited in Nott and Gliddon,
82). Agassiz's co-authors and fellow polygenists Josiah Nott and
George Gliddon choose a differently nuanced term, "*Types*" –
defined as "those primitive or original forms which are independent of Climatic or other Physical influences" – to tell similar stories of racial difference under the rubric of "Mankind" (Nott and
Gliddon, 80).

For all their differences in describing difference, these systems of classification share an underlying cultural logic. The urge to quantify difference – blackness, the primitive, the alien – encodes increasing anxiety about the meaning of whiteness itself, the emptiest, most unstable racial signifier in ethnographic discourse at large. "What is meant by the word '*Caucasian*'?" Nott and Gliddon all but rhetorically ask. "Almost every Ethnologist would give a different reply" (Nott and Gliddon, 88). The idea of an "Anglo-Saxon" character, identity, temperament – so prevalent and available a notion in James's early positionings in and against styles of cultural performance – comes increasingly to depend for its very survival on narratives of exchange between the "savage" or alien and the most highly evolved *homo sapiens*, Anglo-Saxon "Man" (Brinton, 278).[16] Leisured travel, armchair anthropology, the genre of travelogue and quantitative science in Anglo-America thus conjoin in elaborating whiteness – the distinct features of "the so-called white race of man" (Nott and Gliddon, lxviii) – as a cultural problematic. Seizing on the body of otherness, ethnographers no less than literary travelers took the measure not primarily of blackness and difference but of themselves, and of the myths of whiteness that their increasingly disciplinary activities represented and sustained.

This mutual constitution of cultural and racial subjects, through the force of what David Theo Goldberg has called "race creation," has become a commonplace of current racial theory (Goldberg, 83). What interests me here, however, is the ways in which James's texts betray an increasing awareness of the various roles – affirmational, contestatory, experimental – that literary culture might play in that ongoing process. *The American*'s Urbain de Bellegarde embodies the ethos of racial discipline and control in an "ethnological" interest in "negroes' skulls"; James himself, under the sign of internationalist literary culture, is equally interested in the measurement and management of the resources of race. Not unlike the ill-fated Roderick Hudson, who makes a "profession of faith" in the "beauty of Type" as the most powerful resource for creating "a magnificent image of my Native Land," James seeks to develop a style of response liberated from genteel norms whose fluency of filiation will redirect the force of the ethnographic project (*RH* 84–5). In his uneven development of this style, James can be seen to manage the vocabulary of race and nation; to suggest, at least intermittently, its provisionality and its limits. If his first impressions work to aestheticize race thinking as a form of literary sensibility, they nonetheless engage Anglo-America's *idée fixe* of race "vitality," themselves revitalizing consummately literary practices as forms of cultural performance and culture-building.

Rehearsing the Ethnographic

From biological truths it is to be inferred that the eventual mixture of the allied varieties of the Aryan race forming the population of [the American nation] will produce a more powerful type of man than has hitherto existed, and a type of man more plastic, more adaptable, more capable of undergoing the modifications needful for complete social life. . . . [T]he Americans may reasonably look forward to a time when they will have produced a civilization grander than any the world has known.

– Herbert Spencer (1883; cited in Youmans, 19–20)

In 1875, James published a brief review of *Italie, Sicile, Bohême: Notes de Voyage* by Auguste Laugel, French historian of Anglo-Saxon history and Republican commentator on French politics for the *Nation*. Itself a work of ethnography-cum-travelogue, Laugel's text exemplifies the power of racial and cultural typologies to describe styles of literary performance; its author, James asserts, exhibits a characteristically "French" adroitness in "the art of putting literary material into form," a "French" sensibility of "the picturesque aspect of things" (LNT 152; *LCi* 468). Less typical of the author's national temper and urbanity as a "general observer" is his habit of "constantly strik[ing] the moral note, the note of reflection." But these "moral impression[s]," as translated and negotiated by James, suggest very specific cultural projects on the part of both writers. Quoting at length from Laugel's passages on a " 'debased' " Naples and its " 'degenerate race,' " James favors an elegiac idiom strikingly close to his own: " 'you cannot live in the past; you are too much jostled; you are overcome by the continual fever, the sterile activity, the indefatigable and idle curiosity which stir so many thousand beings' " (LNT 152; *LCi* 469).

The energy of the present; the "jostling" of the body by a material culture with a bustling life of its own; the embrace of purposeless activity and of "idle curiosity": these keynotes will be managed with more pointed intentionality in James's later writings. Here, however, they function to emphasize the instrumentality of Laugel's sense of belatedness. The author's mourning, not for ancient Italy but for his own French culture, mired in a decline evidenced by France's military defeat at the hands of Prussia in 1870, is the salient point of James's interest – or so the ventriloquism of the review's ending suggests. In lieu of general comment on the nature of travelogue, or summary disposition of the merits of Laugel's aesthetic sensibility, James closes his own brief text with an awkwardly dense direct citation:

> 'What a jest is history, if you look only at the outside – at the stage-setting! But there is a secret, terrible force . . . an unconscious force tending as a still more unconscious force drives it; history is an ordered succession of chances; it moves always towards something necessary; it uses everything, tribunes and kings, monarchies and republics, barbarians and civilization. Whither is it leading us? Whither is aged, worn-out Europe going? Whither our Latin races? Whither France . . . ?' (LNT 152; *LC1* 471)

The "secret" and terrifyingly deep "unconscious" of "history" – an obvious euphemism for natural selection – "uses" the material of civilization equally with that of barbarism, reducing the achievements of the highest cultures to an evolutionary "jest." This indifferently "ordered succession" poses a haunting threat to the project of cultural observation itself, as "essential" facts of human nature reveal their biocultural fragility, as "our Latin" (or Anglo-Saxon) "races" succumb to the "terrible" pull of "chance," as the "Europe" and "France" of imperial greatness are led via the sport of a restive Darwinian Nature into racial exhaustion and decline.

These leitmotifs of cultural preservation and regression and the fate of Western Man are worth aligning with the local facts of James's career. In the very moment in which he decisively "take[s] possession of the old world," claiming to "appropriate it" for a permanent transatlantic exile, he gives voice in a number of texts to a post-Darwinian vision of "worn-out Europe," its heritages succumbing to the rising tide of racial competition and extinction (*Letters* 1:484). But the anxieties of racial survival James records, in shifting notions of the "Latin," the Anglo-Saxon, and the European, do more than replicate genteel race thinking; they create space for the American cultural critic who – despite the infamous nullities recorded in the decorous prose of James's *Hawthorne* – capitalizes on the iconography of the New World, and of its raw materials of human production, to rewrite the narrative of racial decline. Not unlike *Madame de Mauves*, published the previous year in the *Galaxy*, James's review of Laugel explores the possibilities for his self-representation of the narrative of faltering European "type" (*Tales* 2:298): pitting an American "moral" imagination –

the "Puritanic soul" – against French "blood" of "the very finest strain" (*Tales* 2:288, 303, 290), James's tale concludes with the suicide of the philandering "*grand seigneur*," who "blow[s] out his brains" in anguished tribute to the energetic and "radical purity" of his "essentially" American wife (*Tales* 2:306, 347, 289, 285). Like his own heroine, James entertains the romance of cultural exhaustion in numerous texts of travelogue in order to reconstitute the *données* of "race and instinct" as aesthetic or imaginative resources, through which the enterprise of "general culture" – of Spencer's "civilization" – can be renegotiated and redeemed (*Tales* 311).

For James, the cultural narrative of racial decline has further advantages; it enables not only his appropriation of national mythologies but a developing challenge to racialized norms of masculinity. The latter motive underlies James's engagement with the ethnography of retrogression and the primitive, as evidenced in his review of a volume by J. Thomson, *The Straits of Malacca, Indo-China and China: or, Ten Years' Travels, Adventures, and Residence Abroad* (1875). Booked by James as "a vigorous Englishman," whose account brims with narrative "energy" and "high animal spirits," Thomson enacts a stridently manly style of Victorian exploration. Beginning his trek in Siam, venturing into Cambodia, Hong Kong, Canton, Amoy, Foochow, Nanking and other exotic ports of call, Thomson "sail[s], adventurously over death-dealing rapids, some thirteen hundred miles up the great Yang-tse" (TIC 279, 280; LC2 1306–7). The point of this heroic travel is to record the habits of various racial types in the form of "data" for ethnographic study and for the colonialist project of racial management. James obligingly parrots Thomson's accounts of the Chinese – "who seem to combine in an ingenious manner most of the vices of civilization and of barbarism, and to possess few of the virtues of either state" – and on the aborigines of Formosa, the Pepohoan, "peoples" of reputed "cannibalistic tendencies," who turn out when Thomson "plung[es] energetically" into their midst to be adept at conjuring tricks and fascinated by "the author's cigar" (TIC 279, 280; LC2 1306, 1309).

But the real point of Thomson's venture, and of James's review, is a concern with whiteness rather than blackness, yellowness, or other shades – a concern, that is, with the fate of a signature Anglo-Saxon virility in an era of increasing racial competition and exchange. The sole narrative virtue of Thomson's text for James is "the vivid and entertaining picture" he creates "of life and manners in the commercial stations of the Malay Peninsula and Indo-China." Twenty-five years before Conrad's *Heart of Darkness*, the exotic outposts of European civilization – "Malacca, Singapore, Saigon, Macao, and Hong-Kong" – have already become representational sites for shaping and sustaining myths of white manliness. There, James recounts, "among hosts of perfidious Malays and counterplotting Chinamen, the English, the Americans, the French, the Germans, and the Dutch are measuring their mercantile wits against each other, competing and outbidding, and contracting luxurious tropical habits and irritable tempers" (TIC 280; *LC2* 1307–8). But James, remarking Thomson's nostalgia for "the golden age of these picturesque communities," displays less anxiety about racial contamination than interest in atavism and decline as a "counterplot" to the myth of manliness. In "fiercer" competition among themselves, Europeans and Americans exhibit the ills of "contracting" as a way of life, rather than merely those occasioned by "luxurious tropical climes"; the activities of "competing and outbidding" carry to a fearful extreme "the feverish uproar of the City and of Wall Street." For quite different reasons, Thomson and James are both fascinated with "extinct civilizations" and their "impressive relics": on the site of racial conquest, "the relapse of the people into a primitiveness bordering in some quarters on the condition of the lower animals" ineluctably links the "retrogressive" with the "progressive," white manliness and the competitive ethos with more primitive "tempers" (TIC 280; *LC2* 1308–9).

I have argued thus far that James's engagement with the topoi of race progress and decline is intermittent but intentioned; that he begins to explore the possibilities of appropriating narratives of race in service of more flexible cultural filiations and performances. His initial success is best measured against moments in which James more unself-consciously replicates the thought modes of contemporary ethnography. In an 1874 review of P. V. N. Myers's *Remains of Lost Empires: Sketches of the Ruins of Palmyra, Nineveh, Babylon, and Persepolis*, for example, James assertively treats the mythology of excursion under the sign of the aesthetic. He begins by lamenting a gap between Myers's "excellent" opportunities – his "distinctly" exotic adventures on a raft at Mosul, floating down the Tigris to Baghdad, weathering a prolonged hurricane – and his "decidedly disappointing record," whose prose "recall[s] in equal measure" the styles of "the newspaper reporter and the pietistic 'tract' " (RLE 65; *LC2* 551–2). But the view of "ruined cities" offered by the text, for all its "very dim spectacles," makes it a worthwhile diversion for the armchair traveler. Despite Myers's "rather tame" style and his failures "in the way of entertainment" and "sense of detail," his narrative nonetheless takes the measure of civilizations inaugurated by Caesar, "a power in which we are still interested, as the great initiation of our modern world." By far the most "copious" sections of the text, James notes, are discussions of Nineveh, "the Chaldean record of the Deluge," and "the Tower of Babel as an historical fact"; "pictorial" interest and "graphic description" are crudely displaced by concerns about "the literal veracity of the Biblical recital" of these events, to which the "historical fact" of racial origins and hierarchy can be traced (RLE 65–6; *LC2* 551–2).

The only notable moment of Myers's account, or indeed of James's remarks on its lapses in observation and "style," is an anecdote virtually buried in the drift of James's perfunctory prose. Myers, he notes, "gives an interesting report of the magnificent ruins of Persepolis, where he found 'Stanley, *New York Herald*, engraved between the eyes of one of the colossal bulls, in letters as bold as the Ujiji expedition' " (RLE 66; *LC2* 553). The author in question is of course none other than Henry Morton Stanley, whose "Ujiji expedition" resulted in the infamous rescue of David Livingstone – *and* in the era's most powerful icon of a redemptively energetic style of muscular Anglo-Saxon masculinity. Stanley's succinct text of self-promotion, which gives resonant expression to the full range of ethnographic preoccupations with racial destiny, might usefully be called the signature of whiteness and its cultural desires and designs. Engraving his name and mission with no-nonsense hubris on the face of Persepolis's stone, the traveler nicknamed "Stonecrusher" and "Smasher of Rocks" by African tribesmen leaves his calling card, staking claim to the spoils of vanished empire in the name of literary journalism, manly adventure, and the culture-building "genius" of the Anglo-Saxon race (Bradford and Blume, 22–3).

Read against other moments of scrutiny in the excursion mode, James's account of the heroic traveler *par excellence* is striking in the faithfulness with which it replicates these *données*. Stanley behaves here not as a monitory figure for the excesses of the "mercantile" mind or the populist literary "entertainment" it promotes so much as a model for enterprising and energetic race renewal. Attacking the literal face of cultural "extinction" and decline right "between the eyes," posed heroically against the "ruined cities" of "our" civilizational "initiation," Stanley is allowed, if cursorily, to stand for an energy of defense against the historically resonant threat of cultural – and biocultural – loss and decline (RLE 65–6; *LC2* 553).

Yet there is also a sense in which Stanley stands in for James himself, not in the guise of "enquiring reader," but as author in the mode of excursion. Leaving his signature on behalf of the *Herald*, which underwrote his rescue expedition in the interests of boosting its mass market appeal, Stanley undertakes a populist enterprise of nation-building that vigorously exploits the ethnographic idiom and its figural resources. A virtual icon of tough-minded boot-strapping, he was enthusiastically claimed as a representative "ra-cial" or national figure by both British and American audiences well schooled in nation-building plots of adventure and affirma-tion. Although he became a naturalized U.S. citizen, even request-ing in a moment of grave illness during an African expedition that he be allowed to "die under the American flag," it was early "ascer-tained" by canny news scouts that Stanley was of Welsh extraction. Having escaped a workhouse school in Britain with ingenuity adver-tised as Dickensian, he pursued his destiny with an energy irresist-ible to American readers in the guise of the Algeresque: after work-ing passage on a ship from Liverpool to New Orleans, he fought for the Confederate Army, was taken prisoner under General John-ston, escaped the Federal camp by swimming a surging river and made his way back to England, only to return to the States to fight on behalf of the Union. Opportunistic, bent on indulging and pro-moting his own ethos of "orde[r]" and adventure rather than "exter-minating the slave trade" or promoting social good, Stanley em-bodies manliness as a paradigm of racial romance, a myth of the (alternatively British and American) "Anglo-Saxon spirit" liberated from genteel norms, free to declare its fitness in the conquest of exotic races and climes (Kingston and Low, 389, 384, 402, 477).

For James, forging a cultural politics in and against modes of national character, manliness, and "refinement," the allure and dan-gers of this romance might be equally powerful (*Letters* 1:300).[17] Although many of his essays of excursion exploit the ethnographic idiom so as to forestall the designs of white manliness, his reading of Stanley accedes to that plot – or rather, it accedes to the fanta-sized possibility Stanley figures, of exploiting the mobility of race and nation as resources for distinctive acts of culture-building. James's invocation of the great white hunter taking the bull of Persepolis, and the project of cultural acquisition, by the horns, is at once identificatory and combative: if Stanley enacts a strenuous, self-affirming ethos of whiteness that James's internationalist per-formances seek to challenge, he nonetheless successfully capitalizes on the mobility of his own origins and of whiteness as a cultural project to forge a signature mode of cultural production. James's own performances in the mode of excursion will increasingly attempt an analogous feat, mobilizing the ethnographic theater of race as a resource and a site for the making of a differently Anglo-American style of self-representation and response.

Presuming Africa: Manliness, Heroic Travel, and the Signature of Whiteness

While James's off-handed citation of Stanley's calling card reflects burgeoning anxieties about racial competition and survival, it also constitutes an introduction to a series of his own reviews attending to Africa as cultural theater, published in the *Nation* between 1875 and 1877. The fraught mythology of the Dark Continent would seem a far distance from James's politely ironic essays on the art of travel. But that rich text affords James a focused opportunity to mimic broadly ethnographic gestures of racial discipline and liberation. Engaging the conflicted designs of whiteness on Africa, he experiments with contextually "Anglo-Saxon," American, and Anglo-American styles of response, and with an awareness of their performative force within the culture of genteel and nation-building excursion.

This larger interest is on view even in James's relatively perfunctory "notices," including a review of *Four Thousand Miles of African Travel: A Personal Record of a Journey Up the Nile* (1875). Written by Alvan Southworth, Secretary of the American Geographical Society, the memoir chronicles his mission to sail up that primal river "in a magnificent dahabeah," trek across the Nubian desert to "ascertain Sir Samuel Baker's fate and to look at the country with liberal eyes" (FTM 361; *LC*2 600–1). By way of beginning, James gives an account of the germ of Southworth's trip that might serve to represent his own point of psychic and rhetorical departure: "One day," James writes, "as the author of this volume was indulging in a reverie in the vestibule of the Grand Hotel in Paris, he was tapped on the shoulder by a friend and invited to stroll down the Boulevard." Engaged in that leisurely activity, the "two gentlemen 'met acquaintance after acquaintance, bowing and passing on.' At last they were stopped by a 'portly man' who had been in Egypt, and who talked about that country with such gusto that they all grew hungry." Over a well-drawn bottle of "Chambertin," in the elegant comfort of "Bignon's," the author finds himself seduced by his own "desir[e] to see Egypt"; he allows himself accordingly to be " 'directed toward the East' " (FTM 361; *LC*2 600–1).

James's reconstruction of the germ of Southworth's adventure reads like a revised version of the plot of his then-current novel, *The American*, whose typologically American principal likewise re-

sides at the "Grand Hotel," strolls down the Boulevard des Capu-
cines, and finds himself – in "reverie" at least – "think[ing] of the
far East," in the indulgence of "great ideas" of conquest and self-
development (*American* 51, 115, 59). The confluence of the two
plots is hardly accidental, given the entanglement of these disparate texts with evolving norms of Anglo-American racial thinking.
Both "records" suggest the appeal of contact with the primitive, in
the waking dream of bourgeois culture, as a theater of self-
affirmation, affording possibilities for the expression of hungers
and "desires" only dreamed of in the relative freedom of Paris. The
arena of Africa, of the "East," holds open possibilities for the ultimate "indulg[ence]" of the *flâneur*'s "hung[er]," not for *charcuterie*
and Chambertin, but for increasingly transgressive forms of racial
contact, sensation, and release.

James's review, albeit cursory, unwittingly opens a glimpse onto
these kinds of "reverie." He notes as "rather odd" certain peculiari-
ties of "Mr. Southworth's style," including the latter's vision of
Egypt as "a 'hermaphrodite land, half savage, half civilized' " (FTM
361; *LC2* 600). He also describes the author's failed attempt to
convince a "Turkish nobleman," "to whom he made a 'serious
proposition,' " to "conduct him to Mecca in disguise" (FTM 361;
LC2 601). Apropos of the "slave-traffic" and its "helpless . . . human factors," James narrates the author's exploits at "Khartum,"
where, "wishing to investigate the mysteries of the slave-trade, he
pretended to desire to purchase a small thirteen-year-old Abyssin-
ian." The latter " 'was covered,' he says, 'with a single loose garment
[and] directed to denude herself of this; but I instantly interposed,
not wishing to allow even a traveller's curiosity to insult the child's
purity of person.' " James's anecdotes seem at least partially calculated to suggest the mapping of Africa as an arena in which the
Anglo-Saxon "traveller's curiosity" of racial erotics can be indulged
at will. "Pretending to desire," in the "disguise" of the racial other
he observes, the righteous explorer can covertly stage his own fantasies of foray across apparently inexorable boundaries of gender
and race, embracing the "savage" and "hermaphrodite" as both the
expression of a racialized id and liberation from its norms of purity
and restraint (FTM 361; *LC2* 601–2).[18]

Hand in glove with such fantasies of transgression, which both
shore up and erode notions of the racial virtues of the Anglo-
Saxon, go equally adventitious narratives of manly restraint. *Across
Africa*, the record of Captain Verney Lovett Cameron's exploits as
"the first European who had ever succeeded in crossing tropical
Africa from east to west," records the obverse of Southworth's se-

ductive *flânerie* (AA 209; *LC2* 820). Booked by James as "the record of a really heroic achievement," Cameron's account might more accurately be called a strenuous defense of whiteness as a form of heroic discipline. In a neat counterpoint to Southworth, Cameron travels under the auspices of the English Geographical Society, with the specific mission of coming to the aid of Livingstone "for the further prosecution of his researches." Before achieving that end Cameron has first to undergo what James calls "a journey fertile in miseries" and in contact with the "squalid" realities of the " 'black continent.' " With a certain relish, James rehearses the innumerable hardships of this strenuous form of travel-cum-self-denial: "The people, apparently, are detestable – filthy, stingy, mercenary, false, cruel, and devoted to making every step of advance impossible to you; the climate is in the highest degree baleful, and the 'sport' . . . makes no great figure." Even the vaunted "charms" of the African landscape are rendered irrelevant by "the nature of African travel" and the forms of contact it imposes; "The charms of a good beef-steak," James concludes, "are generally more striking" (AA 209–10; *LC2* 821–2).

Heightening "the perpetual friction which the African traveller apparently has to undergo" are "hired blacks" habitually "deserting and leaving him in the lurch, stealing, getting into trouble, and multiplying infinitely his difficulties," not to mention "the thousand miseries of camping for upwards of two years among savages of great personal foulness" and "revolting" habits (AA 210; *LC2* 822–3). But as even this brief narrative suggests, the rewards of such strenuous "friction," for the "really heroic" character, are a reaffirmation of the vitality of whiteness itself in the face of the "squalid," "foul" character of the primitive it manfully resists. Although Cameron enjoys "few adventures of the classic sort" – escaping ambush by natives' arrows, watching "a leopard tumble out of a tree with a monkey in his clutches" – he reaches Kawele, "near Ujiji," safely, where he takes "possession of Dr. Livingstone's papers" and thereby preserves the testimony of Anglo-America's missionary project for all posterity. His text may well deploy "no great literary art," but, James notes, it nonetheless sustains "a simple manliness and veracity which secure the sympathy and admiration of the reader" (AA 210; *LC2* 825). In ongoing contact with the "miseries" and "iniquities" of "tropical Africa," the "detestable," "filthy" practices of its "savag[e]" peoples, Cameron safeguards the ideological " 'enterprise' " of Anglo-America: he confirms, by enacting, an authentic, incorruptible "manliness," whiteness in its most unadulterated form (AA 209–10; *LC2* 821, 825).

These brief and anonymous essays usefully sketch what numerous readers of the colonial condition have identified as the bivalent role of Africa in the theater of racial excursion. On the one hand, the Dark Continent maps as a space of liberatory dreamwork or "reverie" in which transgressions of the stultifying norms of genteel masculinity can be staged, "invited," "directed" under the sign of indeterminacy. On the other, it is constituted as an arena of trial in which these very inducements can be manfully resisted by a "heroic" racial apparatus that shores up unstable distinctions between whiteness and blackness, manliness and effeminacy, progressive and degraded races. In their constructions and reconstructions of Africa and Africans, Anglo-American standard-bearers stage a wide range of responses to the demands of modernity, from anxieties of racial collapse in the face of increasing competition and social mobility to the pleasures of identification with a fantasized primal authenticity.

James's reviews not only suggest the performative character of Anglo-Saxon "nature" as staged in the culture of excursion; they begin to exploit that performativity in gestures consequential for his more canonical, literary, and conspicuously European travel writing. In taking up *The Last Journals of David Livingstone in Central Africa, from 1866 to his Death, Continued by a Narrative of his Last Moments and Sufferings* (at best a somewhat unlikely subject for his review), James avails himself of a signal opportunity to mobilize the instability of whiteness as a resource for defining a distinctive style – intentionally Anglo-American, "cosmopolite," and modernist – of culture-building. Stanley himself describes Livingstone's journals as a book "no boy should be without," and it is as such, as a virtual primer of white manhood, that James ultimately addresses the text (Stanley, cited in Torgovnick, 26). Extoling the "energy" and "genius" of the "heroic" mode, James nonetheless reveals in various foreshortened local gestures an awareness of the possibilities for alternative performances of race and nation opened by the "sentimentalism" of its race thinking (*LC2* 1141, 1143–4).[19]

Arguably, the very brevity of James's review serves a certain purpose in this regard, pointing up the racial logic of excess in renderings of Africa and in Anglo-America's missionary efforts to master it. He begins by pressing the intractability not of the African jungle but of the body of evidence offered as the white man's "record" of its conquest: "in the absence of available writing material, Dr. Livingstone was at times reduced to the most awkward devices – such as scrawling with extemporized ink on old scraps of English newspapers," producing a "ponderous volume" difficult to "decipher" (LJ 175; *LC2* 1141). Livingstone's editor, Horace Waller, suggests at greater length both the excess of Livingstone's text and its inadvertent testimony to the process by which the body of Africa becomes an arena for the forging of whiteness. Not only does Livingstone's manuscript intersperse "lunar observations, the names of rivers, and the heights of hills" with "map routes of the march, botanical notes, . . . carefully made drawings," "calculations, private memoranda, words intended for vocabularies, and extracts from books"; it includes "two or three tsetse flies pressed between the leaves" along with "some bees, some leaves, and moths" (Waller, 3–4, 329–30). In a critical salvo, James neatly identifies the resulting master text with the unregenerate continent it aspires to convert: "As the work stands," he comments, "it bears no small analogy to the pathless forest, intersected with large districts of 'sponge,' through which Livingstone himself had often to pursue his own uncertain way" (LJ 175; *LC2* 1141).

Professing formalist dismay at the baggy monstrosity of a life's work delivered "*verbatim*" from the author's "formidable" notes, James's figure also defends against what he calls "an extreme veneration for the writer's memory," a mythology of "character" that shapes "the doctrinal side" of African exploration (LJ 175–6; *LC2* 1141–2, 1143). The very editor who has been piously derelict in "his duties" opens the volume with telling claims in this regard. Livingstone, Waller writes, is "not only . . . the first to set foot on the shores of vast inland seas" but the genius "who, with the simple appliances of his bodily stature for a sounding-pole and his stalwart stride for a measuring-tape, lays down new rivers by the hundred" (Waller, 6). In taking the measure of Africa, "laying down" Africa as text, the white man takes the measure of his own racial fitness. Livingstone, then, not only maps but maps onto Africa, embodying the heroism of the white man "alone, . . . with no adequate means of self-protection, practising no deception; everywhere appearing in his true character" (Chambliss, 44).

James's interest in probing the relation between Africa as material text and the cultural body of whiteness is increasingly evident in certain managed absences or lapses in the essay. Most striking are his renderings of the iconic moments in the Livingstone mythology, including the climactic moment of Stanley's swashbuckling rescue:

At Ujiji, to which place he made his way back laboriously, in a state of great destitution and exhaustion, [Livingstone] met Mr. Stanley. This episode figures very briefly in his journals, though it was evidently a very welcome one. Naturally, it completely re-equipped him, and the reader really feels a kind of personal relief when he perceives that the exhausted old man obtained some more quinine. (LJ 176; *LC2* 1145)

James's litotes displaces the heroizing mode of the already infamous opening gambit: "Dr. Livingstone, I presume?"[20] His narrative transfigures the triumph of whiteness in darkest Africa as a cautionary tale of racial "exhaustion"; Stanley's swashbuckling enterprise of relief is displaced by the polite "personal relief" of the charitable reader, himself "pain[ed]" by "the very fanaticism" of Livingstone's missionary "enterprise" and the forms of racial theater it promotes (LJ 176; *LC2* 1145).

A similarly deflationary motive appears to govern James's account of Livingstone's death during a difficult trek back to Lake Bangweolo:

> His health fails rapidly; he makes great marches in spite of it, and only gives up the attempt to advance when his hand is too weak to trace the entries in his diary. The story of his death is compiled very successfully from the statements of those two faithful servants who made their weary pilgrimage back to Zanzibar with his remains. They found him on his knees in the attitude of prayer, beside his bed, with life extinct. This was extremely characteristic. (LJ 176; *LC2* 1145)

James's succinct rephrasing of the hagiography, in which "great marches" and "faithful servants" give way to "life extinct," resituates Livingstone's missionary labor in the ideological climate of post-evolutionary race thinking. It thereby forestalls the motives of Waller's representation of the event, which would make copious appearances in widely varied popular texts celebrating the culture of empire. This latter version gives great scope to what James gingerly calls the " 'sentimentalism' " of Livingstone's relations to "his negroes" (LJ 176; *LC2* 1144). The canonical Livingstone, even in death, embodies "the perseverance, doggedness and tenacity" – "native" to "his race" – that "characterize the Anglo-Saxon spirit" (Kingston and Low, 402). Serving in his rightful and destined role as enlightening master, Livingstone effects community, hierarchy, and all the properly sober virtues of submission among "Ethiopia's dusky children":

> Early on the morning of May 1, a[n African] lad came to Susi [Livingstone's personal bearer] and called him to 'Bwana,' for 'I don't know if he is alive!' Susi, alarmed, ran to fetch the rest. Six men entered the hut, and found their brave leader kneel-

ing by his bed – his body stretched forward, his hands under the pillow. He was dead!

Far away from home and friends, in the heart of the inhospitable African continent, David Livingstone ended his noble life in a manner befitting its course. (Kingston and Low, 410)[21]

James conspicuously ends his review with a salute to rather more impersonal virtues: Livingstone's "unshrinking pluck," his "singleness of purpose and simplicity," his "faculty of universal observation and of what we may call geographical constructiveness" (LJ 176; LC2 1145). Such abstracted praise dovetails with other salient lapses in recording a local resistance to the "romance" of missionary "manliness" (Chambliss, 299, 6). Among his criticisms of the editorial piety that has reproduced "every line" of Livingstone's diaries and memoranda looms the question of propriety or tact in "some omissions Mr. Waller might very safely have made." In particular, James adverts to "religious reflections and ejaculations intended solely for" the "use" of Livingstone himself, "an ardently sincere missionary . . . doing his work with the eye of God constantly upon him." In the context of this vocation, James argues, "it seems a rather cruel violation of privacy to shovel [Livingstone's] sacred sentences, written in the intensest solitude, into the capacious lap of the public, in common with all sorts of baser matter" (LJ 175; LC2 1141–2).

Oddly enough, however, James himself opens a direct view in the following paragraph onto Livingstone's private "ejaculations," his " 'waking dreams' " of "discovering some monumental relics" of the Ethiopian city of Moses: " 'if anything does remain, I pray to be guided thereto . . . if I could bring to light anything to confirm the Sacred Oracles, I would not grudge one whit all the labor expended' " (LJ 175; LC2 1143). Such "private" meditations interpenetrate and frame every daring act of "geographical constructiveness," from the shores of Lake Bangweolo to the coast of Zanzibar. In general, Livingstone's texts of Christian "manliness, love for men, and zeal for Christ" (Chambliss, 6) are far less "ardently sincere" or embarrassingly pious than James's comments lead us to expect. In a typical birthday entry, Livingstone writes: "Almighty Father, forgive the sins of the past year for thy Son's sake. Help me to be more profitable during this year" (Livingstone, 216). In another birthday prayer to "My Jesus, my King, my life, my all," he asks to be allowed to "finish my task," to be "favor[ed]" to "discover the ancient fountains of Herodotus; and if there is anything in the

under-ground excavations to confirm the precious old documents . . . , the Scriptures of truth" (Livingstone, 414, 417). Meditating elsewhere on "the atonement of Christ," Livingstone celebrates the "everlasting love" and "mercy" of his divinity, who
"works by smiles if possible, if not by frowns," and concludes that
"pain is only a means of enforcing love" (Livingstone, 453–4).

The relative conformity and predictability of these pietistic meditations, along with James's inconsistency in dismissing and then
citing them, raises questions about both the nature of his embarrassment and the logic of the "ejaculations" to which it pertains. Arguably, James's superfine delicacy mimes the Gordian entanglement
of missionary culture with unbridled fantasies of "profitab[ility]"
and "enforc[ed] love" – the "waking dreams" of the burdened
white man – sustained in the erotic and psychic theater of Africa.
James, in other words, is not protesting a dangerous category confusion of genuine piety with "baser matter," but voicing skepticism
about "the energy" of missionary "character" and the cultural performances it endorses (LJ 175; LC2 1141–2). His figures counter
the ethos of Anglo-Saxon manliness with the posture of embarrassment: the very text of unimpeachable imperial piety becomes
"ejaculat[ory]"; the narrative evidence of geography, ethnology, zoology, and personal contact with the body of Africa, "baser matter,"
"shovel[ed] . . . into the capacious lap" of a "public" hungry for
"sensation" and racial self-confirmation (LJ 175; LC2 1142).

Locally, then, James can be said to turn against itself the vocabulary of what one historian of Darwinian culture has called the " 'too
offensive for description' school of ethnography," which exults in
the shock value of primitivism exposed, of cultures with "manners,
beastly; religion, none" (Stocking, 153). Livingstone's journals
themselves abound in such prurient piety in the guise of ethnographic observation. He comments at length, for instance, on the
tattoos of the Rovuma women, "lovely belles who displayed their
proportions with shameless freedom." In his professional judgement, the "adorn[ments]" of the "hips displayed uncommon skill,
and were surpassed only by the eccentricities which were traced
along those posterior convexities which our refined conventionality
blushes to denominate – but African belles are not ashamed of
their buttocks" (Livingstone, 431–2). As one of his numerous biog-
raphers suggests, the record of Livingstone's missionary project
allows the reader to indulge a titillating interest in the savage instinct for "blood and cruelty" vented literally "under the shadow of
Christian mission stations" (Chambliss, 34). Everywhere in the
theater of Africa, Anglo-Saxon culture-building takes a certain

erotic charge in, and of, "licentious sensualities and fearful atrocities, which" it "dare not record" (Stocking, 90). Locally, James takes
up the convention of the unspeakable as a gesture of racial self-
affirmation and makes it speak for its own limits.

This logic of speaking the unspeakable from within accounts for
another, less evident lapse in James's performance. From the "baser
matter" contained in the "ponderous volume" in question, he sin-
gles out for critique "the rather sensational and not particularly
valuable illustrations with which the volume is adorned" (LJ 175;
LC2 1142). The images in question, etchings prepared by one "Dr.
Kirk," document the ethnographic and ideological imperatives of
Livingstone's ongoing mission with a certain unintended thorough-
ness. For the most part they predictably replicate the iconography
of excursion: bands of submissive villagers paying homage to their
white visitors; ritual hunting, dancing, and greeting postures; nu-
bile and bare-breasted female models displaying endlessly fascinat-
ing variations in ornamentation – tattoos, liprings, teeth filings and
hairstyles. Not indeed particularly valuable, they represent Africa
with such indifferent technical merit as to confirm their production
en masse in London rather than *in situ*. In fact, many of these illustrations could easily have been found accompanying a wide range of
texts on African travel, so generic is their ostensibly precise ethnographic substance. Kirk does detail numerous images of the "terrible scenes of man's inhumanity to man" (Livingstone, 387) enacted
along the routes of the slave trade, including abandoned slaves tied
to trees, stabbed, and left to die as well as smoking villages and
scenes of intertribal massacre. But these images are for the most
part curiously antiseptic, given the intensity of Livingstone's pious
abolitionary fervor, his vaunted "sympathy" as the racial conscience
of "the white man" (Livingstone, 413; Figure 1.1).[22] *Prima facie*,
James's deliberately moralized language, which charges the text's
images with the "base[ness]" of sensationalism, would appear inappropriate to the objects in question.

Given his obvious familiarity with the iconographic logic of Africa in the texts of "other great African travellers – Speke, Grant,
Burton and Baker" (LJ 176; LC2 1143), his claim merits speculation. Among the travelers with whose texts James is familiar, Speke
unself-consciously represents his "pleasure" in the "prospect" of
Africa as the sensation of "those more intense and exciting emotions . . . called up" in view of "commercial and geographical" conquests to be made (Kingston and Low, 186). Samuel Baker celebrates the "wonderful progress" visited on the African continent by
the "extraordinary" energy of "individual Englishmen," asserting

Figure 1.1 The Massacre of the Manyuema Women at Nyañgwe: *The Last Journals of David Livingstone in Central Africa*, 1875. Source: University of Virginia, Alderman Library.

that the diffusion of Anglo-Saxon modes of "security" and control has made the white visitor "safer in the deserts of Nubia than in Hyde Park after dark" (Kingston and Low, 365). Samuel Verner, a later and more self-consciously entrepreneurial trafficker in Africa, likewise extols "[t]he expanding genius of the Caucasian race" and the distinctly American style of progress and pleasure that is its "invincible" racial "heritage." Testimony to that genius, in his reading of racial virility, is the fact that "a tourist can shoot an elephant in mid-Africa and carry it's [sic] tusk to the snows of Switzerland in less than a week's time" (Verner, 3).

Arguably it is this nation-building version of manly pleasure – expressed in the dictum that "Progress is the law, the instinct, the necessity of the Caucasian mind" (Van Evrie, 74) – rather than the erotic exploitation of African bodies, that strikes James as "rather sensational." Far from protesting the impropriety of the text's images of blackness, the scandal of nude and comely African women circulating among Livingstone's polite readership (and for that matter his own), James can only logically be taken to voice unease with the version of whiteness the *Journal*'s illustrations promote. Kirk's most vivid images bespeak not the evils of slavery so much as the violently primitive condition of the darker races, supplicating for schooling in the white man's progressive "genius," characterological manliness and moral discipline. Along with the supremacy of the Anglo-Saxon, Kirk's etchings confirm the progressive destiny of white "enterprise," booked not merely to countermand "[t]he evils which we have seen" in remotest Africa but to direct the enormous "energy" of racial manliness into acts of imperial heroism worthy of "mighty hunters," "the true Nimrod[s]" of their age (Livingstone, 94, 333). Branding this genre of racial pieties "sensational," James reads the primitive as the grounds for a narrative of whiteness whose "progressive" character he will later – as in his interventions in the discourse of literary realism – more confidently appropriate and revise.

A final lapse in James's reading sums up the import of his skepticism about forms of filiation and character staged in the theater of Africa. In his penultimate paragraph James gives voice to Livingstone's abolitionary fervor: "To the abominations of slavery . . . , Dr. Livingstone alludes frequently and in terms of deep disgust; they haunt him, he declares, by day and by night; they are the 'open sore' of the land, crying aloud to heaven to be healed" (LJ 176; *LC2* 1144–5). Ministering to the "enslaved Manyuema," James notes, Livingstone observes two natural phenomena as yet undiscovered by the white man: the "strange disease" of "literal broken-heartedness," and "the soko, a large monkey, with much analogy with the gorilla." This animal, in James's recounting, is of "amiable disposition"; it even, "from Dr. Livingstone's account, seems painfully human."

In fact, the good doctor's account suggests quite the reverse. In one of his most extensive passages devoted to natural history Livingstone asserts: "the soko is an ungainly beast. The most sentimental young lady would not call him a 'dear,' but a bandy-legged, potbellied, low-looking villain, without a particle of the gentlemen in him." Although the human "natives" of Manyuema are "well made, lithe and comely to behold," the soko "would do well to stand for a picture of the devil" (Livingstone, 323). Contemporaneous readers of both popular and scientific ethnographic documents would immediately have recognized Livingstone's easy displacement from African native to the "type" – fervently adverted to during the 1870s as the Irish "problem" came to a head in urban America and as Charles Parnell assumed leadership of the Home Rule movement – of the bestial Irishman; some would have shared the sentiment voiced by a professor of ethnography then touring the United States, offering the advice that America "might solve our racial problems if every Irishman killed a Negro and got hanged for it" (Gould, 27).[23]

But the virtual diatribe of natural history fails to end here. Livingstone continues over two pages of text, in a remarkable figure of anthropomorphosis that powerfully exposes the anxieties vested in his missionary race work: "He takes away my appetite by his disgusting bestiality of appearance. His light-yellow face shows off his ugly whiskers and faint apology for a beard; the forehead, villainously low, with high ears, is well in the background of the great dog-mouth; the teeth are slightly human, but the canines show the beast by their large development." From the "yellow" "flesh" of the soko's feet, to the tips of its nimble fingers, with its "villainously low" forehead and prognathous jaw, the beardless soko "stand[s] for" the degraded body and race character of miscegenous union: although "represented by some to be extremely knowing," successful at "stalking men and women while at their work, kidnaping children and running up trees with them," the soko's essential quality is a "low cunning" and not a "formidable" courage or intelligence (Livingstone, 323–4).

If Livingstone's text gives voice to anxieties of racial purity in a narrative of species difference, James's review oddly mimes the gesture of displacement. Its narrative movement from the "droop-[ing] and pin[ing]" Manyuema, suffering the "strange disease" of brutally enforced alienation, to the "large monkey" native to the shores of Lake Tanganyika, unwittingly suggests the protocol and governing narrative of ethnographic research, designed to provide objective data for confirming the great chain of being that whiteness superintends. More to the point, however, is James's succinct reformulation of Livingstone's virtual outburst; the "villainously low" and degraded creature, a present link between whiteness and blackness previously unseen by Western eyes, becomes "painfully human" (LJ 176; LC2 1144–5). Why, we might ask, does the soko make its appearance in James's essay at all? One is tempted to read the reference as a deliberate reversion on James's part to a presciently Darwinian Manyuema proverb that Livingstone himself cites and dismisses: "Soko is a man," the saying goes, "and nothing bad in him" (Livingstone, 325). Although ultimately noncommittal, James's local critique-by-imitation of Livingstone's reading of the soko and its "character" registers a heightened awareness of the racial politics of excursion – and of the possibilities of exploiting "the doctrinal side" of Anglo-American ethnography to underwrite his own performances as literary internationalist.

These possibilities receive most productive expression not in James's responses to such narrowly ethnographic texts as Livingstone's or Cameron's, but in the elegantly aestheticized body of work on a nearer "Eastern" theater of ethnographic desire and discontent. Between 1869 and 1882, during the period of his most rewarding negotiations of internationalist cultural politics, James published an important series of essays on Italy, and in particular on Venice, that "Siren of the South" whose carnivalesque mysteries banish "the rhythm of the Connecticut clock" and the "wear[iness]" of Yankee sobriety (IH 112, 138, 281–2). Adopting orientalist fantasies of liberation through contact with Eastern "mystery and romance," James refines what will become his signature ethos of refusal, a style of response forged in shifting filiations with the "queer" text of the asiatic other (Curzon, 10; IH 13). Like James's writings on Africa, these essays appropriate powerful icons – here genteel rather than popular – of racialized manliness, cultural acquisition, and control. For the pious heroism of a Livingstone and the aggressive Anglo-Saxon genius of a Stanley, they substitute the culture-building figure of John Ruskin, whose readings of Italy-as-orient James will deliberately frame and reject as performances of cultural mastery. In rehearsing Ruskin's orientalizing topoi – the allure of the masquerade, the erotics of veiling, the seduction of impenetrable mystery – James revises their performative force so as to strike postures of overmastery, a resistance to alternatively

"New England," genteel, and "Anglo-Saxon" norms of race and nation (*IH* 282, 77) on which his hallmark bids for aesthetic "freedom" will crucially depend.

"Langour Perpetual": Oriental Italy and the Anglo-American Unmanned

Between 1877 and 1895, a period roughly spanned in James's career by *Daisy Miller* and the failure of *Guy Domville* on the London stage, George Curzon, Marquess of Keddleston, made two journeys around the globe and numerous visits in the precincts of a fantasized "East." When not on safari or excursion, Curzon served as Conservative MP for Southport; he later became Britain's Indian Viceroy and Foreign Secretary as well as President of the Royal Geographic Society, in which capacity he delivered ethnographic lectures that drew attendance by Edward VII. His "passion for travel under the most primitive, difficult and dangerous circumstances" can be characterized as a direct response to the decidedly racialized propriety whose colonial agent he so successfully became; ironically, only the liberating *frisson* of immersion in the oriental can erase "the brand of respectable mediocrity" with which he feels himself, as agent of orientalist policies, to be hopelessly "stamped" (King, xii). Curzon's account of his adventures evidences a purer version of Anglo-Saxon masculinity – he has "shot *Ovis Poli* on the Pamirs" and "nearly foundered in a typhoon off the coast of Annam," been "reported as murdered in Afghanistan" and "arrested as a spy in Khorasan" (Curzon, 5) – but it also exults in the glories of passing as an asiatic. Even as he "form[s] an opinion on the Eastern responsibilities and destinies" of the empire, Curzon roams a porous boundary between the disciplinary authority of the English mission and the miming of an "unblemished Orientalism" from Angkor Wat to the Taj Mahal (Curzon, 3, 15).

For American fellow travelers in the psychic precincts of orientalism, the possibilities for liberation – specifically, for freedom from the laws of the bourgeois fathers – are even more pointed, because less obviously central to the work of producing national institutions and character.[24] In his account of orientalism as the "psychic basis" of a *fin-de-siècle* antimodernism that becomes a virtual "ruling class cultural hegemony," Jackson Lears considers the exemplary career of William Sturgis Bigelow, whose ambivalent relations to the strenuous manliness embodied in paternal authority took the doubly marginalized form of a rarefied, high cultural orientalism. Embracing esoteric Buddhism through apprenticeship to an *Ajari*, a teacher, of the Mikkyo sect in Japan, Bigelow actively sought liberation – "the peace of limitless consciousness unified with limitless will," or "NIRVANA"[25] – from the demands of competitive individualism. Although ultimately appointed a lecturer at Harvard and recognized as a scholarly authority on Buddhism, Bigelow in Lears's reading never achieved either a renewed allegiance to high bourgeois conventions of American manhood or a satisfactory renunciation of its ideals. After his death, half of his ashes were placed in the family cemetery in Mt. Auburn; the rest were buried in the Homoyoin temple on the shores of Lake Biwa (Lears, 225–34).

To consider James's deliberately aestheticized essays on Italy in this broader Anglo-American context – remembering, for example, that he set sail for Europe in May of 1872 on a Cunarder named the *Algeria* – is to suggest their continuity with orientalism as a performative structure of racial affirmation and nation-building. But it is also to note the self-consciousness with which James exceeds it. While professional orientalists like Bigelow and Curzon remain deeply ambivalent about the forms of release they purchase through identification with the so-called feminine and occult races, James more deliberately reckons with the consequences of orientalism's oneiric logic of passivity and failed control. Writing to John LaFarge in September of 1869, during his first Eastern foray, he experiences Italy from the outset as the stage for a drama of cultural authority. Overwhelmed by "far more 'impressions' than I know what to do with," he fantasizes a local "companion to help . . . dispose of this troublesome baggage." If Venice "is quite the Venice of one's dreams," it "remains strangely the Venice of dreams, more than of any appreciable reality" (*Letters* 1:134). In this moment of first impressions, the East resists psychic penetration and the Anglo-Saxon traveler's habits of acquisition and control. Ruefully recognizing that he "shall never look at Italy" – "Venice, for instance" – "but from without," James privately recalls Ruskin's recommendation that "the traveller . . . frequent and linger in a certain glorious room at the Ducal Palace, where Paolo Veronese revels on the ceilings and Tintoret rages on the walls, because he 'nowhere else will enter so deeply into the heart of Venice.' " These visual objects will play a crucial role in James's ultimate redirection of Ruskin's cultural politics of immersion and penetration, whereby the strenuous manliness of the latter's orientalism, like Livingstone's pious heroism in Africa, underwrites James's rather more "queer" forms of racial identification and response. Initially, however, James can only admit that "I feel as if I might sit there forever (as I sat there a long time this morn-

ing) and only feel more and more my inexorable Yankeehood"
(*Letters* 1:137).

In James's published, urbanely crafted essays on Venice, this
kind of displacement becomes the hallmark project of the impressionist, relativist, internationalist observer, learning to negotiate his
"Americanness" and the resources of "European" art (Tanner,
160). On the threshold of Italy, poised to cross the virtual Rubicon
dividing modern Italian Switzerland from Italy's dream-world of
"colour and costume, romance and rapture," James describes the
experience of drifting on a "huge Anglo-Saxon wave," one of "five
thousand – fifty thousand – 'accommodated spectators'" (*IH* 94,
95). But unlike his "romantic" countrymen and the "medley of
Saxon" speakers clutching their Baedeker's and Cook's itineraries,
James actively courts a posture of passivity, "loafing" in the "immense new Hotel National and read[ing] the *New York Times* on a
blue satin divan" (*IH* 96, 98). Ironically adverting to his own "accumulated sensibility," this "almost professional cherisher of the
quaint" overturns the force of the "good American" and "the usual
Anglo-Saxon" character: "Mark how luxury unmans us! I was already demoralised" (*IH* 98, 100).

The point of James's orientalizing excursions is neither a form of
cultural hegemony through antitourism, as James Buzard has argued, nor an elitist diatribe against commodification, but precisely
this demoralization, an unmanning that puts in abeyance racialized
and nationalized norms of acquisition and control.[26] With repeated
forays in Italy and in the "curiosity-shop" of Venice – that "peep-
show and bazaar" of "peculiar conditions" – James appropriates
orientalist figures of desire and anxiety; he seeks thereby to redirect an ethos of Anglo-Saxon manliness writ as resistance to immersion in the realm of asiatic indolence, and as expropriation of Italian artifacts and history for the cultural education of an ascendant
Anglo-Saxon bourgeoisie. Beginning in earnest with his essays on
Italian subjects for the *Nation*, the *Atlantic Monthly*, and the *Galaxy* in
1873, James's records of his impressions exploit tensions within
these orientalist projects, imagining Italy as a site of racial masquerade, a locus for the trial of unconventional appetites in whose satisfaction the postures of genteel Anglo-American strenuosity can
ultimately be superseded. In the "irresponsible" accounts of the
"charmed *flâneu*[*r*]," Italy figures as a theater of the "insidious" and
"perfidious, fertile in pretexts," where the attitude of "langour perpetual" critiques and supplements the imperatives of Anglo-Saxon
manhood (*Letters* 2:285; *IH* 128, 32, 108).

James's international fiction, it bears recalling, often trades on less revaluative orientalist designs. From "The Last of the Valerii" (1874), which features an atavistic "young Latin" whose reversion to blood worship expresses an "ineffacab[le] . . . race-characteristi[c]" tracing "back through all the darkness of history" (*Tales* 2:260, 275, 272), to "The Impressions of a Cousin" (1883), with its oriental swindler, the "Caliph" and wandering Jew, his international tales of Eastern exchange treat the beguiling erotics of the oriental as sinister, endemic to uniquely American forms of agency, purity, and freedom.[27] Even in *The American*, the sensuous optimism and erotic liberation afforded by orientalist fantasies are shadowed by the dangers of racial crossing. Christopher Newman outpaces the genteel racism and insularity of Tom Tristram's Occidental Club, no less than his own "intensely Western story," in part by indulging liberatory fantasies that keep "the names of Eastern cities under my tongue: Damascus and Bagdad, Medina and Mecca" (*American* 52, 115); he "talk[s] about Rome and the Nile" and entertains the fantasy of letting loose "in the gondola or on a dromedary" (*American* 101, 58). But Newman's ambiguous self-transformation, from "great Western Barbarian" to something of a "languid Oriental" cosmopolite (*American* 68, 66), is itself melodramatically forestalled by the more dangerous resources of an orientalized Catholicism, which immures the spotless Mme de Cintré within "the blank walls of Eastern seraglios" in the Faubourg St. Germain, the Rue d'Enfer and the "Chinese penitentiary" of Fleurières, hopelessly subject to the brutal discipline of her "Grand Turk of a brother" (*American* 79, 346, 119). Alluring yet sinister, the erotics of veiling and disguise labor in this more ritual fantasy to confirm the nature of the white man's burden, as a cultural logic – a "national typ[e]" or "mould" – of strenuous renunciation, higher self-affirmation, and fair play (*American* 34).

In James's writings on Venice, however, orientalist figures serve a markedly different purpose, staging alternatives to such ethnographically determined gestures of resisted identification. On the site of its "cross-fire of influences," where "peculiar conditions" of "decadence" and "spectacle" overwhelm "the devouring American," the activity of looking itself becomes both "strenuous" and eroticized, transforming the American man of "woefully shrunken and *bourgeois*" mores into the "man of the world" (*IH* 201, 5, 49, 39, 44, 19). In particular, James revises the imperatives of post-Ruskinian modes of engagement with Italian visual artifacts, miming orientalist gestures of immersion in a racially typologized languor, passivity, and purposelessness so as to reconstruct forms of the Anglo-Saxon character. Unlike those of antimodernists and colonial agents, however, James's narratives of racial masquerade ulti-

mately labor not to discipline racial alterity or the ambivalence of
the orientalist, but to redirect discipline itself under the sign of the
aesthetic, through which gesture alternative styles of racial and
national affirmation can be tried.

James's orientalizing project culminates in his publication, as the
newly lionized author of the "real American" masterwork *The Portrait of a Lady*, of his most extensive Italian essay, "Venice," in the
Century of November 1882. Framed by texts representing American
genteel culture and the self-affirmational desires of its bourgeois
readership – that is, by a portrait of Florence Nightingale, and by
William Dean Howells's infamous "puff" essay, "Henry James,
Jr." – "Venice" can be seen to embrace a studied "peculiar[ity]" that
registers unease with the cultural framework in which it appears
(*IH* 5). Although Howells recommends James to the magazine's
polite readership as a writer of "finished workmanship in which
there is no loss of vigor," one who unites "vivid expression and
dispassionate analysis" (Howells 1882, 25–6), a different and far
less manly style of response governs James's own essay. Trading on
the tropes of orientalism, James employs the belatedness and excess
of Venetian pleasures as a mode of forestalling both Howells's literary propriety and a Ruskinian ethos, ultimately racial and nationalized, of renewed cultural vitality.

Adopting the style of languor and belatedness, James begins his
carefully plotted essay by confessing his own "impudence" in taking up the subject of Venice, about which "[t]here is notoriously
nothing more to be said . . . Every one has been there, and every
one has brought back a collection of photographs." Bathed in an
excess of "high-coloured" sentiment, the Grand Canal owns "as
little mystery" as "our local thoroughfare, and the name of St.
Mark is as familiar as the postman's ring" (*IH* 1). As he records his
own impressions, the theme of belatedness recurs: flaunting his
own failed desire "to be original" among "a herd of fellow-gazers,"
James admits that "There is nothing left to discover or describe,"
in a site where "originality of attitude is completely impossible"
(*IH* 5). But unlike the genteelly Anglo-Saxon visitors of William
Wetmore Story's *Roba di Roma*, who "carr[y] a Murray for information and a Byron for sentiment, and fin[d] out by them" the
appropriate postures of appreciation "at every step" (Story, 1:6–
7), James embraces this fate, and the freedom from such a culture
of "information" and "enlighten[ment]" it affords (*IH* 1). Undi-
rected in his "pleasure," the "sentimental tourist" can abjure
"strenuous thinking" in the embrace of mere "spectacle" and "superficial pastimes" (*IH* 3).

In fact, the apparent project of all James's Venetian excursions is a perverse redirection of "strenuous" energies in the apparent pursuit of "encage[ment]" rather than liberation (*IH* 5). He imagines himself, at least intermittently, not as a more liberated or responsible traveler than the "English and American" and European "barbarians" in "full possession," but as analogous to the "helpless captives" led by *valets-de-places* "through churches and galleries in dense irresponsible groups" (*IH* 7). James, however, unlike this "horde," capitalizes on the chance to "accommodate" himself to Venice's "peculiar conditions." Only by giving in to the latter and forming new "habits" of "an undesirable and unprofitable character," he suggests, will the visitor "feel the fulness" of Venetian charm. When "[y]ou are tired of your gondola (or think you are)"; when "you have walked several hundred times round" the enclosed space of the Piazza and "have begun to have a shipboard-feeling – to regard the Piazza as an enormous saloon and the Riva degli Schiavoni" as a tiny "promenade-deck"; when the Piazza "has resolved itself into a magnificent tread-mill" – then, the "peculiarity" of Venetian "conditions" begins to do its work: "You are obstructed and encaged; your desire for space is unsatisfied; you miss your usual exercise. You try to take a walk and you fail, and meantime, as I say, you have come to regard your gondola as a sort of magnified baby's cradle" (*IH* 5–6). Then, James notes, the self-respecting visitor will be tempted to "cal[l] for the bill," but must perversely "pay it and remain." Embracing the enclosure, the enforced belatedness and passivity, unique to Venice, the sentimental traveler inaugurates a "peculiar" form of voluntary bondage (*IH* 6–7).

In James's accounting, the rich reward of that state of reception is the pleasure of surrender to Venice's "happy accidents" and caprice. Coming "to personify itself, to become human and sentient and conscious of your affection," Venice instills a "desire to embrace it, to caress it, to possess it" that will "finally" be realized: "a soft sense of possession grows up and your visit becomes a perpetual love-affair" (*IH* 6–7). But if Venice plays the part of the veiled mysterious woman adept in the arts of desire, this "creature," who "varies" with "a thousand occasional graces" and an "always interesting" beauty, apparently belies the orientalist logic of "possession" altogether, enjoining on the spectator a passivity and openness to psychic penetration. "The only way" for the willingly "helpless captiv[e]" to "care for Venice as she deserves it" is to expose his own sensibility, to "give her a chance to touch [him] often – to linger and remain and return" (*IH* 4). By "living there from day to day," willing victim to her "high spirits or low," her "pale or red, grey or pink, cold or warm, fresh or wan" face, he "invite[s] her exquisite influence to sink into [his] spirit" (*IH* 4, 6).

Tellingly, the erotics of this fantasized bondage to Venice momentarily give way to the reactive voice of Anglo-Saxon refinement, in a sudden tone of bourgeois "disappoint[ment]." The "whole precinct of St. Mark's," James goes on to note, is seasonally full of "savage Germans" and other national types, as well as *valets-de-place* who "infest" the Piazza. As for the "ancient sanctuary" itself, its "condition . . . is surely a great scandal"; the activities of the "pedlars and commissioners" plying their "unclean" trade on "the threshold" of its "sacred dusk," a mark of the "dishonour" pervading the Venetian "bazaar" (*IH* 7–8). Here James's orientalist tropes distance him momentarily from the styles of response they more broadly enable. The "scandal" in question is neither – as James suggests in a feint of some length – the vulgarity of ongoing, "shock[ingly]" inept restorations to St. Mark's, nor the larger "lapses of taste" occasioned by the "march of industry in united Italy" (*IH* 8–9), but rather the implications of his own foray into the economy of cross-racial desire and identification. In effect, James's momentary outbreak of indignance against the vulgar and the "crude" ratifies the dislocating possibilities of his embrace of passivity and bondage as an "amorous" function: "rank[ing]" himself "among the trooping barbarians," he eludes the imperatives of Anglo-American manliness, sobriety, and self-"possession" (*IH* 10).

Reflexively scandalized by the vulgarities of the oriental bazaar and of the variously nationalized "barbarians" therein, James nonetheless explores the possibilities for self-invention afforded by the orientalizing gaze, provisionally liberated from the demands of racial and cultural mastery. In particular, his gestures of belatedness and self-"encagement" perform distancing from what he calls "the Ruskinian contagion" (*IH* 2), which denotes not only a narrower mode of moralized response to Italian visual objects but a strenuously active style of culture-building. Against Ruskin's hallmark icons of sincerity and spontaneity, James takes up postures of "irresponsibility" and failed "originality of attitude"; embracing "superficial pastimes" and the charms of surface alone, he forestalls the missionary fervor of Ruskin's activity as interpreter of Venice for the Anglo-Saxon imagination (*IH* 4–5). Elsewhere, in the more neutral psychic territory of Florence, James will stage direct confrontation with a Ruskinian aesthetic and with the forms of cultural affirmation it promotes.[28] In "Venice," however, the "ill-humorous" text of Ruskin occasions a stance – not unlike that afforded by Livingstone's piety in the theater of Africa – that capitalizes on the unstable racial logic of orientalism from within (*IH* 2).

On site, James takes up the Ruskinian offensive by remarking: "it is Mr. Ruskin who beyond any one helps us to enjoy" (*IH* 2). The absence of a grammatical object is suggestive, since alternative forms of enjoyment, pleasure, and self-consciousness are precisely at stake. Championing the value of a richly varied experience of Venetian alterity over a nostalgic horror of "the latest atrocities perpetrated" by vulgar restoration, James advises "one hour of the lagoon" as antidote for "a hundred pages of" Ruskin's "demoralised prose." Wielding Ruskin's own terms against him, James decries the "inconceivable want of form" in the text of an author who "has spent his life in laying down the principles of form and scolding people for departing from them." Even more tellingly, he suggests that the "contagion" and "ill" humor of *Stones of Venice* result from a fretful want of the very vitality and manliness privileged therein: the "queer late-coming prose" of the text is not only "demoralised" but "pitched in the nursery-key," "addressed to children," like the harangue "emanat[ing] from an angry governess." If Ruskin has "made her [Venice] his own," he has done so in spite of a "narrow theological spirit," a "moralism *à tout propos*," a set of "queer provincialities and pruderies" unlikely in a reader of such authentic passion (*IH* 2–3).

Undermining the Ruskinian mode of response and "pleasure" in figures asserting the "force" of liberal manliness, James perversely proceeds to displace and supplant Ruskin's provincial "queerness" with a more cosmopolitan queerness of his own. Ruskin "helps us to enjoy," the essay suggests, precisely by enabling "us" to be demoralised, freed from the "theological spirit" and pious "pruderies" inscribed in the Ruskinian mode of possession (*IH* 3). Taking his own measure against the imperial "genius" Ruskin exerts, James gives free play to the "peculiar conditions," the "queer incidents of a Venetian installation" (*IH* 5, 11). In place of the "queer provincialities" of Ruskin's "love disconcerted and abjured," James sets an icon of his own "amorous" and orientalizing invention: "When I hear, when I see, the magical name I have written above these pages, it is not of the great Square that I think," nor of "the wide mouth of the Grand Canal," nor "of the low lagoon," nor even of "the dark chambers of St. Mark's." Instead, the "fond spectator" sees "a narrow canal in the heart of the city," from the vantage point of a gondola "pass[ing] under a bridge" that has "an arch like a camel's back." Thereon a "girl" veiled beneath the "old shawl" wound around her head stands poised "against the sky as you float beneath" (*IH* 2, 10, 13). A walled garden, "out of which" protrudes "the long arm of a white June rose," and "a great shabby facade of Gothic windows and balconies" complete the langorous picture; "[i]t is very hot and still," with "a queer smell," the "whole" strangeness "enchanting" (*IH* 13). This "queer" identification with orientalized passivity and feminization, often taken by latter-day readers to stand for a more narrowly psychosexual politics, here affords James "peculiar" possibilities of "floating," not only beyond conventional gender divides but across boundaries of history, nation, and race.

Throughout the essay, in its more disciplinary modes of art historical criticism, the same performative motive can be said to prevail. Against the "strenuous" quality of Ruskinian observation, James adopts postures of response that deliberately "unma[n]." He capitalizes liberally on the vaunted inaccessibility of Venetian visual artifacts, orientalizing his aesthetic encounters so as to liberate himself from the demands of cultural acquisition, the dutiful study conducted by the bourgeois Anglo-American citizen of empires gone. Even as James registers *de rigeur* complaints about the conditions of observation in a city where "many a masterpiece lurks in the unaccommodating gloom of side-chapels and sacristies" and "[m]any a noble work is perched behind the dusty candles and muslin roses of a scantily-visited altar," he simultaneously indulges a certain ironic pleasure in the impossibility of going "behind" Venice, celebrating the fact that these venerated objects, "out of sight and ill-lighted" (*IH* 27), shelter "in a darkness that can never be explored" (*IH* 20–1). Like Venice herself, the city's most desirable objects remain tantalizingly veiled, inscrutable; their conditions of "approac[h]" make "a mockery of" the acquisitive traveler's "irritated wish":

> You stand at tip-toe on a three-legged stool, you climb a rickety ladder, you almost mount upon the shoulders of the *custode*. You do everything but see the picture. You see just enough to be sure it's beautiful. You catch a glimpse of a divine head, of a fig-tree against a mellow sky, but the rest is impenetrable mystery. (*IH* 20–1)

James's conspicuously vigorous attempts to "see" become a kind of charade, an overdetermined performance whose point is the demonstrated insufficiency of the manly style of response to Venice's impenetrable essence. The comic excess of this oft-repeated miming suggests James's investment in the failure of mastery, typi-

cally occasioned by the orientalized "mystery" of its object of desire. If the "position" of "the mightiest" of Venetian paintings,
"sacred" and profane, is "an inconceivable scandal," in the vernacular of bourgeois acquisition and control, James enacts through
their inaccessibility an awareness of the limits of that cultural design. "[A]pproaching the magnificent Cima da Conegliano in San
Giovanni in Bragora" – the site of Cima's *Baptism of Christ* (1492),
remarkable for its lyric iconography and luminous realism – the
viewer must "renounce all hope" of actually seeing the canvas,
which remains shrouded "[b]ehind the high altar" and darkened
by time; "bethinking yourself of the immaculate purity that shines
in the spirit of this master, you renounce [the painting] with chagrin and pain." But to attempt more aggressive visual acquisition is
eminently futile. Inevitably "[y]ou make the thing out" only "in
spots," and although "you see it has a fulness [sic] of perfection,"
"you turn away from it with a stiff neck" and unfulfilled desire (*IH*
21). This posture of overmastery focuses James's interest in racial
as well as cultural mastery; it comically literalizes such popular and
characteristic descriptions as Walter Besant's of the Anglo-Saxon
race: "We are . . . as we have always been, a masterful race," "a
stiff-necked, unyielding race," "a tenacious race . . . a people which
if it settles down anywhere, means to go on living as before and to
make other people live in the same way" (Besant, 130–1). Looking
in Venice, James embraces a posture of "encagement" that attacks
not the condition of Venetian artifacts but this strenuously racialized version of culture-building.

Nowhere is the pleasure of staging such failures of possession
more sensuously immediate than in the case of James's exemplary
Venetian, Tintoretto, whose theatrical and psychically complex
scenography demands a flexible posture of response. "It may be
said as a general thing," James writes, "that you never see the
Tintoret. You admire him, you adore him, you think him the greatest of painters, but in the great majority of cases your eyes fail to
deal with him" (*IH* 21). If "many of his works have turned" to literal
"blackness and are positively rotting in their frames," his whole
oeuvre exhibits the more challenging darkness of a "genius . . .
dense and difficult to breathe" (*IH* 21, 22). "At the Scuola di San
Rocco, where there are acres of him, there is scarcely anything at all
adequately visible save the immense 'Crucifixion' in the upper
story." Even this "huge composition," which contains "many pictures" in itself, strains to their limits the totalizing habits of the
bourgeois sight-seer; "it has not only a multitude of figures but a
wealth of episodes; and you pass from one of these to the other as if

you were 'doing' a gallery" (*IH* 21). Daring, enormous, breathtakingly energetic, the fantastically vibrant composition of the "Crucifixion" gloriously exceeds the etiquette of the Ruskinian gaze. If "no single picture in the world contains more of human life," "no other vision" induces so "intense" an experience of dislocation (*IH* 21–2).

James underlines the value of Tintoretto's style to his own performance of orientalist tropes by imagining at some length the attempts of the self-affirming bourgeois "traveller" to confront that style. The Scuola remains "one of the loneliest booths in the bazaar" precisely because "most visitors find the place rather alarming and wicked-looking" (*IH* 22). Daunted by the "fitful figures that gleam here and there out of the great tapestry" crowding its massive walls, "depressed and bewildered by the portentous solemnity" of the Scuola's "gorgeous and ill-lighted chambers," the viewer seeking to confirm such conventional pieties as those recorded in the 1886 *Baedeker's* – which finds Tintoretto annoyingly "perplexing" and prefers Titian's "glowing rapture" and "jubilant delight"[29] – is overcome "by the echo of" his "lonely footsteps on the vast stone floors." "[W]ith a sense of release from danger," he "take[s] a hasty departure," comforting himself with the "sense that the *genius loci* was a sort of mad white-washer who worked with a bad mixture, in the bright light of the *campo*, among the beggars, the orange-vendors and the passing gondolas." The ventriloquism of this passage transforms the interior of Venice's "loneliest" site into a lurid den of Gothic "danger," in which the alarmed visitor, against his will, catches "strange glimpses of unnatural scenes" (*IH* 22). In the deep structure of orientalism, such a traveler can forestall the appeal of Tintoretto's "wicked-looking" images as well as the power of his own "alarm" by dismissing the objects on display as products of a "bad mixture," committed on the scene of a more-than-Venetian otherness (*IH* 22).

To be sure, James on occasion echoes the tone of bourgeois bewilderment with less self-consciousness. But the episode at the Scuola is carefully plotted, a fact that becomes obvious in connection with James's earlier style of looking at the same visual artifacts. In "Venice: An Early Impression," published in 1872, a younger James with "a fine healthy romantic appetite" returns to test his initial impressions of *la Serenissima* with a marked confidence in "[t]he mere use of one's eyes" (*IH* 54). Surveying "the smaller of Tintoret's two great Crucifixions," the canvas at San Cassano, he evinces a breezy "self-possession," occasioned by his newly achieved awareness of the painter's "mysterious lapses and fitful intermission," his "impotence" rather than "magniloquence" (*IH* 57). Despite these lapses, Tintoretto takes the viewer "to the uttermost limits of painting," beyond the "straining . . . genius" of "Bellini, Veronese, Giorgione, and Titian"; he "never drew a line that was not, as one may say, a moral line" and thus for James is, *tout court,* "almost a prophet" (*IH* 57, 58).

Underlying James's confidence of approach – not to say the vaunted "moral" interest of his art historical criticism – is a vocabulary of the same holism and accessibility that his later Venetian excursion resists in the orientalist idiom. Here, the images of Tintoretto occasion precisely the "self-possession" undermined in those figures of lurid inaccessibility: "Before [Tintoretto's] greatest works," asserts the "healthy romantic," "you are conscious of a sudden evaporation of old doubts and dilemmas"; from this vantage point, even "the eternal problem of the conflict between idealism and realism dies the most natural of deaths" (*IH* 58). In this posture, "natural" unities rather than "unnatural scenes" prevail. Tintoretto's capacious "genius" effects resolution rather than dislocation; aesthetic and psychic "alternatives are so harmoniously interfused that I defy the keenest critic to say where one begins and the other ends." In his *oeuvre* at large, "the homeliest prose melts into the most ethereal poetry – the literal and the imaginative fairly confound their identity."

Far from inaugurating the psychic dissonance James stages at the Scuola, the "intensity" of *this* Tintoretto occasions the experience of boundaries dissolved, oppositions "interfused," difference "confounded"; "one's observation of his pictures" seems "less an operation of the mind than a kind of supplementary" and continuous "experience of life" (*IH* 58). With an "unequalled directness of vision," the "author of the Crucifixion" lays bare "the great, beautiful, terrible spectacle" of human trial: "It was the whole scene that Tintoret seemed to have beheld in a flash of inspiration"; "it was the whole scene, complete, peculiar, individual, unprecedented, that he committed to canvas" (*IH* 59). The enlightening "flash" of his genius here stands opposed to the "[i]ncurable blackness" of "the great collection" at San Rocco, whose "tragic beauty" is "dimmed and stained" by "rapidly increasing" physical "decay" rather than spiritual "gloom" (*IH* 59–60). In a comparison that "throws a doubly precious light" on James's own shifting motives, the "tender" observer of the earlier essay assesses the character of Tintoretto's work by linking him with the indisputable master of English cultural history: Tintoretto "*felt,* pictorially" the human "spectacle . . . very much as Shakespeare felt it poetically" (*IH* 60, 56, 59).

At stake in this claim is not the value or acuity of James's art historical criticism as such, but the shifting logic of his performative culture-building. The same "genius" that enables an experience of psychic wholeness, powerful insight, and confident self-possession in the earlier lexicon of bourgeois mastery becomes the vehicle for James's later enactment of dislocation and failed gestures of racial self-affirmation. Seeking something very much like the confirmatory pleasure enabled by Shakespeare as Anglo-Saxon icon, the alarmed visitor of James's later essay finds his desires irrelevant to the inscrutable, brooding "genius" of orientalized passion and decay. Although Tintoretto unfailingly remains both exemplary and unique for James in the pantheon of Italian painting, the revision of his own earlier response suggests that his doctrine of the picturesque increasingly takes as its deeper subject the cultural politics encoded in styles of aesthetic response. Representing himself as subject observer, willingly frustrated, overwhelmed, and "encaged," James turns the orientalizing fantasies of Anglo-America against themselves, partially detaching the project of cultural critique from the national and racial imaginaries it serves.

James's essay on Venice is exemplary, in my reading, in its performative redirection of explicitly "Anglo-Saxon" and American styles of acquisition and response. Mining the ethos variously staged in official tourist culture and in Ruskin's readings of Venice, James works to detach the orientalizing gaze from the cultural politics of racial mastery, turning it unabashedly onto the inner theater of race and nation staged in the exile's contact with Venetian queerness. Unlike the orientalists whose performances he revises – agents of colonial power gone native, and American sons of the bourgeoisie seeking withdrawal from the demands of modernity by passing as orientals – James in Venice is never intent on becoming the putative other, but rather in constructing a cultural position from which otherness can be more pleasurably and freely experienced, and against which the limits of conventional filiations – of family, gender, nation, culture, race – can be tested and contested. Looking ineffectually at Tintoretto and Cima, or drifting languorously in his gondola in the care of a powerfully handsome and "brown-skinned" gondolier (*IH* 54), James unmoors the ethnographic *Gestalt* from the projects of strenuous manhood and of Anglo-Saxon renewal, taking it to a self-undermining extreme. In this body of work, its performative logic is pressed in service of James's attempts to revise racial and national typologies, to construct an open-endedly modern, internationalist, self-consciously shifting style of cultural subjectivity and response. In later writings

James's management of vocabularies of race and nationhood, and his staking of sites for their performance, will take notably different form. Here, in the texts of travel and racial contact with which he inaugurates his career, James builds on ethnographic thinking to create his own first impressions of, and on, a shifting Anglo-American culture at large.

2

"PREPARATION FOR CULTURE": ANTHONY TROLLOPE, THE AMERICAN CENTURY, AND THE FICTION OF FREEDOM

[W]e young Americans are (without cant) men of the future. . . . We are Americans born – *il faut en prendre son parti*. I look upon it as a great blessing; and I think that to be an American is an excellent preparation for culture. We have exquisite qualities as a race, and it seems to me that we are ahead of the European races in the fact that more than either of them we can deal freely with forms of civilization not our own, can pick and choose and assimilate and in short (aesthetically etc.) claim our property wherever we find it.

– James to Thomas Sergeant Perry, 1867 (*Letters* 1:77)

[T]he good health of an art which undertakes so immediately to reproduce life must demand that it be perfectly free. It lives upon exercise, and the very meaning of exercise is freedom.

– James, "The Art of Fiction" (1884)

In 1861, the American physician Josiah Nott, a fervent apologist for slavery, lecturer in "niggerology," and co-author of the enormously popular textbook *Types of Mankind*, argued that Southern secession was entirely justified by the Declaration of Independence, "the chart by which the Anglo-Saxon race sails."[1] Such rhetoric was common coin among pre-Darwinian popularizers of polygenism (the argument to diverse, separate origins of human races); the latter held that, unlike Anglo-Saxons and other individuals of European "race," "Negroes are not *men*, in the sense in which that term is used by the Declaration of Independence" (Frederickson, 85–6). While this unstably racialized version of freedom wielded enormous conceptual power in prewar American ethnography, it circulated with renewed currency in postwar debates on the fate of America's social body. Through Reconstruction and beyond, nation-building claims for the distinctive collective identity of America and Americans would continue to seize on this characterological idiom, positing as innate and hereditarily determined an "idiosyncratic" Anglo-Saxon trait: the "love of liberty," an unmatched capacity for "democracy itself" (Frederickson 98, 101).

Such Herderian rhetorical stances were, however, hardly the unchallenged preserve of apologists for racism. Rather, they became a site of contestation over the terms of nation and culture on which emergent literary institutions held significant sway. Kenneth Warren has recently argued that debates about cultural enfranchisement for African-Americans in the postwar nation were powerfully mediated for genteel Americans by the literary discourse of realism, emerging in such preeminent vehicles as the *Century*, *Atlantic Monthly*, and the *Nation*. More broadly, literary realism redirects the heightened characterology of freedom, self-consciously imagining itself as an arena for replaying and resolving the vexed problematic of cultural union. If "[t]he ground" of the field of cultural endeavor staked by such journals as *Harper's Monthly* and the *Century* "is strewn with dead and dying reputations," it thereby maps the stakes for literary performance in postwar America (Tebbel and Waller-Zuckerman, 73–4). Claiming for fiction not only a "close-[ness] to the facts of life" but the power of more enlightened culture-building, its promoters critically construct realism as a social genre whose aim is the renewal of a distinctly American character, in literary genres and vehicles offering "good reading [that] serve[s] the social good" (Tebbel and Waller-Zuckerman, 74; Warren, 48; Wilson, 41).

James's participation in this cultural project is at once more vexed and more pointed than Warren and other readers have recognized. By critical consensus, the *Portrait* and other texts of the middle "phase" of his career are only intermittently or ambivalently realist; they realize scant dividends on the generic currency in which they half-heartedly invest.[2] Indeed, James himself would somewhat querulously defend the romanticism of his putatively realist texts, asserting in his 1907 preface to *The American* that "it is as difficult . . . to trace the dividing line between the real and the romantic as to plant a milestone between north and south" (*AN* 37). A more relevant geography might map the lines of division and unification between his American and Anglo-American resources in the early- and mid-1880s. Doubly placed in American realist debates *and* in a wider sphere of contestation over "English" letters, James's realist gestures can be seen to contest the value of the particular, and particularly American, strategies of culture-building they rhetorically mimic and institutionally engage.

It would be helpful at this juncture to recall the professional context of those gestures. By 1883 James had quite successfully inaugurated his program of freely "choos[ing]" and "assimilat[ing]" varied "forms of civilization" so as to claim for his own particular property ("aesthetically etc.") the fiction of contact between the American and European "races." His success was to be crowned in December of that year by the publication of James's first collective edition, a "*charming*" fourteen-volume set organized according to categories of cultural difference and exchange (*Middle Years* 67–9; *Letters* 2:410–11). Pride of place in its transatlantic pantheon was given to *The Portrait of a Lady*, which James himself had earlier described as "an *Americana* – the adventures in Europe of a female Newman, who of course equally triumphs," in the spirit of irrepressible liberty, over "the insolent foreigner" (*Letters* 2:72).

Drawing on the cultural capital the edition consolidates, James enters the precincts of realist culture-building in 1883 with particular designs on the idiom of freedom, whose mobility becomes newly urgent to his stagings of a more broadly Anglo-American form of cultural filiation and performance. Throughout the 1880s, realist doctrine constituted for James an arena in which to test the kind of culture-building and the varied gestures of racial self-declaration to which his writings on Italy – more narrowly concerned with the willfully irresponsible "free[dom] to follow capriciously every hint of entertainment" (*IH* 149) – give unencumbered play. Responsive both to a closely American cultural context and to transnational cultural ideals influenced by the work of Renan and Taine, James's critical interventions in American realism posited a different version of freedom: freedom as the definitive value of a more liberally defined Anglo-Saxon "race," achieving its highest expression in the exquisite self-stagings of a self-consciously Anglo-American character.

I want here to consider two of James's most important literary critical performances in this idiom: "Anthony Trollope," published in July of 1883 in the *Century* magazine, and (secondarily) "The Art of Fiction," which appeared in *Longman's* in September of the following year. In influential studies revaluating James's cultural politics, John Carlos Rowe and Warren have respectively problematized the intentions of "Trollope" and of James's uses of realist doctrine. But neither, I argue, accounts sufficiently for James's complex positioning within and between national and nation-bound literary traditions. The essays in question – the first produced in an American context, the latter in an English – are intricately interwoven with disparate strands of race thinking through the performative rhetoric of freedom. James's larger argument for the novel's autonomy can be seen in these contexts of production to exploit and redirect resonant tenets of racial character, destiny, and redemption. Adopting distinctly American and English ethnographies of the "Anglo-Saxon" race and its power to survive newly urgent racial challenges, James reimagines the novel as a culture-building enterprise capable of forestalling more narrowly defined versions of racial and cultural identity.

This very gesture is itself, it must be noted, performatively internationalist: in "Trollope," James declares himself heir to an English literary tradition within a vehicle of American literary politics, negotiating anxieties of racial and national destiny specific to both cultural sites; their difference will be put strategically under erasure in the more magesterial conduct of "The Art of Fiction," with its designs on an explicitly Anglo-American reading public and cultural formation. But this reordination of cultural resources in what Rowe has called James's "American synthesis" has been largely obscured by critical understandings of realism as an alternately "American" or "European" genre (Rowe, 58).[3] The American context of post-Reconstruction racial anxiety in which "Trollope" appears informs James's strategic idiom of cultural type and futurity in "The Art of Fiction," just as "Trollope" 's gestures of genealogical realignment and "transumption" make possible the intermittently racialized Anglo-Saxon cultural "synthesis" staked out in the later text.[4]

Bringing these essays together under the sign of realism as a second-order ethnographic discourse, I argue that James enters into American realism wars in such a way as to complicate the notions of national tradition and literary culture they consolidate. Rather than working through a nation-bound anxiety of influence in "Trollope," James more complexly uses the figure of that literary ancestor to construct a racialized model of Anglo-American identity and letters. Rejecting more narrowly national models advanced by Howells, Thomas Perry, and the literary institutions they promote, James imports an American cultural typology into an aestheticized discourse of the novel's freedom of reproduction and reproduction of freedom. His resulting texts of literary doctrine ultimately fail on their own terms, in a very specific sense; they fail, that is, to work through the aesthetic consequences of James's culture-building enterprise without recourse to the versions of race and racial character they work to complexify or undermine. But if James's notion of a newly conceived "Anglo-Saxon" cultural order will, by the end of "Trollope," collapse into narrower, more strenuously racialized versions of cultural possibilities, its ironies nonetheless proliferate suggestively, tell against themselves, with important consequences for his ongoing cultural performances.

My ultimate aim, then, is to yield a heightened sense of the performativity of these critical texts vis-a-vis fluid structures of nation, culture, and race playing out in the arena of the literary throughout the decade. Wielding tropes of fixed race character, James paradoxically instances the multiple and shifting identifications of race and nation to which such tropes can be put in service. The rhetoric of freedom, so definitively powerful a feature of his *oeuvre* and its reception, is ultimately forwarded in these texts not so as to declare James's allegiance to genteel critical notions of social order and national character, but at least in part to secure his own freedom of broadly racial self-invention. Capitalizing on his own long "preparation for culture," after the international "phase," James negotiates the terms of literary nationality, "deal[s] freely with forms of civilization," by redirecting realism's characterological anxieties and concerns.

Freedom Texts: "Anthony Trollope" in the Century

> It all comes back, in fine, to that respect for the liberty of the subject which I should be willing to name as *the* great sign of the painter of the first order.
>
> – James, "The Lesson of Balzac," 1905 (*LC2* 133)

It would be useful to begin by asking in what sense James's signature pleas for the freedom of the novel as a cultural act – freedom from "being marked out or fenced in by prescription," a larger "freedom to feel and say" (AF 54) – might reflect a post-Reconstruction rhetoric of cultural identity and agency. How do his articulations of freedom in the early 1880s underwrite or shape his distinctive role in an emergent Anglo-American literary culture? How does the vocabulary of freedom, so central and so resistant to paraphrase in James's realist doctrine, open a view for the genteel transatlantic audience of his own collective edition onto the contested landscape of American identity and self-definition?

The *Century* essay on Trollope poses and begins to answer these questions. At its narrative and critical center, James formulates a sweeping indictment of his predecessor's literary practice that suggestively links the art of the novel, the freedom of the novelist, and his status as representative figure of a community constituted through fluid histories of culture, nation, and race. "I may take occasion to remark here," he begins,

> upon a very curious fact – the fact that there are certain pre-cautions in the way of producing that illusion dear to the intending novelist which Trollope not only habitually scorned to take, but really, as we may say, asking pardon for the heat of the thing, delighted wantonly to violate. He took a suicidal satisfaction in reminding the reader that the story he was telling was only, after all, a make-believe. He habitually referred to the work in hand (in the course of that work) as a novel and to himself as a novelist, and was fond of letting the reader know that this novelist could direct the course of events according to his pleasure. . . . These little slaps at credulity . . . are very discouraging, but they are even more inexplicable, for they are deliberately inartistic . . . It is impossible to imagine what a novelist takes himself to be, unless he regard himself as an historian and his narrative as a history. It is only as an historian that he has the smallest *locus standi*. (AT 390)

In "The Art of Fiction," James will reiterate this claim in a similar register: "as the picture is reality, so the novel is history"; "[t]o represent and illustrate" the "action of men" with "the tone of the historian" is the "sacred office" of the novelist (AF 51).

By all critical accounts, both essays appear to be pressing a claim about the limits of the realist contract, and the instability of its tacit consensus about a shared and accessible social reality (Rowe, 70–2; Jones, 129–30). But this putative appeal to the necessary limits of realism (which reads in "Trollope" as a monitory corrective to the careless freedoms of the latter's literary practice) implicitly puts at stake the "*locus standi*," or distinctive status, of the novelist – the "historian" and guardian, in his imagined community, of a shared, continuous civic life (AT 248). What is at stake, then, in this narrative of authorship is precisely the "property" by which the cultural community constitutes itself: a freedom of imagination and invention whose exercise comprises the transformative power of the novelist's art.

When located in its immediate context – the pages of Richard Watson Gilder's *Century* magazine, penetrating in 1883 "into almost every cultivated household in the United States" and committed to the prosecution of genteel "thought and feeling" (Ziff, 102; Tebbel and Waller-Zuckerman, 68) – "Trollope" 's professed concern about historianship and the writing of cultural communities is clearly legible as a historically specific performance, a meditation on the journal's progressive cultural politics of "new Americanism" (Nagel, 295–7; Brodhead, 109). Warren has argued at length that James's fictions provide exemplary evidence for the ultimately repressive, complicit force of the *Century*'s commitment to genteel forms of political consensus, order, and decorum – a commitment which, he asserts, undermines the most radical impulses of white liberalism. Indeed, in Warren's reading, James (along with William Dean Howells, Albion Tourgée, and other less influential proponents of realism) is in effect cast as the protagonist of one of his own ambivalently realist novels, unable to ratify his most expansive and inclusive cultural ideals or to alter the cultural conditions that impede their realization. But Warren, I would argue, has under-read the particular complexities of James's textual performances, the multiplicity of contexts to which they respond, and the work they do there. Addressing both American and Anglo-American cultural typologies, trading on both English and American resources, James in the *Century* and at the moment of "Trollope" employs realism's racialized idiom of freedom precisely so as to contest the forms of cultural commitment and value to which the *Century*'s deployment of realism ultimately contracts.

The contents of the volume in which "Trollope" first appeared typify Gilder's unfolding cultural designs on the American character and American political union. Having himself served in an artillery unit during Lee's attack on Gettysburg and as a postwar correspondent in Newark, Gilder programmatically pursued "the question of sectional reconciliation" as crucial to the urging of "sacred decencies" of progressive uplift and reform (cited in Ziff, 128–9). Introducing the use of the half-tone photographic plate and the practice of commissioned articles, Gilder "capture[d]" exclusive Civil War reminiscences, socially conscious and meditative fiction, and even a biography of Lincoln, which would, he opined, "have a great moral and political effect in . . . unit[ing] the North and South as never before" (Gilder, 175–6; Tebbel and Waller-Zuckerman, 75). The opening pages of the July 1883 volume of the *Century* take as their point of cultural origin another martyr to the cause of the Union, the figure of John Brown. A newly executed and uncharacteristically sober portrait of the abolitionist adorns its initial verso page. Interspersed with earnestly genteel essays on rose-breeding, the native petroleum industry, and the "native element" in American fiction are reminiscences from wartime Washington and previously unpublished letters of Emerson. In illustration of dominant realist princi-

ples, the volume includes new installments of William Dean Howells's *A Woman of Reason* and of Joel Chandler Harris's *Nights with
Uncle Remus.*[5]

But the *pièce de résistance* for the *Century*'s, and thus James's, readers was surely the volume's central essay, "Recollections of the John
Brown Raid." Coauthored by "A Virginian Who Witnessed the
Fight" and "A Radical Abolitionist," the text offers strikingly different views of that definitively nation-building event. Alexander
Boteler, a states' rights Congressional representative from the
Sheperdstown district at the time of the raid, struggles to accommodate a righteous outrage with his retrospective historical consciousness of Brown's preeminent role in the theater of American national
identity. He begins somewhat oddly; citing Frederick Douglass's "eulogistic address" on Brown of 1881, he gives voice to a contestatory
version of the insurrection that celebrates its reprisal of the rhetoric
of American freedom:

> 'John Brown began the war that ended American slavery, and
> made this a free republic. Until this blow was struck, the pros-
> pect for freedom was dim, shadowy, and uncertain . . . When
> John Brown stretched forth his arm the sky was cleared . . .
> [and] the armed hosts of freedom stood face to face over the
> chasm of a broken Union.' (Boteler, 399)

Boteler himself goes on to characterize Brown's insurgency quite
differently, as "the first outrage perpetrated on the old flag," "the
first forcible seizure of public property," and "the first overt move-
men[t] to subvert the authority of the constitution and to destroy
the integrity of the Union" (Boteler, 400). His memorial act of
recounting puts at stake precisely the uniquely American habits or
properties – primary among them "freedom" – whose active exercise will sustain the emergent modern nation. Brown becomes a
flashpoint for Boteler's tale of the American tribe; he is by turns a
"deluded," unscrupulous, "insurrectionary" marauder, and a "self-
sacrificing" examplar of distinctly American "manliness" and brav-
ery (Boteler, 400, 402, 410).

In certain respects Boteler proves a more effective historian of
American national culture than he intends. Although he clearly
purposes to figure Brown's "cowardly conspirators" – particularly
the African-American participants in the insurrection – as "mur-
derous" in "character," he describes in graphic detail the death of a
black raider whose throat was "literally cut from ear to ear" by a
proslavery defender; the latter had fitted his musket with "a six-
inch iron spike" (Boteler, 404, 402, 406). Taking equally unflinch-

ing liberty, Boteler describes the attempted surrender by one "mu-
latto" conspirator, which was met by a crowd of white residents who
precipitously "began to knot their handkerchiefs together" in
preparation for carrying out the unofficial " 'law' " of the land
(Boteler, 407). By way of discrediting Brown's radical revolutionary
theology, Boteler mordantly attacks his absence of "scruples against
taking" horses and other slave-holders' "property." Yet he records
without the slightest self-consciousness his own eagerness to take
"possession" of Brown's spear at the moment of the surrender "as a
relic of the raid" (Boteler, 410). Throughout Boteler's account, the
moral property of freedom and freedom of property – the picking
and choosing of implements of culture – contend as governing idioms for constructing American citizenship and nationhood.

In a move that will be echoed by James's parting shot in "Trollope," in a very different staking of cultural identity, Boteler ultimately makes "historical" sense of the raid only with recourse to
racialized figures of exhaustion and disease. Recalling his private
interview with Brown after the latter's capture, Boteler invokes the
logic of the sentimental death-bed scene; lying wounded in view of
a jostling crowd whose prurient "curiosity" can only be contained
by military force, "the old fanatic" seems "to be in a dying condition." But at the entry of a Catholic priest, sent to "administe[r] the
last consolations of religion," Brown becomes "violently angry,"
manifesting an almost unnatural "vitality" that belies his copious
wounds. The "earnest gaze of the gray eye that looked straight into
mine" gives way to the specter of a monstrous "countenance,"
"smeared with blood," resembling "that of some aboriginal savage
with his war-paint on." Countering Brown's seductive appeal in the
role of representative American, Boteler imagines him as father to
a cycle of unleashed "horrors" and "terr[ors]" who ends his infamous career by reverting to savage type (Boteler, 410–11). This
"national history" thus concludes with a gesture that confirms cultural Union in the inscription of Brown as an uncannily original
figure of America.

The respondent to Boteler's essay, Franklin Benjamin Sanborn,
identifies himself as one of a small band, including Douglass, Theodore Parker, Emerson, Bronson Alcott, Thoreau, and Thomas Rus-
sell, that "raised money to aid Brown" in executing his plan to
"emancipat[e]" slaves "by force" (Sanborn, 412). Sanborn is in fact
uniquely situated to comment on Brown as American phenomenon: editor, biographer, journalist, and educator, he formed his
own transcendentalist school at Concord and taught the children of
Emerson, Hawthorne, Horace Mann, and Brown (some of whom

would accompany the latter on the Harper's Ferry raid).[6] Sanborn's inclusion in this number of the *Century* not only confirms its progressive and nation-building designs, but also serves to point up the performative force of James's uses of realist discourse under the sign of the "Anglo-Saxon." Participating in an evolving idiom central to the Emersonian inheritance Sanborn embodies, James redirects its forms of cultural commitment into a wider and distinctly Anglo-American sphere.

More locally, Sanborn's account confirms the nation-building force of the *Century*'s debate on Brown. His account diverges predictably from Boteler's, but the two share a central concern for Brown's meaning as a *"historic"* force in the shaping of American "character" (Sanborn, 414). The ultimate aim of Sanborn's recital will be to "make real to ourselves the despotism which a few slaveholders then exercised over the rest of mankind in this country" – including "six millions of white people, nominally free" but subject to political powers that constrained "more than half the free people" of the so-called "free" states (Sanborn, 411). Literally instrumental to this political, cultural, and legal enslavement, for Sanborn, was the figure of then-U.S. Supreme Court Justice Roger Taney:

> Through the mouth of Chief Justice Taney, who simply uttered the decrees of the slave-holding oligarchy, they had made the Supreme Court declare that four million Americans, of African descent, had practically [i.e., de facto] 'no rights which a white man was bound to respect'; and they exerted themselves in every way to give due effect to that dictum. (Sanborn, 411)

Sanborn refers, of course, to the notorious decision authored by Taney in the case of *Dred Scott v. Sandford* (1857), which turned (with curious relation to James's notions of the novelist's standing) on the legal doctrine of *locus standi*: the right of an individual, based on a legally defensible interest, to appear before a body of justice and make claims for its resolution. As Sanborn suggests, Taney's opinion strategically seizes on an amalgam of cultural and legal figures for liberty and the character of citizenship, rewriting the doctrine of standing to "prove" that a former slave and African-American, *even if free*, "could not possibly" be a citizen of the United States, that "political community framed and brought into existence by the Constitution," or legally claim the privilege of personhood under the law.[7] In Sanborn's recounting, the *Scott* decision becomes a decisive causal event: it "was given by Taney in 1857, and it led at once to the execution of John Brown's long-cherished purpose."

For my own purpose, what signifies is Sanborn's canny identification of the perversity of the standing doctrine within the *Scott* decision, which jeopardizes a version of history and of unified cultural character similar to that hazarded in "Trollope." Depriving "four million Americans of African descent" of legal standing, legal protection, and civil rights at a stroke, Sanborn's Taney induces an epiphantic "conviction" among "Northern men" that, in John Quincy Adams's words, "the preservation, propagation, and perpetuation of slavery" was in fact the dearest project, "the vital and animating spirit," of America's nation-building institutions, to be pursued without regard for the health of the republic. More decisively than any other proximate cause – the election as President of Buchanan ("the most complete servant of the slave power who ever held" the office), the breaching of the Missouri Compromise, the battles over slavery in the territories – Taney's willful revision of the standing doctrine, and its implied figures of the citizen, threatens the will to freedom of the American Union and the representative power of its animating texts. If the slave-holding oligarchy can "give due effect" to, make real de facto and de jure, an arbitrary and legally indefensible "dictum" of American identity and citizenship, then the fate of the American people and of the unified social body that ratifies its distinctive "spirit" is gravely endangered (Sanborn, 411).

Sanborn quite clearly establishes the centrality of this characterological concern to his cultural history. The "merit and fate of John Brown," he claims, was "to see and act upon the sad knowledge that slavery and our national existence were incompatible" (Sanborn, 411). Sanborn's idiom here is neither socioeconomic nor narrowly political. He suggests that Brown's essential motive was to contravene the intertwined fictions of American identity and its textuality authored by Taney, on which the fate of "freedom" for all Americans and thus of "our national existence" would ultimately turn. Brown, in other words, "chose the side of the nation against slavery" – chose the grim project of "emancipation by force" – in a desperate bid to sustain the larger "freedom" that gives authentic expression to the American character, and on which American public life depends for its viability and self-understanding. "It is in this broad way," Sanborn fervently insists, "that the Harper's Ferry raid must be looked at" – as a "measure," in both senses, of American freedom, "not as a midnight foray of robbers and murderers" (Sanborn, 412).

Sanborn's justification of "our instinctive sentiment" about Brown's heroism and his recuperation of the "higher elements of [Brown's] character" tender an implicit argument to the American character at large and the dependence of "our national safety" on its just expression (Sanborn, 414–15). "Young men never knew," he writes, "that we once had statesmen (so called) who loudly declared that negro slavery was the basis not only of our national greatness, but of the white man's freedom" – a deliberate perversion of "the language of Jefferson" and of the national consciousness to which it gives birth (Sanborn, 414). A true statesman, true to a uniquely nation-bound capacity (or so Sanborn implies) for liberty, John Brown rendered service to his country "by his heroic impersonation" of "noble" national traits no less than by effecting "the revolution that has regenerated us politically" (Sanborn, 415). Recalling Thoreau's aphorism – that Brown could never be tried by a jury of his peers, because none such existed – Sanborn claims for Brown a differently representative and characterological status than does Boteler: Brown was "so much . . . in accord with what is best in the American character that he will stand in history for one type of our people" (Sanborn, 415).

The debate over Brown's character, staged by the Century's editors twenty-four years after the raid on Harper's Ferry, clearly has as its final object a revaluation of the American "character," and of an intermittently racialized capacity for freedom understood both to define and to sustain it. John Brown's body, that disturbingly powerful icon of the will to freedom, remains a site on which competing notions of nationhood and the characterology of citizenship and civic life are hazarded. If this context seems remote from James's project, it nonetheless meaningfully frames his conspicuously literary performance. For James's Trollope performs a function ironically similar to that of Boteler and Sanborn's Brown: he provides a textual body, itself representative of a broadly racial "character," over and against which James will elaborate on his own version of cultural union. Returned to the pages of the Century, James's memorial essay on Trollope actively participates in its urgent stagings of cultural property, national type, and collective identity.

Yet, contra Warren, James conspicuously departs in "Trollope" from the institutional terms of the Century's realist project. His immediate concern is to denationalize realism's performative possibilities so as to create a more open-endedly, fluidly "Anglo-Saxon" or Anglo-American cultural subject. Redirecting the distinctly American idiom given voice in the Century for reflecting on the

"safety," destiny, and renewal of national institutions and character
into a broadly vexed, post-evolutionary, "English" context of anxiety about racial renewal and exhaustion, James inaugurates a version of fiction as social practice with a performative power to revise
the terms in which national and racial cultures are produced.[8] By
making "freedom" the property of a newly Anglo-American – that
is, a culturally "chosen" and "assimilated" – art of fiction, he can
implicitly claim for literature a powerful role in the "evolution" of
Anglo-Saxon character and civilization. His productive revaluation,
however, is achieved at the cost of a certain paradox; in order to
produce this markedly mobile genealogy of culture, as the final
sections of "Trollope" will suggest, James ultimately musters an
ideology of fixed racial inheritance, of the subject "born" to his
cultural "*parti*." Dealing freely in the idiom of closed racial form,
James translates the thematic concerns of literary internationalism
into a mode of Anglo-American cultural performance: he promotes both an untrammeled freedom of apprehension for the art
of fiction, and the freedom of his own shifting gestures of racial
and cultural identification.

The Death of the Author: Obituary, Extinction, and Racial Decline

When, a few months ago, Anthony Trollope laid down his
pen for the last time, it was a sign of the complete extinction
of that group of admirable writers who, in England, during
the preceding half century, had done so much to elevate the
art of the novelist. (AT 385)

This opening sentence of "Trollope," with its measured apposition
and emphatic use of the past perfect tense, heralds a new age in
the evolution of the novel. As I have suggested, the "complete
extinction" of prevailing literary models it announces comes at a
particularly opportune moment for James himself, as he redefines
his own mode of production in the internationalist mode. His readers have persuasively assimilated the essay to varied anxieties of
influence (English, novelistic, Victorian), but have allowed the
broader suggestiveness of his idiom to go unremarked. James's
death sentence can be understood, particularly in the wake of the
Century's brooding concerns about national character and typology,
to invoke a mobile post-Darwinian imaginary; the fact of literary
"extinction" adverts both to James's own "step by step evolution" as
producer of culture and to ambient anxieties about racial futurity,

with which the fate of the novel as an instrument of cultural expression remains complexly entangled (*Letters* 2:193–4). The very "inexhaustib[ility]" of Trollope's *oeuvre*, the notable "freedom" with which he "produced" (AT 386), signals the imminent danger – prophesied not only in the ethnographic texts to which James's travel writings respond but in innumerable Anglo-American texts of sociology, criminology, and cultural history – of racial exhaustion and degeneration.

The idiosyncrasies of Trollope's literary output, then, provide James with a figural resource for negotiating the instrumentality of literature as a culture-building act. His treatment of Trollope, responding both to the *Century*'s project of nation-building and to the idiom of degeneration, invokes fraught notions of racial decline and renewal so as to install the novel as a significant force in the shaping of an explicitly cross-cultural identity. Throughout "Trollope," James adopts two related strategies for putting the novel in its proper *locus standi*. Initially, he reads Trollope's indifference to form as the sign of a willing immersion in the rising tides of an indiscriminate consumer culture, which threaten to erode the natural vitality of a transnationally Anglo-Saxon race. Finally, however, he rehabilitates Trollope's practices, insofar as they enable the imaginative recovery of a renewable "racial" character, distinct from that of French writers who have more dangerously misrepresented the value of the literary act. Reading in and against the "English ideal" Trollope embodies, James revives the novel as a resource for public life, even as he works to produce an imagined community of Anglo-American readers in whose name the "transatlantic" writer "naturally" speaks (AT 385, 391, 387).

Notably, James begins his essay by declaring Trollope representative to a fault. The latter "responds in perfection" to the "English ideal" – over and against an implied American canon – that declares it "rather dangerous to be explicitly or consciously an artist." The perfection of that correspondence, James implies, renders his talent "of a quality less fine" than that of his great contemporaries (AT 385). Wanting in a "theory" of the storyteller's art – in fact, James suggests, "Trollope's practice was really much larger than such a theory" – his work utterly lacks "a system, a doctrine, a form" (AT 386, 385). It also lacks any apologetic consciousness of its failure, one James takes some pains to illustrate, to achieve the organic wholeness and "roundness" of finish that "rather minister to illusion than destroy it" (AT 389, 391). If such *insouciance* about the novel as a cultural form is "thoroughly English," it makes Trollope conspicuously derelict in the novelist's first duty: "as an artist,"

James proclaims, "he never took himself seriously," "never troubled his head nor clogged his pen with theories about the nature" of the novel's social agency (AT 385, 386). "[F]rom the first," he "went in, as they say, for having as little form as possible" (AT 385).

This argument to form is from the outset continuous with the *Century*'s idiom of national character, type, and ideal – an idiom on which the expression of his ambitious claims for the social import of the novel as an instrument of freedom will crucially depend. But the traffic between literary form and nation or racial identity is busier, more freighted than James's casual conflation of national and literary canons would suggest. His opening paragraph (which runs to three printed pages) amounts to an extended critique of Trollope's mode of production, in which the compromising of a distinction between popular and high cultural forms implies a compromising of "English" and affectively Anglo-Saxon racial energy. James begins by praising Trollope's industrious habits and his dedication to his craft in an anecdote that plays on that idiom:

> It was once the fortune of the author of these lines to cross the Atlantic in [Trollope's] company, and he has never forgotten the magnificent example of stiff persistence which it was in the power of the eminent novelist to give on that occasion. The season was unpropitious, the vessel overcrowded, the voyage detestable; but Trollope shut himself up in his cabin every morning for a purpose which, on the part of a distinguished writer who was also an invulnerable sailor, could only be communion with the muse. (AT 385)

One dense paragraph later, however, in a "direct" representation of Trollope at work, James opens the closed cabin door and exposes the latter's "plain persistence" as a form of jobbing rather than communion with the muse: "He sat down to his theme in a serious businesslike way, with his elbows on the table and his eye occasionally wandering to the clock" (AT 388, 386–7). Both "plodding" and aggressively prolific, Trollope figures as master of the dogged industry of New Grub Street; his work has "no more pretensions to style than if it were cut out of yesterday's newspaper" (AT 388). For all his "old-fashioned reverences," then, Trollope embodies a new breed of professional writers, corporate apologists for forms of " 'entertain[ment]' " whose vulgarity provokes rich performances of James's literary disgust and embarrassment throughout the decade (AT 386, 389).

But James's figures of Trollopean industry themselves do harder labor than merely miming genteel horror at the corrosive effects of mass production. Arguably, James takes issue with this *modus operandi* so as ultimately to promote forms of cultural "communion" that both presume and transgress stable designations of nation and race. Unlike Dickens, Thackeray, and other novelists in the Victorian mode who (or so the claim here goes) prove themselves "able to wait for inspiration" (AT 385), Trollope actively participates in reducing the work of fiction to deadening and dead-end labor, and thereby jeopardizes a certain form of cultural and racial vitality. Not only did Trollope publish "too much" – his "fecundity," James notes with some aspersion, "was prodigious; there was no limit to the work he was ready to do" – but his works appeared with monstrous regularity, "overlapping and treading on each other's heels" (AT 385). Embodying an expense of cultural energy – a "fertility" that James would later call both "gross" and "importunate" (*PP* 98)[9] – James's Trollope ends by ceasing to "produce individual works; his activity became one huge 'serial,' " "without visible intermission" (AT 391, 385). Writing "for the day, for the moment," in a "mechanical" mode that "betray[s] the dull, impersonal rumble of the mill-wheel" (AT 391; *PP* 120), Trollope ends by pandering to the insatiable appetites of an increasingly "hungry public" (AT 389, 385).

If this subplot of exhaustive industry is all too familiar, James concludes it on a more original eulogistic note. "[T]here is sadness," he writes, "in the thought that this enormous mass" of Trollope's work "does not present itself in a very portable form to posterity"; nonetheless James concedes that Trollope may be one of "the writers . . . whom posterity is apt to put into its pocket" (AT 395). James's immediate reference would seem, of course, to be the difference between Trollope's exhaustively "immense quantity" and the kind of finished perfection embodied in his own forthcoming, " 'choice,' " pocket edition, with its "portable form" and clear designs on literary posterity (*Letters* 2:410–11). In James's idiom, however, the issue of posterity also links up to a version of authorial freedom that clearly sounds the keynotes of contemporaneous race thinking. As Rowe has persuasively argued, the argument to overproduction and sameness in Trollope represents a bid on James's part to unshackle literary art from the fetters of hardened convention – the law of the "[u]sual" case (AT 387) – and actively refashion the experimental energy of Victorian fiction at its best, with an eye to the future of the novel (Rowe, 68–9).

But the stakes for "posterity" and renewal of social energies are arguably higher still, as "Trollope" 's insistent, and broadly Anglo-American, idiom of population explosion – "fecundity," "fertility," and "unnatural" issue – declares (AT 386, 390). For James's representation of Trollope's overproduction suggests not only the marked exhaustion of the novel as a literary form in the essay's moment. It further implies a racial exhaustion – an overwhelming of distinctly Anglo-Saxon capacities and virtues by the "excessive reproduction" of the "least capable, least desirable members of the community" – whose ominous foreclosure is the broader context for cultural production throughout Anglo-America (Lankester, 28:1039).

James's idiom engages these ubiquitous tropes of racial degeneration and decline, which, as George Mosse has argued, work to distinguish between cultural virtues that "le[ad] to progress" and vices that "le[ad] to the extinction of the individual" and "the national community" (Mosse, 35).[10] Edwin Ray Lankester, a well-respected English Darwinian and author of *Degeneration: A Chapter in Darwinism* (1880), asserted of the growing challenge to Anglo-Saxon racial energy posed by the swelling population of urban poor that "we have to look for the protection of our race," including among Anglo-Saxon types "the English branch" (Lankester 28:1039). Three years after the publication of "Trollope," Arnold White (a biogenetic alarmist of international repute) would argue in the widely read *The Problems of a Great City* that England could no longer afford to serve as the world's "rubbish heap" (A. White, 144).[11] Against threats of degeneration posed both by "aliens" and from within, promoters of Anglo-Saxon culture "almost despair of the possibility" of sustaining the Anglo-Saxon "type" at "anything like" the "higher level" of its origins.[12]

In the context of such panic, James's revised version of freedom as a distinct racial property signifies more pointedly. Trollope, James notes, "overworked" his gift, was "prodigious" and prodigal of his powers; "there was always in him a certain touch" – or "infusion" – of "the common" (AT 385; *PP* 99). Diluted by their commerce with "common" sensibilities, his illustrations of character or type are themselves "sometimes of the commonest" (AT 387; *PP* 107); like the progeny of lower types and races rapidly populating Anglo-America's urban spaces, they are "turn[ed] out inexhaustibly," in incessant "succession" (AT 387, 391). Finally, James implies, Trollope's expense of aesthetic material and of English tradition or "character," in the most fraught sense, are intimately conjoined. By the end of Trollope's career, a notable adulteration had set in, and "the strong wine" of his representative genius "was rather too copiously watered" (AT 391). Desperately "repeat[ing]" his own conventional plots and gestures, Trollope comes to "illustrate" by implication the dangers to social arts posed by the imminent prospect of retrogression, reversion, and racial decline (AT 387).

The continuity of James's idiom of exhaustion in "Trollope" with such ongoing speculations about the fate of Anglo-Saxon culture in contest with lower, more "common" genetic natures is more than historically accidental. "Trollope" ultimately puts at stake not only the fertility of the novel as a cultural form but the vitality and capacity for renewal of the transnational, broadly racial, culture it has assisted in creating. If Trollope "repeats" his own plots "freely" and "without rest" (AT 387), his mode of production heralds the imminent decline of an energetic freedom of invention and self-invention – the same freedom taken, in Boteler and Sanborn's accounts of John Brown, as in the Anglo-American idiom of racial decline, to stand definitively for the Anglo-Saxon character. James's partially ironic *post mortem* engages not merely the late (in both senses) Victorian novel but a broader cultural contest given limited play in his earlier travel writings: between the dire potential for the ruin – the "extinction" – of Anglo-America and possibilities for its renewal as a dynamic, self-representing enterprise.

This contest shapes the terms in which "Anthony Trollope" gives voice to its subject's indifference to the literary as a site of engaged and active culture-building. In a canny figural gesture – the only such moment in the essay – James allows Trollope to speak in his own voice, so as to defend his complicity with the new technologies of mass production: " 'Judge me in the lump,' " he is made to plead. " 'I don't pretend that each of my novels is an organic whole' "; " 'I have only undertaken to entertain the British public' " (AT 389). The gross, importunate fertility that overflows the form of the English novel also violates what for James's purposes here is a necessary boundary between literature as an authentic form of civic discourse and exhaustive popular fictions and forms; it undermines the distinctive standing on which James's sense of the novel and its value to "posterity" depend. What makes Trollope so accessible and so popular, according to James, is just his "honest, familiar, deliberate way of treating his readers as if he were one of them" (AT 386). Meeting the reader halfway, on the latter's grounds, Trollope locates his acts of narrative within the community he addresses and represents; he "delight[s] wantonly to violate" the fiction of the author's distinction – from the community, the marketplace, the social body – as a privileged or "free" observer of their governing fictions (AT 390; AF 54).

Understood as the context for James's treatments of Trollope's realism, the Anglo-American anxiety of cultural exhaustion helps make sense of the motives and gestures with which James in this instance defends the aesthetic as a distinct realm of activity. Innumerable readers have commented on the injustice, provinciality, or markedly moralizing quality of James's responses to Trollope in the guise of literary historian. (Such readers could aptly cite a notice in the *Revue des Deux Mondes* that rather misguidedly applauds James at the moment of "Trollope" for an active "horreur de la banalité" [cited in Jones, 123].) But if we understand the contest over literary realism to put that urgently theorized, racially constituted freedom of expression at stake, then the intermittently virtuous tone of James's prose (which registers some of the same "evangelical hostility" and "prohibitory" cast of mind he so effectively deflates) makes shrewder critical sense (AF 66, 50). Miming distinctly American and Anglo-American anxieties of exhaustion given play in the *Century* and in his own earlier reviews of ethnographic texts, James indulges a strategic form of excess. Criminalizing Trollope's literary excess as an affront to the implicitly sacralized potential, destiny, and character of Anglo-Saxon racial energy, he thereby raises the stakes for literature as an arena for cultural formation and performance.

Conspicuously profligate with that resource, James's Trollope turns out to be a bizarre blend of prudish John Bull and philandering libertine. His "practice, his acquired facility" of overproduction, "were such, that his hand" – that organ of erotic and narrative excess – "went of itself" (AT 391). Locally, Trollope indulges an even more dangerous and willful urge. Constantly "reminding the reader that the story he was telling was only, after all, a make-believe," he "habitually referred to the work in hand (in the course of that work) as a novel, and to himself as a novelist, and was fond of letting the reader know that this novelist could direct the course of events according to his pleasure" (AT 390). These onanistic self-interruptions appear to "violate" far more than literary decorum, since they inspire James with the fervor of moral outrage. In his reading, they are not only "deliberately inartistic," but constitute positively "pernicious" – in fact, "suicidal" – gestures of "satisfaction" (AT 390).

It is at this point that James makes the essay's central claim: "It is impossible to imagine what a novelist takes himself to be unless he regard himself as an historian and his narrative as a history" (AT 390). In so doing, he calls attention to the ways in which Trollope endangers not only the fiction of fiction's reality, but the conjoined project of cultural-cum-racial renewal. James's argument to a *locus standi* – quite differently constituted than Taney's argument to standing, but similarly directive in its cultural designs – works to ensure the continuing power and dynamic energy of the novel as "history," the narrative of a nation and national culture. For Trollope to "drop the historic mask" and refuse to treat the production of literature as an act of "historical" representation, James suggests, is to compromise not only the freedom of the artist but the premise of art's representative power as the record of the *ethnos*, the people, the tribe (AT 390). Trollope, in other words, breaches the contract between writer and reader by which both agree, in the interest of deeper social purposes, to treat literary making as a free enterprise, conducted in a distinctly aesthetic arena unbound from the institutions of civic life. Such magnificent deception, worthy of the saving lies told by James's fictional proxies, itself preserves the very possibility of the freely exercised moral imagination – that definitively Anglo-Saxon power – against the stultifying habits of conventional modernity. In James's strategically realist argument, Trollope's form of authorship poses a threat to the provisional *locus standi*, the place of belonging and filiation from which more powerfully free fictions ensue; it leaves both the author and his represented public "nowhere" (AT 390).

Ultimately, this argument to standing employs the ambient idiom of racial character and renewal so as to preserve the possibility for changing the Anglo-American subject of its interest. In "The Art of Fiction," James displays an equally mixed affect of racialized "curiosity" and misplaced bourgeois outrage (AF 49). One measure of its performative intention can be taken by the English context of *Longman's*, in which James's language reverberates as resonantly as it does with the American idiom prevalent in the *Century*. The September 1884 issue in which "The Art of Fiction" appeared included a serial installment of Margaret Oliphant's *Madam* and Bret Harte's "A Blue Grass Penelope," a tale of *camareros* and *senoritas* highly colored for the English reader. The volume also features a commentary entitled "The Chase of the Wild Red Deer"; the author, J. W. Fortescue, celebrates this form of the hunt, "distinct from all other English sports," as an exemplary cultural ritual (Fortescue, 488).

Fortescue's language neatly recalls James's strategic description in "Trollope" of the latter as a representatively English figure, "a novelist who hunted the fox" (AT 393). More significantly, it also suggests how adeptly James adapts the language of racial panic as a tool for constructing literary value in a transnational context. Fortescue concludes his ostensibly journalistic description of the finer points of the hunt with an elegiac gesture of wish-fulfillment toward the greatness of England's Christian, Anglo-Saxon, Arthurian past: "though the outward demonstrations are not now so marked as formerly," he writes, the hunt of the wild red deer "has, perhaps, even a greater hold on the good people of North Devon and West Somerset at the present day than when the church bells were rung at the death of a good stag, and 'As pants the hart' was sung in the parish church on the first Sunday of the stag-hunting season" (Fortescue, 488, 500).

It is precisely in this suggestive context, of English national culture-building under the sign of degeneration and decline, that "The Art of Fiction" resumes "Trollope" 's argument to standing. Once again, James rehearses his complaints about Trollope's shocking admissions of artifice, renewing his war on the latter's concession to the reader in the guise of "trusting friend." These episodes, in which Trollope "admits that the events he narrates have not really happened, and that he can give his narrative any turn the reader may like best," constitute more than a mere "want of discretion" or narrative self-control. They amount to "a terrible crime," a "betrayal of a sacred office" that "shocks me every whit as much in Trollope as it would have shocked me in Gibbon or Macaulay" (AF 51).

James's emphatic (indeed repetitive) attempts to undercut this "vulgarization" make it clear that he again defends as mutually interdependent possibilities the privileged cultural standing of the artist and an ever-evolving freedom of Anglo-Saxon imagination and self-imagination. In order not to "give" either liberty "away, as they say in California" – that space affording apparently limitless room for expansion of the Anglo-Saxon genius – the novel "must speak with assurance, with the tone of the historian" (AF 51). This tone, with its ostensibly contingent claims to neutrality, gives reassuring point to James's own assertion that "there is as much difference as there ever was between a good novel and a bad one: the bad is swept away with all the daubed canvases and spoiled marble into some . . . infinite rubbish-yard," while "the good subsists and emits its light and stimulates our desire for perfection" (AF 51). Throughout "The Art of Fiction," a language of the sacred, of purity and "rubbish," urges a self-evident distinction between "a good novel and a bad one." It simultaneously urges the distinction between a culture of the "commodity" that "discredit[s]" cultural energies through adulteration and "overcrowding," and a civilization that gives free play to the defining propensity – the "very meaning" – of the Anglo-Saxon nature: the capacity for energetic "liberty" (AF 53–4). Here, James's claims for "the good health" of the novel are also claims for the more vital futurity of the "international" culture or race whose cultural history it can be made to represent; the project of "reproduc[ing] life" depends on both the medium's freedom from arbitrary aesthetic "laws" and on the novelist's creative pretense that his art ensues from a space beyond the reach of moribund cultural forms. In concert, these conditions ensure the perfect freedom that, in James's imported idiom, registers "the temperament of" Anglo-American "man" (AF 54).

"The Art of Fiction," then, extends the logic of James's racial idiom in "Trollope" into the wider territory of Anglo-America, and to its farthest productive reaches: the notion of the novelist's privileged standing enables a powerfully imagined renewal of the very character, Anglo-Saxon and transnational, that appears to be under seige. The free imagination, in James's impassioned formulation, not only guarantees the novel's "intensity" and "therefore" the novel's "value," combatting "suppression of the very thing that we are most curious about," but it also militates against the kind of "moral timidity" and "cautious silence" that dominate both "the usual English novel" and the "quality of the mind" of contemporary Anglo-America at large (AF 54, 65–6). If there "is no limit to what" the artist "may attempt as an executant," "[w]e are" likewise "perfectly free to find" the production in question wanting (AF 54, 60); if we undertake "a seriously artistic attempt" of production or reception we must inevitably "becom[e] conscious of an immense increase – a kind of revelation – of freedom." In "the light" of that "heavenly ray," James famously suggests, one "perceives . . . that the province of art is all life" (AF 62). Only by "knowing his place," provisionally imagined as the extrinsic vantage-point of the historian, liberated from definitive structures of filiation, can the novelist vigorously "exercise" the reconstructive freedom of "all his standing-room," and thus protect "[t]he essence of moral energy": the act of "survey[ing] the whole field" (AF 54–5, 51, 66).

With pointed insistence on the "liberty" of the Anglo-Saxon "character" and the value of the novel in ensuring its imminent renewal, "The Art of Fiction" combats the specter of cultural exhaustion to which both it and "Trollope," as I will shortly argue, differently give strategic play. Rescuing the novel from its current embarrassment as "a factitious, artificial form, a product of ingenuity, the business of which is" to entomb "the things that surround us" in "conventional, traditional moulds," James commutes the impending sentence of doom to which that art and its broadly racial civilization have been "condemn[ed]": the fate of "an eternal repetition of a few familiar *clichés*" that "cuts short" progress and "development and leads us straight up to a dead wall" (AF 61). The struggle to describe the project of realism – or more accurately, the paradoxical effort to codify that project so as to ensure

its larger freedom of invention – is party to an ongoing project of
cultural and racial renewal whose terms James seeks to redirect.
Getting realism right in "Anthony Trollope" and "The Art of Fiction" consequently involves a subtle negotiation of race anxieties,
counterposing against them the kind of culture-building art of
fiction James means to inaugurate. Finally, James's idiom implies,
the "perfect freedom" of the justly historicized novel will conduce
to the constitutional freedom of a vibrantly Anglo-American culture, whose "magnificent" racial "heritage" might well be summed
up as just the possibility that the novelist's performance of cultural
standing instances and promotes: "the freedom to feel and say"
(AF 54, 51).

From Decline to Renewal: The Art of Fiction and the Recovery of Anglo-America

If Trollope's art signals the advent of a culture in decline, dangerously content to repeat its own exhausted gestures and forms, it
also provides James the materials for plotting a more sanguine
evolutionary *telos*. Projecting a future for the novel as an organic
entity, that "living thing, all one and continuous" (AF 58), James
figures an ongoing process of natural selection through which the
unself-conscious performances of a Trollope will be superseded by
the higher intelligence of a James, toward the renewal of the
Anglo-Saxon character and culture their fiction superintends. In
his 1905 essay on Balzac, James wields the trope of literature as an
evolutionary institution to mourn the "wasted heritage" of the
novel among a contemporary "family" of novelists (*LC2* 120). In
"Trollope," however, he invokes a distinctly progressive idiom, de-
vising a counterplot of cultural renewal in which the evolving organism of the novel will play a leading role. Even as he deplores Trollope's superabundant excess and exhausted literary designs, James
frames these practices as the conditioned responses of a literary
instinct whose limits will be transumed in the progressive unfolding
of a broadly racial evolution.

James mounts the counterplot of renewal in rhetorical figures
that suggestively imagine Trollope in the guise of lower literary organism. The latter's gifts number "unpretending . . . good sense"
and a "good ear," rather than a penetrating vision; a "happy, instinctive perception of character" – and "human varieties" (*PP* 104) –
rather than deeper apprehension of fine consciences (AT 387). Although he has wide "knowledge of human nature," that knowledge
is "not reasoned nor acquired, nor even particularly studied" (AT

387). Far from adopting a "scientific" approach to human observation, James's Trollope eschews all claims to comprehension of "*why*
people in a given situation" behave "in a particular way." "If he was a
knowing psychologist," James remarks, "he was so by grace; he was
just and true without apparatus and without effort" in the practice of
a realism "instinctive" and "inveterate" (AT 387, 392).

By the same evolutionary token, James asserts that Trollope's
critical performances "are of an almost startling simplicity"; his
capacities, consistent with the state of a less specialized organism,
for the higher strategies "of fancy, of satire, of irony" are "not very
highly developed" (AT 387, 386). Speaking from the vantage-point
of cultivated retrospection, James genially admonishes that "We
must be careful" not to "attribut[e] convictions and opinions to
Trollope," who "had as little as possible of the pedantry," or self-
consciousness, "of his art" (AT 387). For all the felicity of his
"grace," his creatures "g[o] too coarsely to work" in the vehicle of a
"plodding prose" (AT 393). "[S]olid, definite" and "somewhat lumbering," Trollope gives expression to his own imperturbable and
hearty good nature with all the "homely arts" of the lower organization (AT 387–8), displaying the "button-holing persistence" and
"literally truthful pathos" of the genuine "natural" (*PP* 107, 119;
AT 393). In James's revised version of the essay, he names as Trollope's only "masterly" gesture "the large-fisted grip" with which, in
the painting of social portraiture, "Trollope handles his brush" (*PP*
109; AT 388).[13]

James's revision points up the logic of his figures, which render
Trollope as literary ancestor a lower form on the scale of literary
evolution: a natural who achieves fortuitous if "heavy-footed" results through the accidents of an instinctually directed "nature"
(AT 388). Massive, lumbering, unself-conscious, Trollope stolidly
"take[s] up room" in the arena of Anglo-Saxon cultural history (*PP*
112). He thus stands in decided contrast to the Jamesian historian
who succeeds him, who purposively stakes out "all his standing
room" in a bid to liberate the art of fiction from moribund cultural
pieties (AF 51). In James's subplot, the idiom of evolution counters
the mandate of racial exhaustion with an alternative possibility: a
renewal to ensue through the cultivation of the English novel as an
instrument of the higher critical and moral intelligence of the race.
If Trollope appears in the guise of sedulous hack, the novelist-
historian of progressive race history figures another order of
being – of feeling and saying – altogether, toward which "our Prot-
estant communities" (in "The Art of Fiction") and "our English
race" (in "Anthony Trollope") may evolve.

With these figures of evolutionary distinction, James mimes and redirects American realism's vexed – and unstably racialized – ethos of cultural renewal. His readings of Trollope not only anticipate but partially forestall the kind of claims for realism as a cultural form articulated by Howells's *Criticism and Fiction* (1891), a standard-bearing text for willfully sunny modes of culture-building. Obscuring the contestatory dimensions of literary production, Howells imagines the literary mode of each age as "a plant which springs from the nature of a people" and takes "root" in "their character" and "will"; in fin-de-siècle America, Howells argues, realism grows organically from, even as it quickens an evolving racial capacity, an impulse "to widen the bounds of sympathy, to level every barrier against aesthetic freedom, to escape from the paralysis of tradition" (Howells 1891:55, 15). The teleological thrust of Howells's argument is advanced even more methodically in the *History of Greek Literature* published in 1890 by James's friend, Thomas Sergeant Perry, an influential proponent in his own right of realism and progressive culture-building. Celebrating evolutionary theory – the principle of "*growth*" – as "an unfailing touchstone" for literary study, Perry argued that literary development was governed by a Spencerian progress toward coherence and heterogeneity. The value of particular genres for Perry is measured by the power of expression they give to a distinct national-cum-racial character, as the exemplary case of Greek antiquity suggests: "Of no people is it truer than of the Greeks that their literature is not an artificial product, but the race speaking" (Perry, 12). Like the forms of high Hellenic culture, the "movement in letters in the present day" tends "in the direction" of "the freedom which civilization is acquiring"; in this argument, Anglo-American realism too constitutes "the direct expression of a free people leading its own life, untrammeled by inherited rules or authoritative convention" (Pizer, 64).

While James's version of realism engages the same rhetoric of evolutionary progress and racial character, his implied claims for the novel as an instrument of cultural recovery more complexly negotiate these nation-building resources than do Howells's or Perry's arguments. Affirming the value of fiction as a site of Anglo-American self-invention – a mode of "represent[ing] our types very finely" (AT 391) – he suggests that its power of renewal resides in a broadly racialized energy that the history of the English novel puts on offer and at stake. In this respect, too, Trollope's *oeuvre* proves an exemplary case. Instancing the dangers of cultural decline, it also makes available for Anglo-American renewal a certain distinctive "character," a signature moral intelligence waiting to be deployed against racial dilution and corruption. "[S]trong, genial, and abundant," the very "type" of a "thoroughly English" moral imagination (AT 385, 388), Trollope bequeathes to his literary descendents a resource not unlike the racialized form of natural rights created by Taney, or the national character contested in the *Century*'s versions of Brown. In James's text, this racially marked capital underwrites the dedication of the art of fiction to the exercise of that definitively Anglo-American capacity for energetic freedom of invention and self-invention.

Midway through "Anthony Trollope," James stages a recovery of Trollope's literary virtues, thereby forestalling a livelier challenge to the freedom to feel and say posed by a group of writers who show no signs of becoming "extinct": the French naturalists. Elsewhere, as I will argue in chapter three, James selectively declares his allegiance to the "Gallic" project in order to shift the performative terms of the international style. Here, however, he will imagine Trollope as faithful to a moralized, decidedly Anglo-Saxon literary tradition, countering the more serious threat to the novel's nation-building possibilities posed by the French avant-garde. Although the comparison belies James's ongoing critical engagement with the canons of "the Parisian race," and indeed belies his use of broadly naturalist tropes of evolution and decline to represent Trollope in this very essay, it secures his "assimila[tion]" of the English tradition as his own literary property, and makes possible his claims for the social power of the novel as an instrument of cultural renewal – or, in more characteristically Jamesian terms, of "civilization."[14]

Initially, "Trollope" hazards only a passing reference to the "votaries of the new experiments in fiction," noting that they have made things "most disagreeable for the novel reader" who attempts to take in the "unwonted and bewildering sensations" their fiction engenders (AT 386). This left-handed allusion allows James to draw a contrast at Trollope's expense between English timidity and French innovation: Trollope's fiction limits itself to the observation of the "usual" and is therefore "always safe," "sure" to conduct "no new experiments" (AT 236). But by the end of the essay the experimental designs of French fiction serve to magnify Trollope's virtues as practitioner of distinctly English, and more insistently racialized, habits of mind on which the health of the Anglo-American social body depends. His "instinctive" perception of "the moral nature" of "contemporary Britons" counterveils against the "ingenious" quality of the "so-called scientific view" advocated by "the countrymen and successors of Balzac" (AT 392, 387). If Trollope gains his knowledge of human psychology by "grace," he nevertheless employs that knowledge in the service of his "great taste for morals" (AT 387) or "the moral question" (*PP* 105), which he obviously understood, James notes with approval, as "the interest of fiction" and the grounds for its centrality to the cultural work of negotiating community and "character" (AT 387).

Here the idiom of instinct underscores differences, usefully implied to be innate or characterological, between the national traditions James performatively negotiates. "[C]omparing" Trollope's "tone of allusion to many lands and many things" – the "good-natured, moderate" tone – with "that narrow vision of humanity which accompanies the strenuous, serious work lately offered us in such abundance by the votaries of art for art who sit so long at their desks in Parisian *quatrièmes*," James marks a strategic difference: "the difference between the French and English mind" [sic] (AT 386, 392). Although "English" writing, of which Trollope's is the unsurpassed type, resounds with "the echoes of voices that are not the voice of the muse," it nevertheless achieves an imaginative liberality and freedom of invention that the French writers eschew (AT 392). "[O]n the whole," James asserts, Trollope "tells us . . . more about life than the 'naturalists' in our sister republic." Like "our English providers of fiction" at large, and like the national culture he typifies, Trollope is admittedly "inferior in audacity, in neatness, in acuteness, in intellectual vivacity" and in "the art of characterizing visible things." But his work puts on view and into play a definitive capacity for moral energy and liberality of invention. This implicitly racialized power of apprehension constitutes Trollope's contribution to the evolving nature of the English novel: he has been "more at home in the moral world" (AT 392) and "know[s] [his] way about the conscience" (*PP* 124); his representative moral intelligence renders his fictions "sound" and "genial" and "true" (AT 395).

If Trollope abrogates the standing of the novel by colluding with the ethos of the marketplace, he continues to typify a distinctly "English" – and thus racially available – habit or tradition of moral awareness, of imaginative liberality, violated by the obsession of that other European race with the modern urban *demimonde*. James again paradoxically presses this distinction in an idiom of the bourgeois propriety for which he exhibits such trenchant distaste. Comparing Trollope with Zola, he remarks that, "[f]or Trollope the emotions of a nursery governess in Australia would take precedence of the adventures of a depraved *femme du monde* in Paris or London" (*PP* 123). (In other words, Trollope is interested in the domestic virtues, whereas Zola is interested in trollops.) But James's ultimate concerns are substantively obscured by this rhetoric. Naturalist views, with their "gimletlike" narrowness of focus (AT 392), pose a threat not because they freely represent hard drinking and loose women, but because they take liberties with the crucial liberty that a distinctly literary, distinctly Anglo-American, art of fiction seeks to promote. Zola's obsession with "depravities" – the abnormal, the genital, the excretory, and other "polluting things" (AT 386) – insists on the arbitrariness of the made boundaries of social community, and on the functioning of the novel as a *cordon sanitaire* that safeguards that body's purity and sameness. In thus narrowing the project of fiction, James implies, Zola deprives the novel of its "exercise" of a higher freedom to feel and say, to engage and re-make orders of being and telling. Zola is thus guilty of a far more baneful breach of standing than Trollope ingenuously commits, one that James figures in the contestatory difference of racial temperament or "mind." Disparaging the "essentially moral" interest of the Anglo-Saxon tradition, Zola's practice endangers James's supreme fiction: that of the author's distinct freedom of enterprise, which enables him to educate his readers in cultural fictions of community and identity (AT 388).

James's measurement of Trollope against the naturalists thus constitutes a strategic defense of one form of fixed national or racial character over another, in service of his own variously internationalist ethos of apprehension and response. Superior in "audacity," "neatness," "acuteness," "arrangement," the new French writers exhibit all the dubious virtues of Gallic "art" and cunning (AT 392). James twice refers to them as "votaries," thereby invoking the charge of papist sensuousness so dear to the Anglo-Saxon imagination (AT 387). Unlike Zola, Trollope eschews all "artistic perversions"; his is a genius, as the French themselves might say, of the "*honnête*," a confident, healthy openness to the word (AT 387, 386). In the context of this broadly racial difference, Trollope's "simple, direct, salubrious" form of feeling becomes the instrumental property of one who "writes," who "feels," who "judges like a man" (AT 386). If he "has kept the purity of his imagination" so as to embody the "natural decorum of the English spirit," he is nonetheless "best" thought of as "a novelist who hunted the fox" (AT 386, 393). James plays several times on the strong contast between such healthy, "natural" English virtues and the artful dodges of the naturalists, invoking the rhetoric of race difference as a measure of the relative freedom of the two novelistic traditions (AT 395). Trollope's "perception of character was naturally more just and temperate than that of the naturalists"; his "natural rightness and purity are so real that the good things he projects must be real" (AT 392, 395).

This final recuperation of the energetic, decidedly Anglo-Saxon masculinity of Trollope's art as against enervated French styles of depravity, nihilism, and cunning instances both the performative dimension and the limits of James's interventions in realist nation-building. To promote the fiction of freedom, and thus the novel's power in emerging cultural orders, he intermittently reverts to a tactic that echoes Taney's in *Scott*, trading in race as a self-evident category even as he seeks to alter its cultural significance and terms. Adverting throughout "Trollope" to "the European point of view" and "the English world" as distinct from "the American," James lays claim to a "mastered" difference between national "character[s]" as well as a mastery of the "transatlantic" mode and the "delicate organism[s]" it in effect invents (AT 391). Yet he ends his long goodbye to Trollope in the idiom of natural inheritance, with a proclamation that declares the racial sameness of, and his own proprietary rights to, an Anglo-American constituency he has helped write into being: "A race is fortunate," James concludes, "when it has a good deal of the sort of imagination – of imaginative feeling – that had fallen to the share of Anthony Trollope. Our English race, happily, has much of it" (AT 395).

James's parting encomium, making Trollope a credit to his race, neatly circumscribes the "real" of Anglo-America's shared inheritance. Tellingly, he would revise this ending for the essay's republication in *Partial Portraits* in 1888, in a measure of the growing intensity throughout Anglo-America of the idiom of racial properties. There the final line reads: "and in this possession our English race is not poor" (*PP* 133). The revised version renders explicit James's internationalist logic under the sign of realist literary doctrine; the local effect in the play of his homophones ("poor," "pure") is to link the war on cultural poverty with the "possession" of racial purity. Trading locally in the imagination of sameness, James ensures his own *parti* as heir apparent to a tradition of Englishness freely reinvented in and the property of free imaginative feeling. Yet his achieved negotiation of cultural character, possibility, and type, writ as mere observation of national literary histories, obscures the dramatic dynamism of his own cultural politics, the very freedom of invention he assertively seeks to renew. James's performance of literary internationality in "Trollope" thus exacts a particular cost: that of belying its own vitally and culturally transformative power.

In the fiction following closely on "Trollope" and "The Art of

Fiction," James self-consciously pursues this self-generated paradox of literary and cultural generation. Still dealing freely with nation-building resources, he will more complexly imagine the relation between forms of cultural production and the making of nation and race. His most interesting reworking of "Trollope" 's race thinking and of the broadly realist concerns it records is conducted in *The Princess Casamassima*, with which James perversely casts himself in the very role he has so pointedly derided: that of naturalist in the modern urban *demimonde*. Such willful self-cancellations are endemic to James's ongoing self-fashioning, but this one enables a particular project. By taking up the generic formation he has strategically resisted, James gains access to another idiom of racial determinism, differently bound up with emergent literary institutions. Adopting its terms of cultural signification, James will more powerfully work to transfigure the novel's cultural agency, in direct response to popular and genteel forms of representation emerging in competing sites of racial making and performance.

3

"TRYING TO BE NATURAL": AUTHORSHIP AND THE POWER OF TYPE IN THE PRINCESS CASAMASSIMA

> I have been all the morning at Millbank prison (horrible place) col-
> lecting notes for a fiction scene. You see I am quite the Naturalist.
> Look out for the same – a year hence.
>
> – James to Thomas Sergeant Perry, 1884 (*Letters* 3:61)

> 'One must see life as one can; it comes, no doubt, to each of us in
> different ways. You think me affected, of course, and my behaviour a
> fearful *pose*; but I am only trying to be natural.
>
> – James, *The Princess Casamassima* (466)

In the preceding pages, I have argued that James's "realist episode"
(Brodhead, 143) – the eruption in his writing of apparently pro-
grammatic generic interests – redirects evolving Anglo-American
notions of racial character, destiny, and freedom. Here, I will argue
that these very negotiations themselves undergo a certain evolution
during the 1880s, in which a newly focused interest in racial tropes
and race thinking on James's part emerges. As "Anthony Trollope"
and "The Art of Fiction" appeared on opposite sides of the Atlantic, James was composing his "very national, very typical" novels of
civic life, *The Bostonians* and *The Princess Casamassima* (*Notebooks* 20).
Both novels trace the entanglement of civic activity with forms of
mass culture, with which literature vies for the power to direct
nation-building energies and fantasies. Both novels conduct this
project under the sign of naturalism, a genre often characterized,
implicitly or explicitly, as instancing the hard facts of racial determination and the contest between individual will and genetic fate.[1]
Together James's novels can be said to explore the mobility of literary nationality and of racial identity, newly conceived as an active
practice of culture-building and cultural affiliation in two specific
sites: post-Reconstruction urban America and transnational urban
London.

Why, we might ask, does James take up the naturalist idiom at this point in his career? To what ends does he mean to put a generic style so foreign to his *oeuvre* as virtually to discredit his experiments altogether?² His 1909 preface to *The Princess Casamassima* is suggestive in this regard. "The simplest account of the origin of *The Princess Casamassima*," James writes, "is . . . that this fiction proceeded quite directly . . . from the habit and the interest of walking the streets" (*AN* 59). Incubated in "perambulation," the story grows organically from James's " 'notes' " on "the great grey Babylon" of London, notes that are "the ineluctable consequence" of the author's "greatest inward energy: to take them was as natural as to look, to think, to feel, to recognise" (*AN* 59, 76). In turn, James's registered "impressions" of "the assault directly made by the great city" are offered to an imagined reader whose "instinct" on behalf of the " 'natural' and typical" is "justly strong" (*AN* 59, 63–4). Assaying "the very particular truth and 'authority' " of naturalism, James in his own recounting becomes a more focused version of the historian he imagines in the "Trollope" essay, an author committed to "the fruit of direct experience" and thus to the limits of his own partial knowledge (*AN* 76).

But *The Princess Casamassima* tries naturalism with more directed motives than this account suggests. The naturalist idiom of urban heterogeneity and bodily instinct provides James a productive resource for figuring and transfiguring literary nationality itself. Adopting naturalism's mobile idiom of type, James appropriates developing mass cultural narratives of nation, race (in all the unstable senses of the term), and individual character, against and through which the "nature" of literary authority, the destiny of Anglo-American cultural institutions, and the "issue" of the novel as a social genre take shape. Revising naturalism's fascination with nature and nurture, James stages more pointed dramas than are given scope by his critical writings about the identity of the " 'internationally' American" author in an increasingly transnational literary scene (*AN* 277).

The naturalist pretensions of *The Princess Casamassima*, in other words, allow James to conduct performative race work under cover of interrogating generic *données*. Professing allegiance to the doctrine of determined social type, the novel paradoxically privileges self-generative gestures that mimic and enable James's own, rewarding its "unnatural" characters, its dubious "cosmopolites," with curiously productive powers and pleasures. James's mixed representation of these figures registers his own competing investments. Their aesthetic sensibilities – the capacity for "taste" and liberating experiences of aesthetic response – are represented as the heritable faculties of distinct national, class, or racial bodies. Yet these same sensibilities enable James's surrogates to transgress the cultural laws of biology and body forth new narrative and social "mixtures." The scene of naturalist writing thus stages an allegory of James's attempts to alter the terms of his own literary filiation, as he experimentally weds the resources of French and English cultures at a moment when "[t]here is positively nothing to read, in England or France," and "the pen is fruitless and dumb" (*Letters* 3:106). The "ripe round fruit" of James's own cross-cultural performance will be the regeneration of the novel as a distinctly civic enterprise, a theater for the production of Anglo-American "racial" identity and meaning.

In attempting this project of renewal, however, *The Princess* turns out to give scope to other than merely celebratory fantasies about the powers of the author and the distinctly literary status of his labors. James's trial of naturalist typology allows him to confront and partially to repudiate an ascendant literary movement – dubbed "King Romance" by James's contemporary, the folklorist and race theorist Andrew Lang – whose cultural politics turn on fantasies of return to more primally authentic, purer forms of racial nature. Adapting the troubled rhetoric of mastery prominent in male romances of the era, and in discussions of the mass market vehicles in which they appear, James forestalls a racial nostalgia that saturates Anglo-American literary culture in its attacks on the perceived feminization of the public sphere and of Anglo-Saxon institutions.[3]

The Princess undermines this racial panic by pitting Hyacinth Robinson, a "natural" author of romance, against the Princess Casamassima. Her performances of desire, curiosity, and pleasure render irrelevant her assigned role as object of romantic desire, casting her instead as a powerful surrogate for the naturalist author himself. In their contest of authorial styles, the Princess initially wins out; the plot of her constitutional "aversion to the *banal*" takes precedence over Hyacinth's racially mandated "romantic curiosity" (*AN* 74, 61). Her victory gives center stage to increasingly powerful cultural anxieties, writ large in the text of King Romance, about what one of James's anticipatory versions of *The Princess* calls "the 'decline,' in a word, of old England," "on behalf of which . . . so much of the strongest and finest stuff of the greatest race (for such they are) has been expended" (*Letters* 3:67).

Rather than bewail this broadly racial decline, however, the Princess's problematic ascendancy works a double shift. It countervails against the emerging commitment in Anglo-American cultural politics to radically asocial fantasies of renewed Anglo-Saxon virility. And it simultaneously redefines the private sphere appropriated by the novel, the sphere of domesticity, intimate association, and female experience, as a site of meaningful civic activity.[4] Positioning the Princess Casamassima between men as an intended object of homosocial exchange, James fleetingly celebrates an authorial victory of the "novel" over the "noble," of frictional energy and social commitment over narcissistic withdrawal – one that turns out to be contingent on the Princess's problematic "freedom" from binding structures of nation, family, and race. Her victory, acted out in "associations" forged across such barriers, gives definitive shape to James's own performative genealogy, whereby the self-fashioning Anglo-American author – like the "representative" figures at work in the revolutionary "International" – travels freely across typological boundaries, undoing civic agency from the fixity of race or the nation–state.

But finally the *données* of naturalism work to contain the Princess's energetic theatricality, reserving the performative agency of transnational self-invention for the "Naturalist" author himself. Reverting, in effect, to type, the novel awards its heroine a dramatically protean energy only to foreclose against it in the romance conventions James actively derides. Christina Light, hazarded anew as a "striking" figure who can't "resign herself not to strike again" (*AN* 74), must be eclipsed, in an anxiety of culture-building inextricably bound up with authorial desires, challenges, and performances. Her remanding to the canons of romance marks the farthest reaches of James's interventions in the naturalist idiom, but it also suggests how productively unstable are the borders he draws for Anglo-America as a literary and cultural body.

"Every Established Law of Nature": Race, Determination, and Self-Determination

James's strategic enthusiasm for naturalism in the preface to *The Princess* inadvertently calls attention to the *in*stability of the novel's interest in genealogy, inheritance, and type. Retrospectively describing his bookbinder as "some individual sensitive nature . . . capable of profiting by all the civilisation, all the accumulations to which [perception and action] testify," James conspicuously relocates the problem of origins from the arena of biological destiny to that of fictive design (*AN* 60). The "history of little Hyacinth Robinson" is said to begin with a virtual act of spontaneous generation. Like other "presentable figures" that "rise from the thick jungle" with "the brush of importunate wings," that "small obscure intelligent creature" appears on the scene of writing fully formed: "he sprang up for me out of the London pavement"; "so the book . . . was born" (*AN* 60, 59). By displacing his earlier naturalist tropes of genealogical issue, James occludes the novel's focus on racial transmission. He thus obscures the self-interrupting quality of the forms of "truth and 'authority' " that constitute his own authorial activity (*AN* 76).[5]

The motives for such misreading of his text are the ultimate interest of this chapter. Initially, however, I want to think about the shifting work done throughout the novel by a naturalist vocabulary of genealogy and type. From the very outset, Hyacinth's drama advertises itself as a play of "determination[s]," the unfolding of a tragic destiny plotted by "every established law of nature" and given form by the "inheritance" that "darken[s] the whole threshold of his manhood" (*PC* 60, 105). The "law" of genealogical determinism appears everywhere to rule, from the sign feebly hanging between the windows at Lomax Place, which advertises Amanda Pynsent's ineffectual eagerness to undertake "DRESSMAKING IN ALL ITS BRANCHES," to the apparent genetic disorder that afflicts Rose Muniment, leaving her "on her back" and dependent on her sole inherited capital: "the intellect" that "our parents had . . . to give us" (74, 491, 147). Every countenance and gesture, both high and low, emits "a suggestion of race," in its familial, national, and class-inflected forms (136). Indeed the terms of personal fate appear to be contained and teleologically unfolded "all in the family" (59).[6]

Like its preface, however, *The Princess* ultimately belies this naturalist insistence on origins. Its invocation of inheritance is remarkably unstable, a fact unremarked until quite recently by James's critical readers. As Millicent Bell argues, James's identification in *The Princess Casamassima* with naturalism, and in particular with naturalist notions of type, is both limited and strategic. Although apparently "foredoomed" to a double life framed by the warring instincts of the "bastard" and the "gentleman," Hyacinth never convincingly embodies the "mixed, divided nature" – the fatal self-division – dictated by his "blood" (269, 478, 168, 165). The "constant element in his moral life" turns out to be the "extraordinarily mingled current" that renders him *a*typical, "exotic," "original," extraordinary (480, 165, 104, 222).[7] As against Frank Norris's McTeague, swept headlong on the foul stream of an hereditary evil, or Zola's actors, dominated by nerves and blood, Hyacinth is "stamped" not with the "stain" of inherited criminal passion but with the "mystical sign" of a higher sensibility (242, 397, 386) – one that transcends the " 'natural' and typical" altogether (AN 63).

Hyacinth Robinson thus proves an unlikely subject of naturalism: not the issue of an ill-fated *mésalliance*, irremediably destined for precipitous moral decline, but an everywhere "foreign" agent with "exception[al]" and "exquisite[ly] organis[ed]" sensibilities (PC 311, 219, 463). Paradoxically, however, James certifies the authenticity of Hyacinth's "individual sensitive nature" in the very language of racial type it partially displaces (34). The little bookbinder's acts of cultural acquisition and possession – not unlike those James attributes in his preface to the observer of London – are given shape by a logic of racial inheritance as certain elements of his "high bre[eding]," of his class and racial predispositions, predominate (61). Despite their instability as social facts, the "ancient and exalted" bloodline of his unproven paternity and the "French blood in [his] veins" are together taken to account not only for his general "air of race" but for his epiphantic moments of aesthetic liberation, the coming-into-being of his most authentic self (58, 201, 62).

Thus "Mademoiselle Vivier's son," like a latter-day Cinderella, discovers himself at the Princess's pleasure palace, Medley Park. To the manner born, "he already *was* inured to being waited upon"; "he became conscious that there were [no attentions] he should care to miss, or was not quite prepared for." In "breathless ecstasy" at the scope afforded his "exquisite impression[s]," Hyacinth roams the Park only to find it "peopled with recognitions; he had been dreaming all his life of just such a place and such objects" (301). Although consistently "embarrassed" by his own desires (191), exposed as "stammering," tongue-tied, and *maladroit* (198), "Florentine's boy" is nonetheless equipped with good taste, "little French shrugs," and " '*la main parisienne*' " (381, 340, 125). With "his French heredity," he finds it "not so easy . . . to make unadorned speeches" in the presence of the Princess (199). While "all his nerves and pulses plea[d] and testif[y]" to Hyacinth's blood, they signify neither the stolid paternity of "the recreant" Lord Frederick – whose only notable act of sensibility seems to have been his ill-advised dalliance with a *femme fatale* – nor even the galling and "blood-stained" legacy of the Viviers (167). Instead his intelligence and curiosity express a "latent Gallicism," a distinctly "racial" receptivity that enables Hyacinth's remarkable sentimental education in "the finest discriminations, the perception of beauty and the hatred of ugliness" (120, 157).

This idiom of inherited "racial" type enables the redirection of James's signature interest in the self-fashioning of the finely aware intelligence profiting by cultural "accumulations." The point of Hyacinth's story, as James admits in the preface, is not merely "the question of what the total assault, that of the world of his work-a-day life and the world of his divination," would have "made of him," but "what in especial he would have made of them" (*AN* 61–2). What Hyacinth "makes" above all is a series of choices and gestures about his own filiation, his connectedness to racialized and nationalized styles of performance and response. This logic – of racial fate superseded by choice – governs two crucial moments of political expression: Hyacinth's declaration of allegiance to the body of working revolutionaries, and his epistolary recantation of that bond for allegiance to a higher bond of "civilisation."

In the first instance, in the novel's most extended staging of revolutionary exchange, Hyacinth acts out a scene of self-declaration scripted as an access of racially inflected feeling. Outside the Sun and Moon, in "the wintry drizzle" of "the huge tragic city," he finds himself overcome by "the contagion of excited purpose," "seized by an intense desire" of belonging. But his "state of inward exaltation" only serves to expose the fragility of social bodies constituted on claims to any naturalized national, racial, or class identity (*PC* 293, 291). At the moment of his own revolutionary performance, Hyacinth declares his loyalties in an internal contest between "fearfully English" notions of political "duty" and "insatiable" French claims for "greatness of soul" (289–90). What prompts him to speak is the "accusation" of Delancey, the "suppositious hairdresser," which "seemed to leap at him personally," like "a quick blow in the face": "There isn't a man in the blessed lot that isn't afraid of his bloody skin," Delancey charges. "There isn't a mother's son of you that'll risk his precious bones!" (294).[8]

As if by instinct, "Hyacinth found that he had sprung up on a chair, opposite to the barber . . . It was the first time he had asked the ear of the company, and it was given on the spot." The affair puts at stake Hyacinth's legitimacy, or rather his manhood – the question whether he genuinely *is* his mother's son, capable of representing a social body of "*le peuple*" or "the people" at large (294). Declaring his readiness to "do anything that will do any good, anything, anything," Hyacinth chooses a style of response that enables him "for the first time" to "speak for myself." Yet his act of choice is elided by an implied logic of race transmission that codes his unnatural outbreak in terms of type. Even as he declares himself to be "the genuine" revolutionary "article," his performance is received as the work of what readers in the American context might call a paleface, "a genteel little customer"; appealing to the assemblage of the crowded club-room, "[h]e was sure that he looked very white" (295–6, 294).

Later in the novel Hyacinth will more successfully negotiate the force of type via a heroic gesture of self-invention. Writing the Princess from Venice during the conduct of his modestly grand tour, he represents himself as transformed by the acquisition of "historical information." "I can scarcely believe that it's of myself that I am telling these fine things," he writes; "I say to myself a dozen times a day that Hyacinth Robinson is not in it" (394–5). Hyacinth in Venice is indeed least himself, least bound by the determination of his inheritance and most capable of revising his allegiances to it. Abandoning the rhetoric of "mixed" blood, he declares instead for "the things with which the aspirations and the tears of generations have been mixed," the "inestimably precious and beautiful" achievements crowning "the face of Europe" and of "man" (396). No longer speaking "the same language" of class warfare and racial fate, he swears to eschew a moral "intolerance of positions and fortunes that are higher and brighter than one's own" for a purer veneration of "the conquests of learning and taste" (397, 396). Rendering irrelevant the "stain" of his illegitimacy, he concludes the article of his new faith by declaring the "devout hope that if I am to pass away while I am yet young it may not be with that odious stain [of intolerance] upon my soul" (397).

In both instances Hyacinth's expansive gestures of filiation redirect the force of racial determination, employing it as a resource in his unfolding drama of self-determination. His declarations of independence from the facts of type, in both the narrowly political and the more broadly cultural modes, are rendered credible through the force of his inherited "Gallicism," evinced as a predisposition to aesthetic striving. Revisiting Lomax Place after an absence of eight years Millicent Henning exclaims, with all the interest of her instinct for upward mobility, " 'You look for all the world like a little Frenchman! Don't he look like a little Frenchman?' " (101–2). More delicately, the Princess Casamassima remarks, " 'I can see that you are not le premier venu' "; she reads "perfectly in [his] face" the "French blood" that announces his exceptionality (201–2). This variously nuanced quality – evinced as "something delicate that was stamped upon him everywhere," a "mystical sign in his appearance" – inevitably will out (242, 386). To his continual embarrassment, Hyacinth is destined by his "constitution" to be "one of those taking little beggars" who unmistakably signifies his true origins, exactly "like a young man in an illustrated story-book" (61, 210).

The latter analogy underscores, contra naturalist determinism, the ultimate mobility and textuality of "racial" character throughout the novel and the ways in which James understands that character to be mediated by conventions of reading, reception, and literary production – mediated, that is, by the instrumentality of type, in the era of mass fictions of social identity.[9] Advertised as a fixed, immutable fact of nature, performed as a shifting allegiance, Hyacinth's inheritance plays out certain heated cultural contests, most notably that between high and popular styles of culture-building. In one sense, as Bell argues, the "genetic elements" of Hyacinth's double nature are best understood as metaphors for contending literary realist ideologies; for the "significant conflict of philosophies" of democratic equality and exceptionality, she claims, "the conflict in blood may be only a figure" (Bell, 175). In another sense, however, the little bookbinder's mixed inheritance is more than only a figure – or rather, as a figure it implicates the fate of the novel as a vehicle for Anglo-America's racial self-fashioning in *The Princess*'s moment. Daring the "divided," "mingled current" of a purely "Gallic" sensibility and "*le genre anglais*" (*PC* 165, 120, 117), Hyacinth allegorizes James's own project of internationality, in contest with other culture-building enterprises for the power to create representative fictions of character and type. In the fate of Hyacinth Robinson, James redirects the discourse of racial determination he entertains into a critique of predominant genres for constructing the cultural category and meaning of the Anglo-Saxon, thus underwriting his own performances of cultural self-determination.

Trials and Tribulations: The Romance of Type and the Theater of Embarrassment

> I have been seeing something of Daudet, Goncourt and Zola; and there is nothing more interesting to me now than the effort and experiment of this little group . . . They do the only kind of work, today, that I respect; and in spite of their ferocious pessimism and their handling of unclean things, they are at least serious and honest. The floods of tepid soap and water which under the name of novels are being vomited forth in England, seem to me, by contrast, to do little honour to our race.
>
> – James to William Dean Howells, 1884 (*Letters* 3:28)

When Hyacinth Robinson, that "flower of a high civilisation" (165), gains unexpected access to Lady Aurora Langrish's library, he anxiously scans its shelves for tomes of "French literature," particularly the same ferocious works of that "intensely modern school" of "advanced and scientific realists." To his disappointment, he finds only "several volumes of Lamartine and a set of the spurious memoirs of the Marquise de Crequi" – a far different story from the authentic naturalist "history" in which he figures (*PC* 264). On holiday in Paris, he imagines himself "fraternising with Balzac and Alfred de Musset" as he indulges in "a tall glass of champagne" and "a pineapple ice" in "the most dandified" of all Parisian cafés, known to him "from his study of the French novel" (379–80). Installed at Madeira Crescent, he weaves a Balzacian fireside fantasy of marriage to "the most remarkable woman in Europe." Their intimate "intercourse," "interfused with domestic embarrassments" and conducted "often in the French tongue," suggests "the idea of the *vie de province*, as he had read about it in French works" (482–3). No longer protesting her treatment of him as a clever "specimen" (225), Hyacinth happily countenances "[b]eing whistled for by a princess"; this is, after all, "an indignity endured gracefully enough by the heroes of several French novels in which he had found a thrilling interest" (188). Furthermore, the most beautiful woman in Europe makes Hyacinth's most powerful fantasy come true: she gives him "the last number of the *Revue des Deux Mondes*," complete with "a story of M. Octave Feuillet," and thereby confirms Hyacinth's natural fitness for the authentically high international style to which he, like the novel, aspires (307).[10]

These excursions into a cultural avant-garde, which can be "accounted for in no other manner" than as the natural consequence of Hyacinth's racially determined sensibility (480), invariably raise the possibility of negotiating racial type that constitutes the grounds of James's engagement with naturalism. But if Hyacinth figures "the painter of the human mixture," *The Princess* is nonetheless determined to undermine his "romantic curiosity," subjecting him to an ordeal that Joseph Litvak has resonantly called the theater of embarrassment (*PC* 37, 35).[11] The more closely Hyacinth's eager gestures of cultural filiation resemble those of *The Princess* itself, the more firmly they seem to be linked with issues of cultural reproduction or type and fatally undermined. Oscillating between French and Anglo-Saxon canons, between naturalist and romance imperatives, between high and low cultural formations, Hyacinth's project of self-authorship mimes the taxonomic anxieties of the Anglo-American novel in the closing decades of the century, as the latter contests other discursive enterprises for the power to redirect the cultural energies of a more urgently "Anglo-Saxon" social body.

In particular, Hyacinth's racially coded embarrassment rehearses

James's own vivid embarrassments throughout the 1880s – in which *The Princess Casamassima* richly participates – at the hands of the newspaper, an increasingly powerful competitor for the management of cultural type. Throughout the 1880s and 1890s, print culture in Anglo-America was being radically transformed by England's "new journalism" of sensation, and by the aggressively anti-genteel cultural politics of William Randolph Hearst and Joseph Pulitzer's "metrojournalism" in America. One reporter at the New York *Dial* acerbically declared that "The fundamental principle of metropolitan journalism is to buy white paper at three cents a pound and sell it at ten cents a pound. And in some quarters it does not matter how much the virgin whiteness of the paper is defiled so long as the defilement sells the paper" (cited in Ziff, 147). If such sensationalism resulted in enormous increases in the circulation and prestige of mass dailies – Pulitzer's *New York World*, for example, upped its circulation fully tenfold between 1883 and 1885 (Juergens, 50)[12] – those booms also depended crucially on the deployment of human interest journalism, which both predicated and promulgated typological distinctions of persons into different social categories, corresponding to structural divisions between "news," "society," "entertainment," and other forms of cultural expression (A. Kaplan, 25–6; Ziff, 147–8). Increasingly, the print organs of Anglo-America's mass market not only harness the energies and appeal of the realist novel; they vie aggressively for the cultural authority of distinction, through which fictions of national character, progress, and type will be instituted and circulated.

Numerous readers of the realist project have documented the terms of this contest, but the facts of *The Princess*'s production provide a pointed instance of its urgency.[13] In January of 1886, as James completed the novel for serial publication, he received a letter from Edward Tyas Cook, an editor of the *Pall Mall Gazette*. Later editor of the *Westminster Gazette* and the *Daily News*, and biographer of such nation-building icons as Ruskin and Florence Nightingale, Cook was a leading apostle of the new journalism. Actively campaigning to boost readership among the ascendant bourgeoisie and shore up social types for its education, in service of what Cook would later describe as the "larger interests and duties of the country as an Imperial Power," he asked James, Swinburne, and Matthew Arnold to provide a list of "the hundred best books" to be recommended to the *Gazette*'s readership.[14] The program was designed to promote not only a distinctly Anglo-Saxon sensibility, but the priority of newsprint itself as the authoritative source for narratives of cultural identity and community.

With self-consciously heightened gentility James "beg[s] to be excuse[d]," implicitly rejecting Cook's missionary gospel of culture. His "convictions, on the subject," he writes, can be "resolved into a single one" that "may not decently be reproduced in the columns of a newspaper. . . . It is simply that the reading of the newspapers is *the* pernicious habit, and the father of all idleness and luxury" (*Letters* 3:108). James's ostentatiously delicate refusal proves both futile and prophetic, as another more anxious note to the same correspondent testifies. Just two days later, he writes Cook again to "request . . . very earnestly" that his "strictly private" condemnation of publicity – speedily returned to him "in proof" for final approval despite its substance – not itself "appear in the columns of the *Pall Mall Gazette*" (*Letters* 3:108–9). In control of the last word, the newspaperist *par excellence* promotes in the richly responsible author a certain nostalgic romanticism of the sort James attempts to combat. With their "contemptible little" judgements, he confesses, "the idiocy and ill nature of the journals of my time have made me [sublime]" (*Letters* 3:139).

The Princess offers a more plotted entanglement of this particular idiotic and sublime. James links the central drama of Hyacinth's self-knowledge – his acquisition of the "new and more poignant consciousness" of inherited type that literally puts him in a class by himself – with the reproductions of the mass press, and in particular those of its sentimental organs.[15] The result is a continual embarrassment of Hyacinth's genteel style of reading and self-declaration – and the preservation, potentially, of a more culturally engaged high style for James's own performance. Exposing the insufficiency of Hyacinth's "romantic" passions, scripted as the inevitable voicing of "a latent hereditary chord," James registers the fatedness not of racial nature but of the literary enterprise in the realist moment, struggling for the power to "represent" the "immeasurable body" of whiteness in its transnational reading public (*PC* 375, 384).

The determination of identity attaches, then, not to "the state of the account between society" and Hyacinth or to his possibilities for self-determination so much as to the structures of feeling that give them voice (75). Against his strenuous efforts to make his exceptionality count, the novel poses the intransigence of emergent consumer forms of racial and class identity. In a freighted scene of reading, on a "never-to-be-forgotten afternoon," Hyacinth pores over the columns of *The Times* in "the reading-room of the British Museum" (479). "[D]isinterr[ing]" a "very copious" report "of his mother's trial for the murder of Lord Frederick Purvis," he "reconstruct[s] his antecedents, t[akes] the measure . . . of his heredity" (479, 167). Even the restrained style of official culture, encountered in its most austere arena, fails to protect Hyacinth from the power of the *"cause célèbre"* or the "romantic innuendoes" of mass fictions of type. "[W]ith his head bent to hide his hot eyes," the "gentleman born" peruses "every syllable of the ghastly record" (167, 169). Like lower journalistic organs, the latter naturalizes class and racial hierarchies by sensationalizing the perversity of their undoing, narrating as a kind of "monstrous farce" the "poor and hideous" facts of encounter between the daughter of "the wild French people" and "an English aristocrat" (169, 167). This confirmatory "evidence" of type, in both senses, affords a readerly *frisson* against whose seductions Hyacinth must ever be on guard. When he thereafter "sometimes saw the name of his father's relations in the newspapers," he "always turned away his eyes from it" (169). To Hyacinth's chagrin, however, the performance of his "finest sensibilities" is inevitably entangled with conventions of type; even his own best revolutionary rhetoric can do little more than echo "precious phrase[s] out of the newspaper" (169, 151). Aiming for impassioned oratory that represents the reality of cultural experience – "the thing itself" – Hyacinth turns out to be an ironically "genuine article," fated to recapitulate the "drivelling leader[s]" of the mass press (151, 295).

In subjecting its hero to the embarrassment of what James trenchantly calls "newspaperism" – which Hyacinth himself describes as the "insipid [sensationalism] of an age which had lost the sense of quality" (163) – the narrative takes its "little presumptuous adventurer" to book for his romantic self-imagination (*AN* 72). Yet it also evinces a partial sympathy for his tentatively hazarded project. Seeking to overthrow the banal but irresistibly determinative force of the emergent cultural forms that shape his experience of his own "nature," Hyacinth yearns to install a narrative economy that would nurture a different, transumptively romantic plot – one governed by sacred vows, tests of manhood and loyalty, a blood brotherhood of meaningful sacrifice and redemption. He longs, in the narrative's phrase, to speak the "mystic language" of the self-determined "disinherited," joined in "a freemasonry" or "reciprocal divination" of mutual "moral dignity" (*PC* 283).

Rather than merely protest the vulgarity of mass culture, in a textual enactment of the mandarin cultural politics typically assigned to James, Hyacinth's fantasy of acting against type enables a more complex and responsive form of culture-building. He ultimately fails to redirect the "romantic innuendoes" of his assigned role in the narrative or to overcome its ongoing embarrassment of his designs (169). But his very failure is richly significant; it registers a meaningful intervention on James's part in a broadly racial structure of feeling, insofar as Hyacinth's style of response is measured against generic narratives of the fate of the Anglo-Saxon. In the staging of his romantic sensibility, *The Princess* pursues two related and sometimes competing interests: it challenges the defensive project of imperialist romance and its radically narcissistic response to the plot of racial contamination and decline; and it simultaneously particularizes the problem of "feminization" as a challenge not to racial health but to the novel's power to conduct politically meaningful forms of culture-building. A figure of and for racial affect, Hyacinth registers an interest in wider revolutions in literary value, production, and privilege whose issue will revise the Anglo-American culture of type.

The Instinct of Manliness: Racial Romance on Trial

The chief part of our business lies with men who are wearied at the end of the day – certain great captains. They will not bring their womenfolk aboard.

> – Rudyard Kipling, *The Kipling Pageant*, 1897
> (cited in Green, 283)

We are poor tame, terrified products of the tailor and the parlour-maid; but we *have* a fine sentiment or two, all the same.

> – James to Robert Louis Stevenson, 1890 (*Letters* 3:273)

As the scenario of embarrassment suggests, Hyacinth's racial inheritance plays out in conspicuously gendered terms. His legitimacy as central authorial consciousness is virtually certified by his feminization, his "queer mixture," his "fragility of constitution" (*PC* 526, 61); on these, the vaunted "*quality* of bewilderment" itself appears to depend (*AN* 66). "[S]hrinking and sensitive," "delicate and high-bred," Hyacinth divides his readers within the novel on distinctly gendered lines (61). While that intractable "arm of the law," Mrs. Bowerbank, takes "pleasure" in the delicacy of his "refined and interesting figure," an unsentimental Vetch derides him as an hysterical narcissist, "a thin-skinned, morbid, mooning little beggar" with "a fine, blooming, odoriferous conceit" (59, 63, 72–3).

Both readings cast Hyacinth Robinson as the romantic heroine of his own text – precisely the role that the Princess Casamassima

perversely refuses, in turn, to play. Governed by "paralysing melan-
choly," he specializes naturally in the affect of the romantic heroine
(163). As he turns pale and "crimson" by turns, "his heart beat[s]
fast" at her approach (219, 189); he despises his own "trembling
hand" and "too nervous" mannerisms during interviews in which
he "seem[s] to himself to stammer and emit common sounds" (245,
198). In the presence of the Princess, Hyacinth displays a romantic
self-consciousness to whose "provoking" quality she critically calls
attention: " 'you drop your eyes, you even blush a little, and make
yourself small' " (194, 320). Even in his own milieu Hyacinth fares
little more heroically. He "blush[es] and stammer[s]" in front of the
partisan crowd at the Sun and Moon (286); he suffers "a pang in his
heart" (399) and a "tremor in his voice" (446) in the company of the
"manly" and indifferent Paul Muniment (135). In the best tradition
of romantic feminine passivity, Hyacinth finds himself everywhere
"embarrassed, overturned, bewildered" (191).

   I want to suggest that a naturalist idiom of racial type, played out
in the narrative's insistence on Hyacinth's gallicized "delicate constitution," becomes the vehicle for James's positioning of his hero in the
arena of a cultural politics of whiteness, of Anglo-Saxon masculinity
in withdrawal from gathering cultural forces of degeneration. The
insistent feminization – the wholesale embarrassment – of Hyacinth Robinson actively participates in a complex plot of literary
historical engenderment, putting the value of this form of agency at
stake. Purity of racial type and "sinister" forms of masculinity go, in
The Princess's notation of sexuality, class, race, and authorial power,
"hand" in "hand."[16] Certified as the "real thing" by the sensitivity of
his racial nature, Hyacinth intermittently figures a power of resistance to the problematically white and manly agents he confronts on
both sides of the class divide.

   James most obviously mounts this revolution of embarrassment
in Hyacinth's exchanges with the "unmistakably" Anglo-Saxon and
"gentleman[ly]" Godfrey Sholto, who represents a certain "English
type" produced by nature – "a longish pedigree" – and confirmed
by nurture – the "idle, trifling, luxurious" circumstances of "complete leisure" (225, 352). His interest in "specimens" and "curious
out-of-the-way nooks" turns out to be not merely that of the "tout"
or "cat's paw," but a kind of *droit de seigneur*, the erotic license of
"the finest whites": " 'That was rather a nice little girl in there; did
you twig her figure? It's a pity they always have such beastly
hands' " (226, 273–5). Indulging a certain "romantic" curiosity
about Sholto's "chambers" and "enchantments," Hyacinth nonetheless registers discomfort with the latter's race-bound aestheticism.

"[W]ith the conscience of an artist," he notes that "the bindings of the Captain's books . . . were not very good" (232). In this case, one can indeed judge a book by its cover. The inveterate "trifl[er]" and cosmopolitan trafficker in "the spoils of travel and the ingenuities of modern taste" is distinctly if locally "sinister" (352, 230, 353).

Sholto, however, provides an all too easy target for James, as for his latter-day readers. The novel's energy of resistance is thus largely reserved for a riskier embroilment with the "remarkable" Paul Muniment (126). Embodying the homosocial manliness fantasized by such popular writers of racial romance as Andrew Lang, Rider Haggard, Robert Louis Stevenson, and Rudyard Kipling, Muniment provides a foil for the "queer mixture" of Hyacinth's racial inheritance (526). Taken as representative of their cultural politics, Muniment can be seen to play a more coherent and more interesting role in the novel than that usually assigned him: he figures a crucial link between ongoing genre wars and the embattled arena of racial preservation and decline.

Despite renewed interest in the textual politics of *The Princess*, virtually none of James's recent readers has interrogated the credibility of Muniment as a political – or more narrowly, a revolutionary – agent. But as R. H. Hutton noted in a canny review of 1887, Muniment lacks any coherent motivation in such a role. Although he remains "a remarkably vivid presence," James "does not contrive to give us even the faintest notion of the ground on which Paul Muniment had persuaded himself that it was worth [his] while . . . to upset all existing institutions." Muniment, Hutton contends, "is just such a man . . . as would leave political dreams alone, and make his way up the ladder by steady thrift and industry. The great blot on the novel" is its failure "even to hint which side of the man it was that made him a revolutionary; hardly even to make us feel quite sure he is one at all except in appearance. In Mr. James's novel as it stands, Muniment is almost unintelligible."[17]

Hutton's criticism, which usefully resists recent styles of reading the novel, is both apt and revealing. As revolutionary Muniment indeed remains "almost unintelligible." Declaring off the bat, " 'I don't think I care much for plots' " (130), he would as soon succeed by bourgeois self-betterment as by the violent seizure of property. James shrewdly registers this fact of "character"; as Hyacinth's "latent hereditary" sensibility awakens in Paris, Muniment enjoys "a rise . . . at the chemical works" (391). Rejecting the politics of communitarianism or representativeness – " 'A man's foremost duty is not to get collared,' " he proclaims – Muniment reserves his allegiances for himself and for a fantasized "religion" of "supreme duty," a transcendent bonding between "honest men and men of courage" (289). Finally, he embodies no political imagination so powerfully as the emergent romance ideal of escape from the contract of culture, imagined as party to traffic with "unclean beasts" (289). He ultimately "works" not under the sign of the revolutionary will-to-power that would transfigure the civic arena in the image of his own pyschic designs or destroy it altogether. Instead Muniment practices a politics of withdrawal, refusal, and evasion borrowed from the race-renewing fictions of Stevenson, Haggard, and other contenders for the production of cultural types that will, in James's words, "succee[d] most with the English of today" (*Letters* 3:128). Grounded in the figure of Muniment, the variously named charge of the novel – homosocial, homoerotic, "queer" – can be read as a limited engagement with the imperatives of racialized romance.[18]

Apposite in this connection is James's contemporaneous writing to and about Robert Louis Stevenson, a central figure in the romance revival and its politics of race vitality.[19] In numerous letters, James pays tribute "by left hand" to the aggressive muscularity of Stevenson's fiction, which ironically belies the latter's chronic and neuresthenic ill health. Although Stevenson himself is "but a bag of coughs and bones," suffering from an inherited susceptibility to tuberculosis, the body of his work has been "coloured" with his "extreme invalidism . . . not at all"; he "project[s] upon the printed page a suggestion of a young Apollo." In fact, writes James, "the conception that most of your readers catch from your pages" leads them to "se[e] you mainly in want of bloodletting and other emasculation" (*Letters* 3:103). Elsewhere James congratulates Stevenson on a signature narrative virility, an unlimited power of writerly dissemination; consorting with "half a dozen Muses," the latter entertains "a shameless polygamy" (*Letters* 3:207).

James's published essay on Stevenson of 1887 clearly makes a certain capital by negation of just such writerly and race-linked virility. In a markedly measured assessment he describes Stevenson's style as problematically "conscious of" its social "responsibilities"; "it meets them with a kind of gallantry – as if language were a pretty woman, and a person who proposes to handle it had of necessity to be something of a Don Juan" (*PP* 137–74; 140–1). Yet at the back of the "nature" that produces this style is "an absence of care for things feminine. His books are for the most part books without women"; when women do appear, they are "so many superfluous girls in a boy's game" who "don't like ships and pistols and

fights," who "encumber the decks and require separate apart-
ments, and, almost worst of all, have not the highest literary standard" (*PP* 141, 149).

James's review identifies two distinct and crucial failures at-
tendent on Stevenson's "apology for boyhood": the repudiation of
forms of engagement (particularly marriage) on which civic life
depends, and the fantasy of race purification and renewal achieved
only at the cost of withdrawal from culture into a primally authentic, revitalized nature. In the annals of King Romance, "[t]he idea
of making believe appeals . . . much more than the idea of making
love"; why after all "should a person marry when he might be
swinging a cutlass or looking for a buried treasure?" (*PP* 146, 149).
The "odd" absence of real women, let alone odd women, from
Stevenson's adventures is the trademark omission of the manly
writer, one who "does not need, as we may say, a petticoat to in-
flame him" and whose "best effects" are achieved "without the aid
of the ladies" (*PP* 141, 170). Finally, James notes, the only woman in
Stevenson's world who isn't merely a "grown-up gir[l]" is "the delightful maiden . . . whom he commemorates in *An Inland Voyage*,"
who furthers the renewal of Anglo-Saxon power in her agency as
the "fit daughter of an imperial race" (*PP* 149). In carefully chosen
citations from the antidomestic essays of Stevenson's *Virginibus
Puerisque*, James tests the link forged by male romance between
gender trouble and race doctrine: " 'To marry is to domesticate the
Recording Angel. Once you are married, there is nothing left for
you, not even suicide, but to be good . . . How then, in such an
atmosphere of compromise, to keep honour bright and abstain
from base capitulations?' " (*PP* 150–1).

Notably, the homosocial contract of "honour bright," in this
cultural imaginary and imagination of culture, declines irremediably in traffic with the compromising other of Anglo-Saxon manliness. Just as, in Stevenson, the " 'proper [i.e., natural] qualities of
each sex are eternally surprising to the other,' " so the natural
characters of " 'the Latin and the Teuton races' " are eternally
" 'divergen[t]' " – enisled natures " 'not to be bridged by the most
liberal sympathy' " (*PP* 151). In his better-known remarks on Stevenson in the preface to *The American*, James makes quite different capital of the latter's cultural politics, extrapolating from Stevenson's "panting pursuit of danger" to his own "pursuit of life
itself" as an active enterprise in which differently conceived danger "faces us at every turn" (*AN* 32). Here, however, James's carefully gendered versions of Stevenson challenge the "real" motive

of "the romance of boyhood": the recuperation of a racially purified masculinity untainted by, unbound from, the " 'base capitulations' " of Anglo-America's emerging culture of commodity and
sensation (*PP* 146).

At large, then, James's masculinizing gestures record both ap-
probation for the figure whose work has provided "[t]he intensest
throb of my literary life" (*Letters* 3:273) and a contestatory interest
in the culture-building power of literary genres and styles of cultural response. But as serial publication of *The Princess* begins,
James's exchanges with Stevenson register a more obviously combative engagement with the racialized virility of male romance,
conceived specifically as "mental food" for the future chiefs of a
great race (Salmon, 259). Writing "on the subject of the unspeakable [Rider] Haggard" after having finished the enormously
popular *King Solomon's Mines* and "half of" *She*, James unleashes a
self-consciously gallicized gentility against the excesses of manly
Anglo-Saxonism: "Ah, *par example, c'est trop fort!*" (*Letters* 3:128).
Moved "to a holy indignation" by "the fortieth thousand" (an accounting of the novel's run-away sales[20]), he excoriates "the contemptible inexpressiveness of the whole thing," exceeded only by
"the beastly bloodiness of it . . . Such perpetual killing and such
perpetual ugliness!" Deriding Haggard's homosocial fantasies of
race atavism and supremacy, he complains that "the Narrator" is
"addressed constantly by one of the personages of the tale as 'my
Baboon!' *Quel genre!*" With deliciously delicate litotes James concludes, "It isn't nice that anything so vulgarly brutal should be the
thing that succeeds most with the English of today." The self-
indulgent, vulgarly masculinized fantasies of a Haggard "seem to
me works in which our race and our age make a very vile figure"
(*Letters* 3:128).

With nothing less than the cultural imagination of "our" Anglo-
American "race" at stake, *The Princess* takes on the project of King
Romance, embodied in the figure of Paul Muniment. Giving sub-
stantial play to Hyacinth's "drea[m] of the religion of friendship" in a
bond surpassing the love of women, James nonetheless suggests the
limits of romantic typology for productive and culturally engaged
culture-building (*PC* 394). Uniting "a rude, manly strength" with
"superior" intelligence, "the complexion of a plough-boy" with "the
glance of a commander-in-chief" (135, 128), Muniment evokes *par
excellence* the homosocial fantasy of unfettered masculinity. "[I]n-
stinct with a plain manly sense" (414) and alive with "joyous moral
health" (128), notoriously free of sentimental engagement or "passion" (391), he "care[s] nothing for women" or for the insufficiently

robust polemics of the idlers at the Sun and Moon (205). Like his
gallic counterpart, Auguste Poupin, he "delight[s] in the use of . . .
his tools," casually displaying the "brown stains" on his powerful
hands – consistently read as metonymic organs of power, sexual autonomy and authorial privilege – without shame or embarrassment
(125, 128).

Like other male romance heroes Muniment proves irresistible to
the women of whom he has "always had a fear" and a healthy
distrust (453). His ironic reading of his erotic desirability turns out
to ring true: " 'Daughters of earls, wives of princes – I have only to
pick' " (492). Indulging the pleasures of flirtation across class
boundaries with this "tribune of the people" (452), the Princess
Casamassima particularly notes "the size of his extremities" as well
as "his powerful, important head" (449) and "military eye" (452).
Having at last met her erotic match, she succumbs to his corrective
power to withold interest and desire. By contrast, the feminized
Hyacinth, incapable of such mastery, is "not so difficult" or nearly
so well endowed. The Princess notes that he merely "held off a little
and pleaded obstacles" before abandoning his ineffectual resistance to feminine arts: " 'one could see you would come down' "
(425). As Sholto shrewdly predicts, Muniment's impassive "dis-
lik[e]" becomes a source of both erotic and moral fascination:
" 'That's his line, is it?' " Sholto asks. " 'Then he'll do!' " (347).
Weary of men who abandon their natural powers, the Princess
herself declares: " 'But I liked him for refusing' " (425).

Such gestures of refusal invite not only the interest of perverse
and theatrical women but the more complexly performed desires
of Hyacinth as aspirant to high culture. The narrative intermittently suggests that his investment in Muniment, while dangerously
sentimental, is nonetheless heroic, a form of identification or desire
that transcends embarrassment altogether. In other words, James
both derides and partially ratifies Hyacinth's queerly romantic reading of Muniment: "There was something in [Muniment's] face"
that "made Hyacinth feel the desire to go with him till he dropped"
(131). If the little bookbinder "treat[s] himself to an unlimited be-
lief" in his idol, the novel nonetheless fails to expunge its force,
given shape in the sense that "this man he could entreat, pray to, go
on his knees to, without a sense of humiliation" (206, 151).

In effect, *The Princess* sustains Hyacinth's fantasy of "some grand
friendship" even as it undermines his reading of Muniment as "the
best opening he had ever encountered" (206). Ratifying the desire
" 'to get inside of *you* a little' " (443), James honors the romance of
male "compact" as the ultimate fate of his protagonist. During

what we might call their fateful outing at Greenwich, Hyacinth
pays "tribute" to Muniment's "powerful, sturdy . . . nature" with an
"inrush" of "pride" and a "tremor in his voice": " 'It's no use your
saying I'm not to go by what you tell me. I would go by what you
tell me, anywhere . . . I don't know that I believe exactly what you
believe, but I believe in you' " (446). In the "extreme clearness"
with which "the two men's eyes me[et]," in the "vibration in
their interlocked arms," the narrative itself romances the notion
of "a purer feeling than love," transumptive of the "smutches
and streaks" of heterosocial intercourse, "mark[ed]" by traffic in
women, "betrayal," "contagi[on]," and unregulated desire (441,
447, 62).

     If these fantasies are pulled up short it is not, notably, in the
service of reinstating a "natural" or naturalist paradigm of hetero-
sexual generation, but by way of undermining the canons of racial
romance they imply. Hyacinth fatuously misreads Muniment as
leader of men, a natural to stand "at [the] head" of the "exalted,
deluded" mass of revolutionaries, leading it to "pour itself forth,"
"surge through the sleeping city, gathering the myriad miserable
out of their slums and burrows, and roll into the selfish squares" to
"awaken the gorged indifferent" (293). But his misreading has particular point, for it underscores the radically asocial character, the
contemptuous inexpressiveness, of Muniment's race-bearing vitality. The revolutionary bond that Muniment elicits from Hyacinth,
not unlike the self-heroizing "Contrack" forged between Dan and
Peachey in Kipling's "The Man Who Would Be King," is empty of
any culturally productive – or, in James's terms, civic – meaning. In
the end Muniment turns out to be the real naturalist hero of the
tale, a bloodless "brute" without social affinities or sympathies
whose ironic detachment forestalls social agency altogether (579).
In a certain crucial sense, then, the novel awards Hyacinth's fantasies about Muniment the ring of higher truth. A heroic figure
imported from the race fantasies of male romance, Muniment
wields the power of an unfettered, antisocial, free-floating "freedom" that makes him, in the Princess's ironic and apt exclamation,
a "first-rate man" (581). By contrast, Hyacinth's "queer mixture"
renders him constitutionally and productively unfit not only for
violent class warfare, but for culture-building in the style of racial
romance. In and through Hyacinth's overdetermined embarrassment, the novel registers the complexity of James's understanding
of generic politics as a resource for negotiating the cultural power
of type.

"Under the Influence of Women": The Female Naturalist and the Fate of the Literary

What you tell me of the success of [Francis Marion] Crawford's last novel sickens and almost paralyses me. It seems to
me (the book) so contemptibly bad and ignoble that the idea
of people reading it in such numbers makes one return upon
one's self and ask what is the use of trying to write anything
decent or serious for a public so absolutely idiotic. . . . Work so
shamelessly bad seems to me to dishonour the novelist's art to
a degree that is absolutely not to be forgiven; just as its success
dishonours the people for whom one supposes one's self to
write. – James to W. D. Howells, 1884 (*Letters* 3:27)[21]

If James's trial of naturalism undermines the politics of King Romance, it also participates to a certain degree in the latter's anxieties of engenderment. Tightly bound as a text of romance, Hyacinth's "poor little carcass" becomes a fetish over which various
readers and authors, conspicuously female, vie (329). Hyacinth's
reception within the novel, like the reception of the novel – which
leaves James, in his own words, "staggering" under an "inexplicable
injury," reeling from a demand for his work "reduced" to "zero"
(*Letters* 3:209)[22] – pointedly raises the question of the relation between the transnational audience for whom James supposes himself to write and the brute contingencies of actual readership. Who,
in the world of *The Princess*, constitutes "the people," the appropriate type, among whom Hyacinth's story of determined resistance to
determination will circulate?

From the outset Hyacinth is read by a female audience that both
dismisses and reifies his life story – or rather, his attempts to narrate
that story in a meaningfully transformative plot – as puerile fantasy.
The Princess mocks his "famous engagement" with Hoffendahl as a
melodramatic courtship ritual: " 'it's too absurd; it's too vague,' " she
all too reasonably declares. " 'It's like some silly humbug in a novel' "
(485). Rose Muniment, the "pert" and omniscient reader who "see[s]
everything in the world" without ever leaving her bed, similarly
debases Hyacinth's rhetoric of self-determination (151–2). His impassioned declarations, to which she responds with a "fit of laugh-
ter," prove indistinguishable from the self-assertion of the " 'little
man at some club, whose hair stood up' " as he " 'glowered and
screamed . . . almost the same words' " (148). While Hyacinth's story
of "dreadful revenge" deeply "move[s]" Millicent Henning, she

transforms the heroic *agon* of his "base birth" into a vulgarly Algeresque self-interest. His narrated history "produce[s] a generous agitation – something the same in kind as the impressions she had occasionally derived from the perusal of the *Family Herald*."²³ Recalling Hyacinth's own early acts of self-fashioning in contemplation of that lurid journal, Millicent indulges her "agitation" on behalf of the way "he might have 'worked' the whole dark episode as a source of distinction, of glory" (532–3). In so doing, she effectively exposes the generic continuity that Hyacinth struggles to suppress: between his drama of type and the typical plots of the music hall, the penny dreadful, and the matinee, with all their "dreadful common stuff" (204).

All three women turn out to be damagingly canny readers of Hyacinth's narratives and of Hyacinth as text. Their self-possessed responses expose his fantasy of self-determination as such, painfully pressing the continuity of his exquisitely attuned sensibility with the organs of a mass culture whose plots of social filiation he so ineffectually despises. Together, these critical female readers can be imagined to perpetuate a binding sentimental plot, more powerful even than Hoffendahl's conspiracy, from which Hyacinth – and perhaps James, as practitioner of civic realism – can never fully escape. For all these women, across lines of culture and nation, Hyacinth's body serves as a *tabula rasa* on which romantic desires and dramas of fulfillment can be inscribed. So Mrs. Bowerbank confirms, in the deflationary and naturalizing rhetoric of the law: " 'Certainly, in [his mother's] place, I should go off easier if I had seen them curls' " (63–4). In this climate of desire, the pointedly "queer mixture" of racial, national, and gendered "characters" that Hyacinth embodies may become merely another delicate morsel, one that can be heedlessly "swallow[ed]," by "great lady" and "shopgirl" alike, "at a single bite" (526, 37, 99, 270).

The troubling reception of Hyacinth's queerness by both male and female readers within the novel suggests how delicate is its own positioning against the problematically race-bound, escapist energies of male romance and apparently untethered, consumerist forms of fin-de-siècle women's culture. In a moment defined by the anxiety that "*they*" – the fantasized others of a racial and national culture in decline – "keep the books" (552), James attempts to unbind the political energies of the novel from such projects and their sclerotic and stultifying, "sterile" and "frivol[ous]," aimlessly revolutionary designs (200, 433). Paradoxically, he conducts this effort in an internal trial of naturalism, staged in the fate of his eponymous heroine. On the one hand the Princess problematically but spiritedly refuses to be bound within romance plots as fantasized by Hyacinth, dictated by James's generic commitments, and intermittently sanctioned by James himself. Her energy of resistance suggests productive engagements for the novel as a civic enterprise, capable of reforging links among and between competing versions of nation and race. On the other hand the Princess's naturalist commitments turn out to be inseparable from class tourism and racial affirmation of the most self-serving kind; dramatizing the dangers of naturalist authorship, she is made to bear their social costs, and thus perhaps to naturalize James's own culture-building ambitions and gestures of filiation.

I want to think more closely in the following pages about the Princess Casamassima as subject of and to naturalist laws. Initially opposing romantic paradigms with her interest in socially transformative plots, the Princess forges a tentative victory of responsiveness unbound from literary, class, and national "conventions," hazarding the energy of trial, commitment, and novelty over fixed notions of propriety, privacy, and nobility. In so doing she figures, on James's behalf, the problem of self-determination as a performative engagement with textual and social bodies. Finally, however, her particular energies must be recontained in the very idiom of type she appears to undermine, so as to reserve for the "Master" or "Maestro" a determinative agency of representativeness, of speaking "for every one," constituted by a freedom of broadly racial self-invention (332, 228).

In the theater-box where the Princess meets Hyacinth, the narrative frames her as another kind of actress in a melodramatic "play within the play" (193). Yet she nonetheless lays claim to a more productive social role, introducing herself with the assertion, " 'I like to know all sorts of people' " (193). She consistently represents her own authorial interest in "leading spirits," "the people," and "really characteristic types" as a form of political vocation, a way "to know something, to learn something, to ascertain what really is going on" (197). For the woman "married by her people, in a mercenary way, for the sake of a fortune and a title," naturalism as a form of cultural engagement will have high stakes (249). Highest among them will be the authentication of her curiosity as a meaningful form of work, in an era in which such "extremely *disponible*" women are, in James's phrase, "looking for a situation, awaiting a niche and a function" in Anglo-American literature and culture at large (*AN* 73).

Although the novel recognizes the Princess's curiosity as an authorial politics, James ultimately refuses it full credibility as such.

Taking up taxonomies of class and racial type with great persistence, she reserves her keenest interest for Hyacinth "[a]s a product of the 'people,' " and of "that strange, fermenting underworld" of revolutionary passion (332). At Medley – the aptly named country house she has rented in a gesture of characteristically mixed interests – the Princess tells him that she has watched him " 'constantly, since you have been here, in every detail of your behaviour,' " as she becomes "more and more *intriguée*" by the occurrence of such "natural tact and taste" as he displays in an "Anglo-Saxon" (337). Avidly curious about "the realities of his life, the smallest, most personal details" (384), the Princess self-consciously cultivates a naturalist attention to the determining forces of inheritance and atmosphere, indulging her imagination of the little bookbinder as "a representative of suffering humanity" (413).

In a certain obvious and predictable sense the Princess's experiment is made to fail; it implicates her in the very forms of egotism she apparently seeks, through sensationalism or misguided charity, to revise as better opportunities. " 'To observe the impression made by such a place as this,' " she tells Hyacinth, " 'on such a nature as yours, introduced to it for the first time, has been, I assure you, quite worth my while' " (321). The novel reaps its own very different dividends from her enthusiasm. When she concludes by exclaiming, " 'I want to see you more – more – more!' " she appears both narcissistic and damagingly sentimental, misnaming an erotic desire to know the "curious animal" in question as a "passion" for political knowledge (321). The narratives of self-justification she offers become a measure of the Princess's inevitable failure, linking her naive authorial project with self-serving, richly "irresponsible" forms of female desire.

Yet the Princess, displaying all the fine intelligence of the Jamesian heroine, might be said to anticipate such readings and even partially to forestall them. She adopts the posture of naturalism not primarily to indulge a banal erotic curiosity but to improvise from a racialized script of femininity with greater passion and power. Whetting an appetite for the "curious mixture of qualities" that makes Paul Muniment, "a tribune of the people, more interesting to her" (452), the Princess imagines her own desires and interests as socially negotiable instruments. She wants "to know the *people*, and know them intimately," "convinced they [are] the most interesting portion of society" (248). Her "studies of the people – the lower orders" (257), whose forms of life "haunt" and "fascinate" her (248), give outlet to an energetic if narcissistic "passion" for the " 'modern,' " and they do so with particular point (259). Her per-

versely earnest insistence on the naturalist keynotes of type, representative character, and racial fate are intended at least in part to
forestall oppressive claims for the "individual" and the "original,"
which in the heavily plotted world of *The Princess* inevitably impli-
cate canons of romance – fictive laws in which anxieties of femininity and racial panic coincide.

The Princess, in other words, adopts the *données* of naturalism as
a refuge not merely from boredom or the spurious conventions of
a complacent aristocracy but from the narrowness of romantic heroism as a cultural plot, and its foreclosure on genuinely "interesting"
possibilities for women beyond those – marriage, the reproduction
of "noble" class and race histories – she has already tried. Declaring
that she " 'can care only for . . . one *class* of things at a time' " (412,
emphasis added), preferring "everything that was characteristic"
(184), the Princess takes up Hyacinth precisely because she believes
his initial, disingenuous declaration: " 'There is nothing original
about me at all' " (197). For her, he remains "much more interesting" as a representative figure " 'than if you were an exception' "
(198). As soon as Hyacinth "t[ells] her, in a word, what he was"
(337), the Princess loses interest, initially failing to inform him of
her noteworthy change of address from Medley Park to Madeira
Crescent. The novel stages this failure of "interest" not to prepare
for the entrance of Paul Muniment as transgressive love interest
but to register the deeper design of the Princess's naturalist intentions. Once Hyacinth confesses the facts of his "destiny" (338), he
reveals his insufficiency as the "representative" type she desires to
"know" so as to free herself of the burden of typological representativeness. As "constituted" individual, as male romancer seeking a
confidante to whom he can reveal "the things that had never yet
passed his lips," Hyacinth inadvertently urges the romance plot of
pure womanhood, with its fatal female destinies, that her trial of
naturalism is meant to evade (337).

That trial has impressive if unstable results. First and foremost,
the Princess's naturalism deflates Hyacinth's designs – and the
more intermittent designs of the novel – on her highly overdetermined femininity. Cast as the heroine of an ongoing drama of
purity and danger, the Princess is directed to shine for her male
audience with "the essence of her beauty; that profuse, mingled
light which seemed to belong to some everlasting summer, and yet
to suggest seasons that were past and gone" (306). Scripted in this
romantic style as the light of the world, she entrances Hyacinth,
and the reader, with "the noble form of her head and face, the
gathered-up glories of her hair, the living flowerlike freshness

which had no need to turn from the light" (306–7). In the ambivalent affect of James's third-person narration, these figures echo an
idiom of purity that arguably recalls not only the formulas of fairy
tale but the cultural romance of endangered white womanhood,
for which cultural plot Verena Tarrant will also problematically be
rescued and preserved. Fashioned by nature "of some different
substance from the humanity he had hitherto known," the Princess
"conform[s]" absolutely for Hyacinth "to the finest evocations of
that romantic word" (191–2). "[T]oo beautiful to question, to judge
by common logic," she commands all the mysterious allure "natural
to a person in that exaltation of grace and splendour" (195). In
Hyacinth's narrative and in the narrative that gives a certain credibility to his fantasies, the Princess is aptly transported to the "establishment" to which he eventually conducts her: the "Happy Land"
of a romantic "exile" of "refin[ed] . . . intimacy," shared by the hero
and "the all-comprehending, all-suggesting lady of his life" (419–
20, 401).

The Princess's naturalism contests precisely this deeper plot. As
Hyacinth undertakes to school her in proper styles of feeling and
distinction with "an offering" of "Tennyson's poems," bound with
"passion, with religion," "as perfectly as he knew how," the Princess
changes addresses (254); when he reads aloud Browning's *Men and
Women*, with its rich affect of passion and exile, she "pay[s] no
attention" and directs the conversation along more closely political
lines (487). Adopting the authorial style of naturalism, the Princess
mounts a genuinely "interesting" protest against the fate of romantic purity and danger. The Princess, in sum, pointedly refuses to
behave as a princess, an "exalted" being "clothed . . . in transcendent glory" with an undefilable beauty that has "worked itself free
of all earthly grossness and been purified and consecrated" (569).
Her "slumming" in the "*mesquin*, Philistine row" of Madeira Crescent, however limited and "pious," is a gesture deliberately intentioned to "take the romantic out of [Hyacinth's] heroism" (417,
407), to mock a melodramatic imagination that "giv[es] no hostages
to reality" (272). With "an indifference" and "even a contempt" for
his stylized, type-laden veneration, the Princess challenges the privileged uniqueness of the romantic – and indeed the Jamesian –
heroine and her binding within narrative laws of purity and type.
" 'What title have I to exemption . . . ?' " she demands. " 'Why am I
so sacrosanct and so precious?' " (574).

With this ultimately thwarted refusal of her generic and social
destiny, the Princess briefly achieves a redoubtable vitality, a moral
"energy," conspicuously denied virtually every other agent in the

novel (416). "[T]hread[ing] her way through groups of sprawling, chattering children, gossiping women with bare heads and babies at the breast, and heavily-planted men smoking very bad pipes," she takes up not merely a naturalist, or naturally feminine, whim but an experiential "project" that bears a notable and legitimate family resemblance to James's own: that of "br[eaking] out, joyously" into the street, of "see[ing] London" not through the window of domestic sanctuary but first "hand" (415–6).

Here the streetwalking heroine is clearly a surrogate for James himself, who has sought both to experience and transmit the productive "state of bewilderment" occasioned by his "fresh experience of London – the London of the habitual observer" and "pedestrian prowler" (*AN* 66, 77). "[I]rreverent" and invidious, the Princess momentarily achieves the "singularly free and unrestricted" authorial power of filiation James himself hazards; liberated from canons of type, she can "cast off prejudices and g[ive] no heed to conventional danger-posts" (178, 483). Unbound from her fate in the romance of racial purity, she is free to expose as such "the egotism, the snobbery, the meanness, the frivolity, the immorality, the hypocrisy" of high Anglo-Saxon culture itself, to which both she and the novel that contains her remain complexly bound, in part against their wills (433). Possessed of an unmatched "feeling . . . for the *mise en scène*" (233) and a "faculty of creating . . . a tension of interest" (501), the Princess represents a rare freedom of "movement" – that "with which, in any direction, intellectually," as author in her own house of fiction, "she [can] fling open her windows" (483).

But if the Princess's naturalist interests become a strategy for evading the dangers of the romantic will-to-power and the imperatives of racial romance, the novel ultimately redacts them as the product of a purely feminine "resentment and contempt" (251). In an ironic turn of the naturalist screw, her "performance" of a "modern and democratic" cultural politics is fatally discredited as the fitful "exhibition" of naturalism's paramount subject, the "*capricciosa*" or "monster" (310, 251, 400, 227). Truly a member of the female "race," she "swear[s] by Darwin and Spencer" not disinterestedly but with the "force of reaction and revenge," the fury of a woman wronged (251). The Princess anticipates such readings with remarkable acuity but cannot ultimately evade the double bind created by her efforts at self-authorship. Accordingly she tells a skeptical Vetch – who imagines her as "some splendid syren of the Revolution," an "incongruous and perverse" type "of the feminine character" – " 'You think me affected, of course, and my behaviour a fearful *pose*; but I am only trying to be natural' " (465–6).

Throughout the novel the Princess will be read by men (including, intermittently, James) who refuse to take seriously or sympathetically the definitive force of this oxymoron. What would it mean for any woman on exhibition within the theatricalized public arenas of Anglo-American culture to "be" or act "natural"? In what sense does fin-de-siècle female "nature" by definition transgress, even as it reinstalls, fictions of purity of race and type? Is the Princess "trying" some version of femininity, or being put on trial for her failure to observe the "law[s] of nature" itself (60)?

James's narrative appears both to honor, or at least stage, this difficulty and to undo some of its most promising complexities. As interpreted by her own faithful retainer, the aged Madame Grandoni, the Princess's curiosity is emptied of its authorial designs; she becomes merely another natural force or disaster of the sort with which naturalism is preeminently concerned. Beseeched by the Prince to remain with his estranged wife, Madame Grandoni protests her own insufficiency to contain the latter's energies, querying, " 'You must have been in Rome, more than once, when the Tiber had overflowed, *è vero?*' " (238). Never known "to carry out any arrangement, or to do anything, of any kind, she had selected or determined upon" (236), the Princess ultimately proves true to her origins. She exposes herself as an illegitimate agent, a "trumpery Princess" whose every gesture of self-invention is not chosen but determined within a life that "had turned out as badly as her worst enemy could wish" (529, 249).

The faithful *ficelle* thus confirms what the Princess's male admirers within the novel have long suspected: that her unnatural self-authorship is the issue of a femininity left unbound by race or nation – in the laws of marriage, citizenship, and inheritance – or by narrative closure. Her inevitable containment within these laws is the point of the Princess's ultimate *tête-à-tête* with Paul Muniment, who recalls with brutal efficiency the power of "legal advice," "settlements," and "the court" to enforce her marital fate (577). Recalling both his romantic mastery and the forms of "civil" power it promotes, Muniment remarks, " 'I shouldn't in the least care for your going to law' " (578). In so doing, he serves as the agent not merely of the patriarchal state, but of an authorial sleight-of-hand that shores up this form of determination, remanding the Princess to the custody of her husband: " 'you *will* go back!' " (577, 581). With this *dénouement* of the revolutionaries' vulgar plot, James might be said to take the laws of naturalism to book for the shocking irrelevance of the destinies they naturalize – those of ill-fated marriage, domesticity, and cultural reproduction – to women's ambitions, passions, and desires.

Despite such sympathetic engagement, however, the novel conducts its own trial of the Princess as author, turning against her a naturalist insistence on the facts of racial, class, and gender "character" or type. Insufficiently analytic, unschooled in "the principles of economical science," the Princess can only "preten[d] to be sounding, in a scientific spirit – that of the social philosopher, the student and critic of manners – the depths of the British Philistia" (476, 418). Characterologically bound up, as is the Lady Aurora Langrish, with a typology of womanly charity, she can never be more than a "lady-bountiful of the superstitious, unscientific ages" to whom "every sort of bad faith is sure to be imputed" (476, 197). But because she is "not a woman to be directed and regulated – she could take other people's ideas, but she could never take their way" – the Princess poses genuine social danger; she "play[s] with life so audaciously and defiantly that the end of it all" will "inevitably be some violent catastrophe" (476, 418). In the "modern lights" of the sociology and political economy she affects, the former Christina Light can only be found wanting. She thus "pay[s]" in the currency of cultural legitimacy more dearly than she recognizes for her "gathered impressions." With a tenacious resistance to its own feminist identification, the novel awards the Princess an enormous "fund of life," an "energy of feeling," a "high, free, reckless spirit," but – in the naturalist vein – regulates their expenditure as the dangerous, predictable caprice of a fatally "embodied passion" (418, 476).

If *The Princess*'s treatment of its recalcitrant heroine participates in a broader, and often-remarked, ambivalence about women in the public sphere, the instrumentality of naturalism to that affect measures a more precise anxiety. Negotiating the currency of literature as race-text, James reveals mixed motives with regard to his heroine, who is more pointedly adrift between national "characters" and more effectively "disinherited" than even Hyacinth himself (293). Her transgressive character crucially depends on the instability of her cultural filiations, evinced through the failure of naturalist taxonomies to predicate her without friction or unease. Proving that she is indeed "really a foreigner, you know," the Princess can openly master and adapt reigning conventions of Anglo-Saxon gentility, making them "a kind of [quaint and touching] picture . . . in my mind, . . . like something in some English novel" (432). Both nature and nurture contribute to this elasticity of self-imagination;

"American on the mother's side, Italian on the father's," she is the product of "a wandering, Bohemian life, in a thousand different places" and of her failed marriage to a "late-coming membe[r]" of a "long-descended rac[e]" (249, 234). Her cosmopolitan energies, which are ultimately adjudicated as the "issue" of a typological failure of "responsibility," suggest a freedom of narrative and cultural self-invention that underscores the mobility of the Anglo-Saxon cultural agency she redirects. With a "comfortable polyglot" mastery (316), the highly " 'coloured' " Princess conducts a free "tr[ial]" of enormously varied resources from "democracy and socialism" to "illuminated missals" and "horrible ghost-stories" (AN 18, 258, 346). Liberated, albeit problematically, from the exigencies of allegiance to conventions of class, race, or nation, the Princess gives wide scope to an "active, various, ironical mind, with all its audacities and impatiences" (256).

In this untrammeled character she represents James's own designs for and on the fate of "metropolitan culture" (135), and thus figures the deepest interests of the novel with which she shares a title: the possibility of "audaci[ties]" of identification that would enable a more liberating politics for the novel as a social genre (418), and as the representative "record" of what Anastasius Vetch calls "this sodden, stolid, stupid race of ours" (76). Throughout the text James's eponymous heroine is crucial to sustaining this possibility, as she experiments with provisionally untethered forms of authorship and identity. Herself "an accident" in a "world . . . full of accidents" (193), the Princess capitalizes on an instability of filiation that she shares with the novel's most powerful political figures, including Hoffendahl, the "German revolutionist" or "Dutchman" who has masterminded a "great combined attempt . . . in four Continental cities at once" (290, 288). Freed conspicuously of "the manners of this country" or "of any class" (201), the Princess remains the novel's paramount exemplar of its own transnational aspirations, a master of alternative cultural styles in all "the foreign tongues" (423).[24]

But as the novel unleashes the Princess's energy of trial, commitment, and transgression, which labors across ostensibly fixed boundaries of nation, race, and type, it must ultimately reserve the significantly civic power of filiation for the figure of the Maestro himself. The naturalist canons that give shape to the Princess's authorial power of curiosity are thus also made to provide the measure of her failure. When James suggests in Hyacinth's register that "Nature had multiplied the difficulties in the way of [the Princess's] successfully representing herself as having properties in com-

mon with the horrible populace of London" (481); when he inti-
mates in Schinkel's voice that " 'it is the nature of ladies' " to break
faith with the social contract (588); he then claims both the energies
of self-invention and a productively intimate form of nation-
building for his own very typical, very international performance.
Too, that distinctive internationalism must be distanced from virulent strains of the "international" conspiracy popularly thought, in
the climate of suspicion brought to a head by the Haymarket bomb-
ing of 1886, to be threatening "the good old Anglo-Saxon civilization."25 The Princess, then, must stake out its own cultural politics by
disciplining the energies of its cultural double, the anarchist International, displaced in the typologies of naturalism onto the figure
of the Princess.

This logic – which we might, with regard to James's queer relations with his hero, call one of bookbinding – reveals itself most
fully in the novel's climactic episode. The revelation of Hyacinth's
suicide is often dismissed as a melodramatic lapse from James's
naturalist mode or a betrayal of the novel's political interests. But it
can more usefully be understood to record the limits of James's
experiments in race thinking and culture-building under the sign
of naturalism. Working against its own most trenchant insights into
the "nature" of generic and gender conventions, the novel's finale
effectively remands the Princess to the custody of traditional romance. It thereby forestalls the "contagion" associated with the
politics of internationalism (590), and asserts on James's behalf a
more powerful, authentic command of human "nature" and of the
racialized and nationalized typologies in which its histories are re-
layed. Abandoning naturalist pretensions for the plot of romance,
James naturalizes both the failure of the Princess's powerful curiosity and his own custodianship of a distinctly civic imagination, on
which the free play of Anglo-American energy and engagement
implicitly depends.

Reverting to the essentialism of type the Princess has so richly
undermined, James's ending corrects her errors of nature: it be-
stows on her the romantic feeling and genteel passivity she has hitherto successfully resisted in more mobile performances of cultural
self-determination. Earlier in the novel, Sholto notes in connection
with the Princess's "extraordinary nature" that " 'there are some
mysteries you can't see into unless you happen to have a little heart.
The Princess hasn't' " (344). This deficiency will be neatly redressed
in the narrative's closing scene. Under the spell of "her own dread"
before Hyacinth's locked and impassive door, "the Princess wait[s],
with her hand against her heart" (590). As Schinkel breaks down the

door, the narrative briefly inhabits her consciousness, with the effect of underscoring the fatal absence of feminine feeling that has brought her to this threshold. In the "poor" light of Hyacinth's "small room," her real nature is glaringly exposed along with the "something black, something ambiguous, something outstretched" lying on "the small bed"; in the instant of exposure, "she s[ees] everything" (590). Hyacinth's mutilated body – "a mess of blood," "a horrible thing" – evokes "a convulsive movement" and "a strange low cry from her lips." "[Q]uietly and gravely," the ever-efficient Schinkel pronounces judgement: " 'Mr Robinson has shot himself through the heart' " (590). The Princess, who has been dangerously free to remake herself in every venue from Medley Park to Audley Court, is thus indicted as a kind of vampire, an unnatural creature whose parasitic acquisition of a "heart" – the organ of a justly feminine sensibility – occurs only at the dearest expense of the hero's own.[26]

This denouement can be said to secure the trajectory of James's aspirations for the novel; it does so, however, only at the cost of abridging certain of its most powerful insights into the typologies of naturalism and the power of type. Behind the hitherto heartless Princess stands the internationalist author, attempting to intervene productively in the constituted identity of the Anglo-Saxon "race," whose "possible *malheurs*, reverses, dangers, embarrassments" and even " 'decline,' in a word, . . . go to" his own "heart" (*Letters* 3:66–7). Meditating on his shifting and renewed investments in an Anglo-Saxon cultural body at the moment of *The Princess*'s inception, James suggests the power with which national, racial, and literary bodies can be imaginatively aligned, in the "spectacle" – "touching, . . . thrilling and even dramatic," of a "great precarious, artificial empire . . . struggling with forces which, perhaps, in the long run will prove too many for it." To this "struggle" to revaluate national character and institutions within contemporary "Europe," as sustaining fictions of nationhood and racial solidarity "collapse," the Princess herself is finally consecrated and "imput[ed]," even sacrificed (*Letters* 3:67; *AN* 73). Trying to be natural, tried by naturalism, she remains the secret agent of James's interest in the generic management of national and racial feeling, in the service of a fiction more productively civic, more expansively Anglo-American. True to "world-weary" type, the Princess ends by enabling James's ongoing project – the binding of text, nation, and the "immeasurable body" of Anglo-America – as even his hapless little bookbinder fails to do (*AN* 74).

4

JAMES, JACK THE RIPPER, AND THE COSMOPOLITAN JEW: STAGING AUTHORSHIP IN THE TRAGIC MUSE

I am deadly weary of the whole 'international' state of mind – so that I *ache*, at times, with fatigue . . . I can't look at the English and American worlds, or feel about them, any more, save as a big Anglo-Saxon total, destined to such an amount of melting together that an insistence on their differences becomes more and more idle and pedantic and that that melting together will come the faster the more one takes it for granted and treats the life of the two countries as continuous or more or less convertible, or at any rate as simply different chapters of the same general subject.

> – James to William James, 1888 (*Letters* 3:243–4)

[I]n society, as in nature, the structure is continuous, and we can trace things back uninterruptedly, until we dimly perceive the Declaration of Independence in the forests of Germany.

> – Lord Acton, *A Lecture on the Study of History*, 1895 (Simmons, 6)

In the fall of 1888, as Henry James began to compose his "study of a certain particular *nature d'actrice*," the print culture of Anglo-America was sensationalizing a real-life drama, the serial murders of Jack the Ripper (*Notebooks* 28). Staged in London's East End, the site of a heavily concentrated population of immigrant Jews, the Ripper's crimes participate in a heightened theater of Anglo-Saxon character, racial history, and destiny. Animated by gathering "anti-alien" sympathies, the local populace was quick to read the Ripper murders through the lens of racial anxiety. When the body of Catharine Eddows was found by a Jew on September 30, 1888, outside the International Working Men's Educational Club, a virtual pogrom threatened to erupt in the East End. The *East London*

Figure 4.1 Sketch of Supposed Murderer: *Illustrated Police News*, October 20, 1888. Source: The Newspaper Library, British Library.

Observer reported that "the crowd who assembled in the streets began to assume a very threatening attitude towards the Hebrew population of the District. It was repeatedly asserted that no Englishman could have perpetrated such a horrible crime as that of Hanbury Street, and that it must have been done by a JEW" (15 October 1888; cited in Gilman, 117). On a wall in Goulston Street, near the spot where a bloody apron connected with the Ripper had been found, a message was scrawled: "The Juwes are The men That Will not be Blamed for nothing" (Sharkey, 45).

England's official narratives follow a similar script. The description released in aid of the police search described the murderer as a man of "age 37," with "rather dark beard and moustache, dark jacket and trousers," and "black felt hat," who "spoke with a foreign

Figure 4.2 Latest Sketches: Arrested on Suspicion: *Illustrated Police News*, September 15, 1888. Source: The Newspaper Library, British Library.

accent," while the *Illustrated Police News*, a popular crime sheet, figured the suspect in virtual caricatures of the semitic "type" (Frayling, 183; Figures 4.1 & 4.2). Sir Robert Anderson, who spearheaded the massive Ripper manhunt, retrospectively declared:

"One did not need to be a Sherlock Holmes to discover that the criminal was a sexual maniac of a virulent type . . . [T]he Police had made a house-to-house search for him, investigating the case of every man in the district whose circumstances were such that he could go and come and get rid of his blood-stains in secret." The "virulent" and perverse individual who could "go and come" with such stealth would hardly be one of England's own; "the conclusion we came to was that he and his people were low-class Jews" (R. Anderson, 357–8). A high proportion of suspects detained and questioned were Jews, and an "alien" Jewish worker was briefly arrested in September 1888. It was, ironically, the Ripper himself who intervened to suspend the fantasy of racial impurity that could be expunged from the Anglo-Saxon body politic without a trace. In a rhyming missive sent in 1889 to Sir Melville McNaughton, Chief of the vaunted Criminal Investigation Division of Scotland Yard, he wrote with characteristically *insouciant* dispatch:

I'm not a butcher, I'm not a Yid,
Nor yet a foreign skipper,
But I'm your own light-hearted friend,
Yours truly, Jack the Ripper.
　　　　　　　(Kelley and Wilson, 14)

As Judith Walkowitz and Sander Gilman have argued, the Ripper is virtually made to order as an icon for Anglo-America's imagination of the Jew, and itself, at the fin de siècle.[1] In a decade of financial panic marked by radical labor movements and violent strike-breaking, the publication of Thorstein Veblen's *The Theory of the Leisure Class*, massive immigration into Britain and America from Eastern Europe and crises on the Exchange and Wall Street, the Jew conveniently figures the dire threat of over-production and surplus desire in a godless industrial age.[2] In the case of the Ripper narratives, the Jew is made to embody more pointed threats to the continuity of a newly urgent Anglo-Saxon "brotherhood."[3] Jack, as Jew, like the Jew, becomes representative of a deviant civic agency whose virulent corruption threatens the purity of native "Anglo-Saxon" institutions and character.[4]

Thus the February 1886 *Pall Mall Gazette* – with whose editor James had tangled during the writing of *The Princess Casamassima* over the imperialist designs of print culture – warns of "a *Judenhetz* brewing in East London," whose every nook and cranny has been peopled with Jewish immigrants "of the lowest type" (Fishman, 69–70). The *St James's Gazette* identifies Jews in Anglo-America as a distinct "colony . . . steeped to the lips in every form of physical and moral degradation" (Fishman, 70). The New York *Tribune* similarly typified Jews by their linked affinities for waste and trade, placing them "on social terms with parasitic vermin" (Sachar, 154–5). Arnold White, a prominent fin-de-siècle proponent of nationalism and Anglo-Saxonism, more trenchantly deploys the same idiom: "The Polish Jew drives the British Workman out of the Labour market just as *base* currency drives a *pure* currency out of existence" (Fishman, 74). At issue across Anglo-America is the Jews' "remarkable fecundity, tenacity and moneygetting gift," a feared power of multiplication that makes "[t]heir very virtues seem prolific of evil" (Fishman, 75). This newly urgent anxiety of Jewish baseness structures even the "diagnostic" rhetoric of London's first Yiddish socialist journal, *Poilishe Yidl*. The latter not only mimes mainstream Anglo-American journals by admonishing against the "discredit" of Jewish "business enterprises," "deal[ings] in gold sovereigns," and "ge[t] rich quick" schemes, but claims that "The most scandalous English newspaper, which is written to popularise dissolute behavior and demoralise young people, is issued weekly by a Jew."[5]

Ironically, such broadsides on Jewish corruption insist on the "primal" character, the "indestructible type," of the Jew at a moment when native Jews in London had become linguistically and socially indistinguishable from their Anglo-Saxon countrymen, in the decade after Disraeli's great ministry and the Prince of Wales' attendance, on January 14, 1881, at the wedding of Leopold de Rothschild at a London synagogue (Gilman 179, 177, 122).[6] In America, assimilation of an earlier wave of Germanic Jews had been so successful that progressive Jews in the 1890s could argue for the "elevat[ion]" of the "lowest type" of new arrivals, even as others warned that the presence of a population "largely tainted with Orientalism" would become "a standing menace."[7] The Ripper murders, in the wake of such assimilation, occasion a revival and refashioning of the myth of the Jew's debased racial economy as a newly powerful threat to the projects, aspirations, and character of the Anglo-Saxon "world." In this episode in the cultural imaginary of whiteness, the very presence of the Jew threatens a dangerously communicable disease within the racial body.

As the sensational drama of the Ripper murders unfolded, Henry James was laying a contestatory claim to that protean organism. Writing in October 1888 from Geneva, where he had retired to work on "the long thing" that would become *The Tragic Muse*, he articulated another version of internationalist cultural politics under the sign of the literary: the construction of an "Anglo-Saxon total," whose "general subject" would comprise shared racial, linguistic, and cultural formations. With his breathless prospectus, James strategically abandons the plots of national difference on which his earlier fiction and criticism have been founded, miming the "melting together" of English and American traditions proposed by such emergent Anglo-Saxonist enterprises as the Anglo-American League and the Transatlantic Society of America and reified within a genteel American movement "from shirt-sleeves to coats-of-arms" (Gossett, 324; Hart, 181).[8] James's own fiction, he asserts, will be a "magnificent arm" for "taking for granted" this newly Anglo-American "subject"; his literary corpus as a whole will prove so uniquely representative of that redefined "total" that "it would be impossible to an outsider to say whether I am, at a given moment, an American writing about England or an Englishman writing about America." Unlike his earlier self, the traveler contextually eager to preserve distinctive national styles in the service of shifting appeals to his readership, this James "should be exceedingly proud" of "ambiguity" of national origin, "for it would be highly civilized" (*Letters* 3:240).

But James engages the Anglo-Saxonist idiom heightened by the Ripper murders in the service of challenging narrower notions of the "Anglo-Saxon" imagination, risking gestures of filiation with ambiguously "cosmopolitan" figures. The "constitute[d] . . . total" of his own *oeuvre*, with its "pictures of my time," will have, he imagines, particular "value as observation and testimony" of this expansive "Anglo-Saxon" character in the making (*Letters* 3:240–1). Against more defensive notions of type, James's redirected performances in the internationalist mode concern and themselves depend upon, a whiteness whose currency is "convertible" rather than fixed. What James posits for his own culture-building activity is the crucial role of defending against the "object density and puerility" of a degraded discourse of culture, whose "lo[w] level of Philistine twaddle" circulates throughout the Anglo-American press, compromises authentic communication, and "writes the intellect of our race too low" (*Letters* 3:240).

The suggestion that *The Tragic Muse* articulates specific anxieties on James's part about the cultural work performed by the novel in the fin de siècle is hardly a novel one; as several recent readers have noted, the text openly invites us to link political and narrative forms of representation.[9] But that invitation, I argue, depends on and intervenes in racial thinking of the kind narrativized in the Ripper episode, whose importance to the novel's conduct has remained virtually unexamined.[10] James's venture into the theater during the 1890s implicitly engages the project of creating national and nation-building institutions, even as he exhibits deep skepticism about distinguishing between genuinely productive social arts and the rhetoric of the widening public sphere in bourgeois Anglo-America. His texts intermittently sustain the fantasy of a "representative" literature engaged in a revised *mission civilisatrice*, that of reforming the "intellect" of a newly cosmopolitan "race." Like earlier versions, this revised internationalism is sustained by a malleable idiom of race; in *The Tragic Muse*, its enabling condition is tropes of cosmopolitan Jewishness that structure popular and self-consciously Anglo-Saxon responses to the specter of the Ripper.[11] Taking up the fraught figure of the Jew, James gives play to the competing possibilities the Jew embodies: the danger to unified culture, and the very "convertibility" of cultural identity that the newly cosmopolitan author fantasizes for his own performances.[12]

This broadly political project governs James's figures for his heroine, Miriam Rooth, whose racially mandated "unscrupulous power" will enable her to "delive[r]" not only Shakespeare's monologues but the English-language theater, reanimated as a national institution "striving for perfection" and "unburdened by money-getting" (*TM* 278, 75, 326, 325).[13] On the one hand, the novel's representation of Miriam suggests a strong identification with the very "looseness" of her origins, which remain a subject of obsessive interest to all of James's *dramatis personae*. The "blank[ness]" associated with her history and performances constitutes, at least in part, a power of transformative self-invention to which the author of *The Tragic Muse* continues to aspire (457). In an age when "*nous mêlons les genres*," the very ambiguity of Miriam's racial and national origins serves as a valuable commodity in her bid to become the "English Rachel" (249, 141). Her Jewishness is made to signify a promising freedom from determinate cultural identity, a form of transgression that enables the breaching, and ultimately the management, of both narrative and ideological bodies and boundaries. As a polyglot and wandering Jew, an alien within the body politic, Miriam achieves precisely the transformation of Anglo-Saxon resources that James privately fantasizes; her racially coded power of self-representation will turn out to transvalue the collective imagination of the "race."

Simultaneously, however, the radical instability of Miriam's origins enables James to give voice to anxieties about the implications of the public forum she seeks as woman, actress, and Jew. Putting herself on display, and theatrical tradition at the service of the modern contrivances of "humbug[gery]," Miriam articulates the same confluence of dissemination and deviance figured by Jack the Ripper (75). The Tragic Muse, daughter of a "Jew stockbroker in the city" who bequeaths her his instinct for "profit," turns out to represent the "monstrous" proclivities of the proper upper- and middle-class English women who are uncertain how to "receive" her (46–7, 249). Like Miriam, they too are aliens on the civic stage; their activities as speakers, political pundits, independent professionals, and consumers of the novel are booked as discreditable labors in a usurious cultural economy. In James's scripting of their social roles, Jewishness becomes a usefully "convertible" metaphor for the contagion initially associated with Miriam's calling (and inconsistently with his own); it enables him to effect a breaching of class and national boundaries, across which the threat of usury as social disease links various public women as a common representational enemy.

At large, the racial logic of usury becomes a metaphor for more distinctly Jamesian performances, a way of staging the problematic confluence between literary, social, and consumerist modes of producing cultural agency. Implicating his own most powerful representatives, Nick Dormer and Gabriel Nash, in "the new idiom" of vulgarity, James conducts an in-house critique of the novel as a representative and nation-building form (369). Yet even as James's engagement with the racial logic of Jewishness exposes the limitations of newly racialized Anglo-Saxon styles of self-affirmation, his project of intermarriage – between England and America, between political and narrative representation – demands a certain defense against the specter of impurity or miscegenation. In order to reserve the possibilities of Miriam's transformative power of filiation and culture-building for his own narrative art, the novel must ultimately convert its heroine, recuperating her as a genuine actress whose "vulgarity" – and whose Jewishness – have been effectively purged. Notably, hers is not the only conversion undertaken by *The Tragic Muse*, nor do these conversions concern merely the circulation of language. Mrs. Rooth, the "inevitable comic relief," must be transfigured as a Jew in order for the novel to distance its own investment in the production of racial narratives from her baser interest (459); likewise Gabriel Nash, that consummately urbane "cosmopolite," must be exiled from the bourgeois English-speaking universe to which the novel reluctantly contracts, in both senses of the word (331).

Like the partisan readers of the Ripper murders, then, James takes up the mythos of the cosmopolitan Jew at the fin de siècle in the service of reimagining "our race," the Anglo-Saxon subject of a shared and evolving racial history. Engaging tropes of purity and danger, his novel gives play to the feared figure of the Jew in order to sustain its own form of nation-building, one that countervails against narrower versions of the Anglo-Saxon character. Appropriating and rehabilitating the "double nature" of the Jew – corrupt by "type" and unstable in civic identity – *The Tragic Muse* ultimately dramatizes varied possibilities for reinventing national culture and the civic or racial bodies it represents and constitutes.

Reading Race: The Theater of Narrative and Narratives of the Theater

From the opening passage of *The Tragic Muse*, an elastic language of race sets the stage for the work of "observation and testimony" on which the novel's culture-building aspirations depend:

> The people of France have made it no secret that those of England, as a general thing, are, to their perception, an inexpressive and speechless race, perpendicular and unsociable, unaddicted to enriching any bareness of contact with verbal or other embroidery. (*TM* 7)

Throughout the initial scenes set in the Palais de l'Industrie, and more broadly in that mecca of cosmopolite self-indulgence, Paris, both the narrative and the inconsistently distinct narrator exhibit a virtual compulsion to read and produce texts of racial identity. Introducing the Dormer family, the narrator declares that "even the most superficial observer would have perceived them to be striking products of an insular neighbourhood, representatives of that tweed-and-waterproof class with which . . . Paris besprinkles itself at a night's notice." With "the indefinable professional look of the British traveller abroad," these representative characters "were the more unmistakable as they illustrated very favourably the energetic race to which they had the honor to belong" (7).

The same taxonomic notation that classifies the Dormers as "doubly typical" products of their class and nation (8), "as much on exhibition as if they had been hung on the line" (7), also sets the stage for an "exhibition" of sibling rivalry between the English cousins – the painter Nick Dormer and the diplomat Peter Sherringham, whose alternative forms of representation will be placed in contest and in jeopardy. Invoking for the first time the privilege and immediacy of the first person, James's narrator asserts of Nick Dormer that

> I cannot describe him better than by saying that he was the sort of young Englishman who looks particularly well abroad, and whose general aspect – his inches, his limbs, his friendly

eyes, the modulation of his voice, the cleanness of his flesh-
tints and the fashion of his garments – excites on the part of
those who encounter him in far countries on the ground of a
common speech a delightful sympathy of race. (9)

Sherringham, only "middling high," is by contrast "visibly a representative of the nervous rather than of the phlegmatic branch of
his race" (38). Having "taken up the diplomatic career and gone to
live in strange lands," he has "cultivated the mask of an alien" – "an
alien in time, even"; nonetheless, "it would have been impossible to
be more modern than Peter Sherringham, and more of one's class
and one's country" (38). The narrator's casual invocation of racial
type as the grounds of analogy not only inaugurates a developing
contest between political and aesthetic forms of representation; it
also structures the narrative's appeal to collectivity, that fantasized
totality of readers united by "common speech" and the "delightful
sympathy" of shared culture. As part of "the community" that observes Sherringham, we "may" without embarrassment "rest" "our
eyes" on him and anticipate fulfillment of the narrator's promise
that "[w]e shall see quickly enough how accurate a measure" the
fact of "race" takes of "Nicholas Dormer" (38, 9).

James, I would argue, invokes this fluid *Gestalt* of race and nation to create a local community of self-consciously cosmopolitan
readers, capable of negotiating shifting interpretive perspectives
and cultural filiations. Enforcing a vigorous relativity of point of
view, the narrative consistently qualifies the representational claims
it bases on the facts of "type." In the "perception" of the "people of
France," those of England are, "as a general thing," essentially "per-
pendicular," unreadable; such nationalist bromides about race and
nation "might have derived encouragement" on the particular
scene in question, "a few years ago, in Paris," where

> four persons sat together in silence, one fine day about noon,
> in the garden, as it is called, of the Palais de l'Industrie – the
> central court of the great glazed bazaar where, among plants
> and parterres, gravelled walks and thin fountains, are ranged
> the figures and groups, the monuments and busts, which
> form, in the annual exhibition of the Salon, the department of
> statuary. (7)

Setting the stage with virtually comic qualification, James's narrator
calls attention to the performative force of "calling" things by their
cultural, racial, and national names.

Such syntactic punctiliousness can readily be dismissed as characteristic of an evolving Jamesian style, but the narrator's careful management of unstable public identities signifies more pointedly here: it preserves for James himself the possibility of fluid identification within various typologies and constructions of cultural filiation. Throughout the initial scene, James's narrator stages complex engagements with the language of race, projecting a series of alter egos and observers whose readings of race and of the "representative" English subjects on view may or may not replicate his own. Positing in turn a "most superficial observer," watchful "passers-by" in the gardens of the Palais de l'Industrie, "a very close observer," and "[t]he foreign observer whom I took for granted," the narrator allows these "foreign" agents to do the work of putting the novel's English and alien constituencies in proper place (7, 8, 16). "Their" racial performances, nearly perfect to type, make possible "his" own studied relativism, through which the narrative keeps the identity, origins, and national affiliations of its representative spokesman under erasure. James's narrative thereby contextually performs the negotiated version of culture-building to which his cosmopolitan art aspires.

This management of the advertised contingency of race and nation is largely carried out in the formalist transgressions of James's markedly intrusive narrator. On the one hand, that surrogate deftly distances himself from English "insularity" and "inexpressiveness" in his elaborate play with syntax and narrative style, and in his deadpan observation of Lady Agnes Dormer's attempts to negotiate the moral vagaries of Paris. Quite unlike the English *"abrutis"* who have apparently crossed the Channel and come to the Salon in mourning clothes in order to avert their eyes from the statuary on display, the narrator can savor "the genius of France" (8); in particular, he relishes the "state of exhaustion and bewilderment" to which it remains "capable of reducing" the "competent British matron," who responds to the blandishments of an attentive waiter by declaring, " *'nous sommes beaucoup!'* " and countermanding the French bill of fare he offers with orders for *"boeuf braisé"* and "galantine" – proper English food (30, 39).

Just as conspicuously, however, the narrator fails to include himself among the "foreign communities" he imagines into being, whose observers – at home in their own culture and history – he consistently identifies as foreign (7). His "[a]ddiction" to the conditional mode, to careful interpellative "embroidery" of temporal and historical circumstance, certifies his distance not only from the "inexpressive" English, but from the French perspective against which Lady Agnes more militantly and predictably defends (7). No less than that "high, executive woman," the narrator executes maneuvers of difference in order to sustain a certain logic of racial containment (31). Between cultures, languages, nations, he dramatizes his own privileged relationship of alterity to all the types of race and nation he observes. Like Gabriel Nash, the "cosmopolite" who "drifts" from one nation to another, with "*no* profession" and "no *état civil*," like Miriam Rooth, who is free to choose among her national and cultural affiliations, the narrator comprehends multiple forms of *patrimoine* (23, 27). He too is capable of translating across apparently fixed boundaries of race and nation that comically distinguish the "visitors" and tourists 'with narrow nationalist pretensions from those who genuinely expose themselves to the "general sharp contagion of Paris" (19).

But even as the narrator conducts this kind of cosmopolitan exposure, he embodies a certain involuntary movement of defense against the "contagion" inherent to cosmopolitanism itself, linked metonymically with the activities of decadents, anarchists, homosexuals, aliens and Jews.[14] The dual logic of the cosmopolitan accounts much more convincingly than Jamesian doctrines of dramaturgy and center of consciousness for the instability of *The Tragic Muse* as a realist document.[15] Enacting a fantasized transparency to the cosmopolitan Anglo-America he attempts to body forth, James's narrator and surrogate is neither wholly omniscient nor wholly subject to the drama he observes. A more complexly representative historian of the modern self, the narrator remains party to the instrumentality of race as a resource for James's self-invention. His own transgressions of national, linguistic, and narrative boundaries will ultimately be redirected, so as to protect James's project of culture-building against both provincial Anglo-Saxonism and incursion by more virulently transgressive forces. The mobile idiom of type underlies not only the novel's shifting readings of various "representatives" on the public stage, but its own claims to a representativeness that depends in part on the management of race and nation as imaginative resources and boundaries.

This performative culture-building puts James in contest with the most troubling of the novel's cosmopolites, the Tragic Muse herself. Peter Sherringham, conditioned by "years of exposure to the foreign infection" (326), displays the deepest anxieties given voice in the novel about racial purity, particularly as it governs the health of national civic institutions. During Lady Agnes and Nash's initial clash over the relative value of the dramatic and political theaters, Sherringham diplomatically changes the subject; he chooses the "safer ground" of polite euphemism to inquire "if the ladies you just spoke of are English," commenting, " 'Mrs and Miss Rooth: isn't that the rather odd name?' " (44). Told that Miriam is both "more than half a Jewess" and "magnificently stupid," he replies, " 'If she is, she'll be the first.' " Skeptical about her initial success on the stage, he comforts himself with the ironic reminder that she and Dashwood "were by no means coining money" (329). Increasingly under the sway of her "exotic gift," Sherringham amuses himself by figuring "the liberal way she produce[s]" impressions as the spectacle of "a naked islander rejoicing" in the gift of civilization, "a present of crimson cloth" (336).

But Sherringham's genteel racism, which will ultimately erupt in an outbreak of violence structurally akin to that of the Ripper episodes, is obviously inadequate. It thoroughly fails to account for the elusive instability or the psychic interest of a racial otherness that proves both promising and dangerous. Even the predictable impropriety that clings to the Rooths heralds a certain plenitude of national resources, cultures, and traditions from which Miriam remains at liberty to choose. Citizens of all states and none, the two women appear to be "people whom in any country, from China to Peru, one would immediately have taken for natives" (20). The very garments that bespeak Miriam's "exile" from England, gentility, and the bourgeois fashion system – the "light, thin, scanty gowns, giving an impression of flowered figures and odd transparencies" – also flaunt a theatrical power of self-invention, a freedom of intercourse purchased by her history as a "wander[er] in search of . . . cheapness, inured to queer contacts and compromises" (21, 97). A wandering Jew, a self-professed "gipsy" who has "spent her life on the Continent" and "picked up things," Miriam "agitat[es]" for liberating possibilities of self-representation that appear both revaluative and monitory (83, 332, 46).

Like Sherringham, the narrative displays an almost prurient interest in the scandal of Miriam's difference. Imagined initially in a state of near-undress, "the dishevelled one" is nonetheless never "naked" as Sherringham fantasizes, never in any psychic, moral, or narrative sense fully revealed (519, 336). No real exposure of her otherness – her racial origins, her displaced class affiliations – is ever motivated or "reflected"; Miriam is the one figure whom James refuses, in the retrospective language of his preface, to "g[o] behind" (AN 91). At the center of the novel the narrator remarks on this refusal; in a passage that has frequently troubled James's readers, he tendentiously celebrates the "mystery" sustained by the insistence with which "[w]e have chosen" to "regard this young lady" only through the "medium" of "other minds," in the "indirect vision" (*TM* 276). Chief among the "advantages" thereby accrued is arguably the preservation of Miriam's "blank[ness]" of origin and filiation, with the cosmopolitan dangers and possibilities it represents (276, 131). "[C]onstructed to revolve like the terrestrial globe," with "some part or other . . . always out of sight or in shadow," Miriam Rooth achieves a simultaneous resistance to and power of totalization that James imagines as the property of his own culture-building in the "Anglo-Saxon" mode (374). If she can never be "grasp[ed] . . . as a whole," even by the trained "diplomatic mind," Miriam embodies the plenitude of a great round world of *mondanité* itself (374, 64).

Miriam's free circulation in the guise of woman, actress and Jew thus gives play to James's own "new idiom" of the cosmopolitan self, even as it raises the specter of unmanageable "revol[utions]" in type, taste, and civic identity (369, 374). The narrative partially shares Sherringham's *horror vacui* with regard to Miriam's public performances; she remains a veritable "monster" with "no countenance of her own" save "the one that came nearest to being a blank" (130, 131). Like the female freak of the music-hall "shot from the mouth of a cannon," Miriam displays an uncanny plasticity of body and public self alike, as "elastic" and exotic as "gutta-percha" (131). Yet the racial origins expressed in these physical powers of adaptation – "of any complexion you liked" – become equally malleable resources in her bid for narrative and social "authority" (47).[16] Sherringham, who trades on his own "connect[ions] by blood" to enter the diplomatic trade, virtually accuses Miriam early on of being "not English," claiming, " 'You're a Jewess – I'm sure of that' " (391, 140, 141). Unexpectedly, however, she "jump[s]" at the possibility as one "that would make her more interesting," declaring, " 'That's always possible, if one's clever. I'm very willing, because I want to be the English Rachel' " (141).

Like her chosen model, Miriam exploits her own marginal origins as a form of cultural capital.[17] Of indeterminate "character," a thousand faces and numerous names – she begins her career under various "*nom[s] de guerre*," including Maud Vavasour, Edith Temple, and Gladys Vane – Miriam achieves a power of cosmopolitan self-invention that James himself cannot afford to concede (146, 44). Dangerously free to extemporize her origins and public self, Miriam commands "an intensity of sensibility," an "incalculable" array of "incarnations," transforming the theater of civic identity into her own "room with many windows" (383). Woman without a country, diasporic Jew roaming across history and the "globe," Miriam sustains a "free, brave, personal" power to challenge the limits of civic culture. Her successful evasion of the fixed selfhood on which assignments of race, class, and nation crucially depend mounts the clear and present danger of identity denatured, reduced to an infinite regress of roles or signs (Gallagher, 41–2). It also suggests, however, a productive power of political and narrative representation – the power to shape cultural identity in sustaining fictions that can be reinvented as constructively as Miriam's origins. For this latter power, James is in contest with his eponymous heroine. Like the protagonist from whom he distances himself most thoroughly, Peter Sherringham, he displays an opposition of "inclinations" and desires with regard to the Tragic Muse, engaging her racial otherness so as to resist and reclaim its transformative possibilities (*TM* 306).

This contest accounts for the novel's insistence on Miriam's otherness as the condition of her choice of the English language and theater as her medium. Her all-important audition with the *grande dame* of the French theatre, the "incomparable" Honorine Carré, makes it clear that Miriam's greatest resource is precisely her "vacancy," a freedom from the determinate social affiliations that so precisely assign Lady Agnes, Sherringham, Julia Dallow, and the Dormer "girls" to their respective parts (45, 82). Master equally of "English, French, Italian, German," or even "half a dozen languages," Miriam in effect "knows too much" (84, 139, 85). Her first representational decision must be a commitment to one "stage," culture, and history; she must, in Carré's judgement, " 'have a language, like me, like *ces messieurs*' " (84).

Unlike these other actors and agents, however, Miriam is free to choose and reinvent her medium, as the canny ambassador Sherringham recognizes; she is "an embroidery without a canvas," untethered to social institutions that might limit the range of her performance (145). Under the sway of her "blankness" of "nature" – she appears wholly without "a *fond* or background" (145) – the distracted diplomat remains in Paris to give his protogée a crash course in "legitimate indirect culture" and "the formation of a cultivated cosmopolitan taste" (158). Playing Pygmalion to her Galatea, laboring to inculcate her with "the grand style," he takes her to see Versailles and Rambouillet – useful venues for the education of an ambassadress, if not a *femme de théâtre* – and orders her to learn Milton and Wordsworth by heart (158).

The narrative appears both invested in and ironic about this project of education, undertaken in the ultimate service of a distinctly Anglophone cultural accession. Properly educated, the Tragic Muse will "do something for the standard" of the theater and of the English language, which of late "has gone to the dogs" (139). Her career, as Sherringham imagines it, will be not a job but an adventure, a "mission" full of "greatness" to recover the "[p]urity" of English speech from contamination, from the "vulgarity" and "crudity" of "abominable dialects" that threaten its historical integrity and its power to set a cultural "standard" (139, 468). Trained in the style of the great English poets, Miriam will do no less than reinvent the expression of what Sherringham calls "our English personality" (140).

If Sherringham's program echoes the call of fin-de-siècle Anglo-Saxonists across America and England for protection of the sacred patrimony, it differs from these in one crucial respect. His program turns, ironically, on the marked alterity of Miriam's speech, which, as Sherringham remarks in an extended colloquy on the subject, departs from the "conventional" in "the foreign patches," the "little queernesses and impurities" that identify her as one who has "lived abroad too much" (139). James carefully dramatizes this marked investment in the purifying power of Miriam's racial and linguistic impurity. On the occasion of her initial session as a model for Nick Dormer, she engages him in badinage, requesting that he come to see her act. Told that Dormer is "on the point of being married," she responds: " 'Ah, then, do bring your – what do they call her in English? I'm always afraid of saying something improper – your *future*' " (274). Staging the novel's commitment to the power of otherness, Miriam's hesitation more trenchantly represents the instability and the essentially commercial "future" of Dormer's relationship with Julia than the common, pointedly Anglo-French "*fiancée*" could do. But Miriam's "improper" speech, which recovers the power of metaphor as living language, trespasses dangerously on the territory of the novelist himself, who no less than his heroine is "find[ing] a voice" between and beyond national cultures (95). Identified as a woman who has no mother tongue, Miriam remains unnaturally free to adopt and adapt the resources of race and nation in a richly cosmopolitan form of cultural theater.

The determined actress is surprisingly successful in this enterprise. As Miriam develops her gifts, she learns to translate outmoded foreign melodramas into representative texts of the "English personality" and the English stage. Her performances themselves are "a living thing, with a power to change and grow, to develop, to beget new forms of the same life" (336). Racially indeterminate, she learns to harness the unpredictable potential of mutation in the national body. "[F]antastically unit[ing]" the mores of Balaklava Place and Cromwell Road, of bourgeois and "Bohemian," of high and low, in her own "natural abundance," she promotes productive adaptation of the social organism, reconstituting her chosen English public in her own cosmopolitan image (339, 340). A "queer" specimen, "neither fish nor flesh" in Sherringham's inadvertent echo of the mandates of *kashruth*,[18] Miriam performs in a wider theater of identity so as to transfigure the ideological texts that sustain the living state (381, 212).

This power of representation is precisely what overwhelms Nick Dormer as he attends the debut that launches Miriam's "dazzling success" and confirms the value of the culture-building "idea" that "possesse[s] her" (456, 454). Even the vulgar journalistic "licence" of reviews that pander to Anglo-America's publicity machine fails to compromise the "instrinsic" and communicable "magnificen[ce]" of her art (455, 454). Speaking verse on the English stage for the first time, Miriam renders it "unexpectedly exquisite":

> She was beauty, she was music, she was truth; she was passion and persuasion and tenderness. She caught up the obstreperous play in soothing, entwining arms and carried it into the high places of poetry, of style. And she had such tones of nature, such concealments of art, such effusions of life, that the whole scene glowed with the colour she communicated, and the house, as if pervaded with rosy fire, glowed back at the scene. (455)

Unifying narrative and political bodies, Miriam produces in her audience "a fine universal consensus" of response that inaugurates a powerful experience of mutual affirmation: "People snatched their eyes from the stage for an instant" only to "look at each other" as "a sense of intelligence deepened and spread" (455).[19] "[E]xcit-[ing]" her mixed public with the registers of feeling she "communicate[s]," Miriam transforms the local moment "into a feast of fraternity," a ritual of identity and identification so powerful that Dormer "expected to see people embrace each other" (455). Alive with a higher form of contagious feeling, the assembled body becomes subject to a "passion" of affirmation, in the "flutter" and "triumph," the "signals and rumours," the "heated air" of the "spectator's joy" (455, 458). This "shining confusion" of the "fictive" and the "irresistibly real" that Miriam inaugurates "inexplicably transmute[s]" collective identity far beyond the limits of the stage (457, 458). "[A]s satisfactory as some right sensation," her performance virtually creates a unified collective consciousness, a form of self-affirmation that will "feed the memory" of her public "with the ineffaceable" (455).

In Dormer's perception, Miriam is far more than the merely sensational phenomenon touted by the popular press. The images of arousal and nourishment with which he and the narrative celebrate her representational power clearly counter Gabriel Nash's cynical diatribe against "the essentially brutal nature" of a "modern audience"; here that social body is "f[ed]" or nourished with Miriam's art rather than "gorged" with "buying and selling and with all the other sordid speculations of the day" (50). Her brilliant success sustains an ongoing fantasy about the reinvention of a civic body in the image of an animating "idea" – the "idea" to which Miriam is determined to cling "even if it's destined to sink me into obscurity" (470); the "idea that," in Dormer's own developing aesthetic judgement, has historically "won the race" (418). "[L]ike a kind of royalty," "like a young queen on her accession," an "inextricably transmuted" Miriam commands the theater "in state," promoting a "continuity" between the nation's theater and the theater of nation-building (456, 457, 456, 458).

It is fittingly the cosmopolite Nash who provides the language conceding the dependence of this state of affairs on Miriam's decidedly mixed origins. Truly a "capital girl," in both senses of the word, Miriam is capable of performing a particular social "good": an agent of the vulgarity that defines "the modernness of the age," she will nonetheless, Nash concedes, "have brought the ideal nearer" to her audience, have "held it fast for an hour" (376, 375). He therefore counts her among those who have "dropped even the smallest coin into the little iron box that contains the precious savings of mankind" (376). Miriam's own contribution, an appropriately "big gold piece," will " 'doubtless,' " Nash remarks, " 'be found, in the general scramble, on the day the race goes bankrupt' " (376). For both Dormer and Nash this parsimonious form of authorship, troped as racially redemptive, is linked with the resource of Miriam's Jewishness. Usurer *and* authentic "productive force" (497), she transforms even as she embodies the vulgar "publicity" – "populations and deputations, reporters and photographers, placards, and interviews and banquets, steamers, railways, dollars, diamonds, speeches and artistic ruin" (375) – against which Nash and the novel militate. "[E]vil genius" and Jew, Miriam acts the part of *pharmakon* to the health of the civic body, figuring a cosmopolitanism that is both the disease and the cure of its collective life (126).[20] On the stage of race and nation she becomes an "evil genius" who "communicate[s] the poison" of difference, a "bigger dose" of which will cause her public either to "die or get better" (126).

Changing the Subject: Reading Women

James ardently invests in Miriam's transformation from would-be *fille de théâtre* to the legitimate actress who brilliantly performs Shakespeare's Constance and Juliet, "leap[ing] into possession of her means" (*TM* 224). In order for that transformation to be credible, however, certain anxieties about the cosmopolitan Jew within Anglo-America must be allayed. Miriam's racially coded vulgarity is increasingly communicated to other figures in the novel, so that the "shining confusion" of agency induced by her performances can be recuperated for James's own (457). If Miriam's racial otherness is to sustain his imagination of the vitality of public culture in the cosmopolitan mode, it must be exorcised of its contagious strain: the "remarkable fecundity" metonymically linked with the body and cultural economy of the Jew (Fishman, 75).

Increasingly, James displaces the Jew's power of unchecked reproduction onto other women in the novel, in a division of narrative labor that holds open the possibility of literary performances true to the animating "idea" of an organic Anglo-Saxon culture. From Balaklava Place to Julia Dallow's "Place," women appear virtually to govern the conditions of representation in the public sphere. Insistently linked across class and national boundaries, virtually all of the novel's women act as writers or readers of social texts. Lady Agnes, James's most trenchantly conservative critic of the aesthetic life, fulminates comically against the "contagion" – the "horrible insidious foreign disease" – of the stage and of public women as represented in "the charming drawings in *Punch*" (385). Yet she too succumbs to the "rage of self-exposure" after her son's abandonment of the Houses of Parliament, transfiguring herself as another version of the Tragic Muse (171). Even the private, ostensibly domestic filial piety she enjoins on her wayward son – " 'Your father, your father!' " – reveals itself to be entangled with a vulgar veneration of "the newspapers," whose accounts of her husband's political triumphs she "religiously preserve[s], cut out and tied together with a ribbon, in the innermost drawer of a favourite cabinet" (163, 62).

A similar anxiety of category "confusion" informs even the minor female roles in the Dormer family drama. Mrs. Lendon, the sister of Nick's political sponsor and patron, Mr. Carteret, is a "large mild, healthy woman, with a heavy tread" who proves instrumental to the disappointment of Dormer's expectations of inheritance (345). A metonymic figure for the stolid, "curiously fat-faced" citizens of Harsh, she also represents an attenuated public whose "principal interests" are "an herbaceous garden" and "the advertisement-sheet of *The Times*" (165, 345). More dangerously articulate and transgressive is Biddy Dormer's companion, Florence Tressilian. An "old mai[d]" and odd woman, she exhibits considerable freedom of aesthetic judgement as well as of social mobility (514). "Miss Tressilian" inhabits "the dearest little flat in a charming new place, just put up, on the other side of the Park," replete with the most advanced technology of circulation, "lifts and tubes and electricities" (514). "Do[ing]" without a "chaperon," she carries "two latch-keys" and travels "alone on the top of omnibuses"; her name appears "in the Red Book" without benefit of spouse (515). As a social agent and a spectator of Miriam's performance in the theater, Florence conducts her own "cheer[ful] and sonor[ous]" criticism of contemporary proprieties (324). Like Miriam she has found an articulate voice of "enlightened spinsterhood," which threatens to "confus[e]" such good daughters as Biddy Dormer by encouraging them to author and represent their own vulgar and theatrical desires (515, 260).

If other private women understudy for Miriam Rooth's role as an agent of social transgression, rehearsing it in the space of literary institutions, Miriam herself becomes curiously resistant to this particular strain of the disease. Aspiring to reanimate the English drama, she refuses to read even the high cultural English canon prescribed for her by Sherringham. Stubbornly remaining "on almost irreconcilable terms with the printed page," she embraces an ethic of readerly refusal that distinguishes her from other sentimentalized Jewish heroines, like George Eliot's, who remain creatures of the Book, and authenticates her insistent distinction between the living language of the drama and the stale provender provided by "a diet of dirty old novels" and magazines (154, 137).

James will press a similar distinction between the dead letter of texts disseminated without license and the animating power of fiction authentically aware of its cultural obligations. In service of this difference, the novel increasingly displaces the casuistry associated with women as readers and speakers in the public sphere onto those women with the most overtly political designs, Julia Dallow and Mrs. Rooth. Despite the firm generic and class distinctions that separate their performances, James unites these characters through the similarity of their representational aspirations, which register and resemble his own. For this reason both must ultimately be made subject to the violent force of "comic" and metaphoric conversion, whereby their continuity with James, and the convertibility of their desires and his own, can be expunged or obscured.

Mrs. Rooth provides the novel's "inevitable comic relief" in the enactment of her romantic cultural aspirations (459). In virtual exile within her native land, she is the paradigmatic voracious reader; her mode of literary consumption suggests her investment in the honorific trope of fiction as spiritual nourishment rather than mere entertainment. In Miriam's recollection of their dire "café" life, Mrs. Rooth literally lives on the sustaining power of fiction, which liberates her imaginatively from the realities of poverty-induced "wander[ing]," lived out "in places . . . where there was only really room if we were in bed" (47, 137). Awaiting money "sent out from England" that "sometimes . . . didn't come for months – for months and months," Miriam's "mamma" remains "always up to her ears in books":

> 'She knows every *cabinet de lecture* in every town; the little cheap, shabby ones, I mean, in the back streets, where they have odd volumes and only ask a sou, and the books are so old they smell bad. She takes them to the cafés – the little cheap, shabby cafés, too – and she reads there all the evening.' (137)

Physical deprivation makes "no difference" to Mrs. Rooth; her fictions "serv[e] her for food and drink." Faced with the prospect of "nothing to eat," she habitually begins reading "a novel in ten volumes" – "the old-fashioned ones" that "las[t] longest" (137).

Through the strong but narrow lens of Peter Sherringham's perspective, these reading habits appear dangerously to conflate sexual and textual desires in pursuit of female pleasures that can only end in conspicuous, unchecked consumption. Insisting on the most punctilious bourgeois bromides about respectability, class distinction, and the "precious" value of "the ideal" (151), Mrs. Rooth plays the role of chaperone to Peter and Miriam by stationing herself out of view with "an armful of novels" on "a bench in the park, flanked by clipped hedges and old statues" (158). Indoors she similarly preoccupies herself with old romances – "the earlier productions of M. Eugene Sue, the once-fashionable compositions of Madame Sophie Gay"²¹ – rather than the romantic interests of her daughter's "*Cher maître*" (334).

These female texts, "works that Sherringham had never read, and as to which he had vaguely wondered to what class they were addressed" (157), turn out to be dangerously vulgar, linked in their affect to the apparatus of "circulation" that promotes the shrill prominence of woman's "voice" on the public stage (261, 96). Tumbled about in "odd volumes from the circulating library (you could see what they were – the very covers told you – at a glance)," Mrs. Rooth's "familiar fictions" speak volumes (382, 461); they confirm "untidy" and "irregular" arrangements, "the barbarous absence of signs of an orderly domestic life," and a theatrical freedom of female self-invention (381–2). Characteristically appearing in "limp garments, much ungirdled" (157), with her "unbuttoned wrapper" and "large tinsel fan" (381), Mrs. Rooth embodies the reading woman who demands of "any life" that it "yield her" the "two articles" necessary and sufficient to autonomous female pleasure: a "sofa" and a "novel" (157).

Judging such female texts by their covers no less than his compromised representative, Sherringham, James gives play to the threat posed by public women whose desires resist the benign management of his own revisionary *mission civilisatrice*. More immediately, however, he distances that project from Mrs. Rooth's fictive practices, which closely concern her genealogical anxieties. By exposing her "refined, sentimental, tender" fantasies of racial origin as such, James in effect authenticates his own (150). Flaunting her status as a "Neville-Nugent of Castle Nugent," that "domain of immeasurable extent and almost inconceivable splendour" not "to be found in any prosaic earthly geography," Mrs. Rooth trespasses on the territory of the aspiring cosmopolitan novelist (48). Delighting "in novels, poems, perversions, misrepresentations and evasions," she indulges in the same kind of "blazonry" that enables James's imagination of a newly "convertible" currency of cosmopolitanism (150). Militating against the "genteel fable and fantasy" that Mrs. Rooth consumes and produces, he builds his own genealogical castles in the air, taking similar advantage of the opportunity for self-invention provided by a cultural history in which his literary ancestors are, in Miriam's ironic echo of his earlier claims, "almost extinct" (150, 138).

If Mrs. Rooth's readerly self-indulgence poses a certain challenge to James's representational design, it merely rehearses the larger problem of "free" women who enter the public sphere as political agents, claiming therein a privilege of self-representation that resists authorial management. Julia Dallow, the "refined and quiet" widow who has inherited the most "intelligent collection of beautiful objects . . . in England in our time" but "doesn't care a rap about art," is arguably the most unattractive woman of privilege in the entirety of James's canon (67, 12, 10). A figure that *The Tragic Muse* refuses to motivate generously or go behind, Julia occasions a notable failure of sympathy in her own regard, not because she keeps bad faith with vulgar party politics but because she unleashes a monstrous power of multiplication with grave consequences for civic culture. "[M]ade for" that "public life" in the grand, gentrified style afforded her by the gifts of "blood," Julia nonetheless bears the contagion of usury deflected from Miriam Rooth in recuperation of the latter's promising alterity (168).

Initially the narrator represents Julia in mixed terms that suggest an uncertainty about how to script and dispose of her political desire. "[F]ine," "refined," "extremely slender," moving with an "air of resolution and temper" and "extreme delicacy of line and surface," Julia enters the narrative in the double role of political pundit, who insists that Nick Dormer "stand" for Parliament, and of romantic lead, with "hair like darkness," "eyes like early twilight" (67). The incompatibility of these generic markers signals Julia's complex relation to speech in the public arena – will she command or inspire it? – as well as a certain anxiety on James's part about that relation. The narrative consistently undermines her acts of communication as cynical maneuvers, throwaway gestures in the mode of political "trash" (76). The phrase links her securely with Miriam; unlike the latter, however, she is given no ironic self-consciousness or wit to redirect its critical force. If Julia's mouth resembles "a rare pink flower," it also appears "too small" for the utterance of any but "hollow, idiotic words," the canting platitudes and "humbug of the hustings" (67, 75). Unlike Miriam Rooth, who successfully converts from *fille de café* to legitimate English actress, Julia never achieves an authentic voice; she remains imprisoned within the compromised language of the public arena, where "speech [is] not in itself a pleasure" (65).

Yet Julia closely resembles the transgressive woman of the theater in other ways. Divided from Miriam by the prejudices and privileges of her class, she nonetheless exhibits the same dangerous propensity for freedom of movement. During her initial encounter with Dormer in Paris, Julia dismisses her carriage, the symbolic machinery of her social power, in a mood of "liber[al] dominan[ce]," and proposes that they take to the boulevards, rich with "the tokens of a great traffic of pleasure," "profusion of light" and "pervasion of sound" (72). In her own national element, she proves similarly restless. Not unlike the "dreadful Miss [Fanny] Rover," a *cabotine* who openly "has" innumerable lovers, Julia resists masculine regulation, indulging a troubling habit of "wandering about" (338, 174). During the period of Dormer's standing, she exerts a disturbing power of physical and narrative conveyance. Seated discreetly in "her low, smart trap," she "move[s] in a radiance of ribbons and handbills and hand-shakes and smiles," "of quickened intercourse and sudden intimacy," "carrying" Dormer from place to place (160). The "composed picture" Dormer mentally paints to stand for his own political life is "inveterately Julia and her ponies:

Julia wonderfully fair and fine, holding her head more than ever in the manner characteristic of her, brilliant, benignant, waving her whip, cleaving the crowd," "carrying him to his doom" (179). Cracking "her whip in the bright summer air," Julia figures the specter of women seizing governance of the conditions of circulation, impressing on the novel no less than on Dormer "a perception of what women . . . in high embodiments" may "do" (161, 179).

Like the actresses and Jews she despises, Julia Dallow embodies a transgressive potential that undermines but also, insofar as it can be differentiated and managed, enables James's own. Dismissing her genteel political rhetoric as empty vulgar "rot," James sustains a vivid fantasy of healthier forms of civic representation (75). At a decisive moment in Nick Dormer's career, when he has just been elected "member" for Harsh and simultaneously begun to remake "the bed of his moral existence," he encounters one of Julia's social entourage on her estate. Mrs. Gresham, "a lady who received thirty letters a day," appears on the scene only to reveal the terms that will govern Dormer's ensuing "proposal" to the woman on whose financial and political capital he reluctantly draws: " 'Julia lives so in public,' " she remarks. " 'But it's all for you . . . It's a wonderful constitution' " (174). In a revelatory moment of suspended meaning, Dormer "fail[s] to seize" Mrs. Gresham's "allusion"; he interprets the remark as "a retarded political reference, a sudden tribute to the great unwritten instrument by which they were all governed" (174). Like Sherringham, who can formulate "no analogy whatever" to the person of Miriam Rooth (213), Dormer falters before the possibility of an authentic analogy between the female body and the national body, between woman's "constitution" and the power of social representation and containment.

Yet Julia continues to raise precisely this possibility, and most powerfully at the very moment when Dormer connects the "concluded affair" of his political standing with the "abyss of intimacy" her political aspirations have opened up (179). "[A]fter leaving Mrs. Gresham," Dormer finds Julia wandering at the edge of her lake, carrying a monthly "review" that contains an essay by one "Mr Hoppus," entitled "The Revision of the British Constitution" (179, 181). Here James as well as his representative, Dormer, contest Julia's cultural aspirations; the revision of the British "constitution," of the Anglo-Saxon social body, is precisely what *The Tragic Muse* puts at stake. Dormer predictably derides Julia's investment in this "periodical literature" in order to fortify the boundary between authentic discourse and language circulated baselessly, without reference to value: " 'But *is* that what we are in for – reading Mr

Hoppus? Is that the sort of thing our constituents expect? Or even worse, pretending to have read him when one hasn't? Oh, what a tangled web we weave!' " (181). Fulminating against the blatant theatricality of the political arena, where "pretending" sustained by "horrible ambition" is the order of the day, Dormer adverts to the purity of his own narrowly nationalized cultural designs (181).

Julia, however, refuses to abandon her political text or the forms of identity and empowerment it sustains. When Dormer "irrelevantly" requests that she let him carry what he ironically calls "your book," she "forbore to give it up, and they held it together" (181). More directly, she defends periodical culture as a source – like Mrs. Rooth's "circulating" novels, like Miriam's popular theatrical texts – of knowledge and power: " 'People are talking about it. One has to know. It's the article of the month' " (181). In a transparently aggressive gesture, Dormer "stupid[ly]" forgets "Mr Hoppus" in "the temple of Vesta," the island summer-house where he proposes marriage (189). Ever resourceful, Julia tells him it "doesn't signify," since she has a "copy" at home – "the one that comes every month" (190). His agitated response – " 'Every month – I see' " – and Julia's arch reply – " 'Did you suppose they come every day?' " – call further attention to the "periodical" quality of political narrative, reiterating a troubling link between mass culture and menstruation, the body politic and the reproductive female body (190). This prospect forces Dormer to change the subject with nostalgic vengeance. Surveying the nearer prospect of Julia's estate, he remarks, " 'Delightful English pastoral scene. Why do they say it won't paint?' " (190). Here Dormer voices questions that James's idiom of racial convertibility more generally opens up: what, in fact, will define the "English," and more broadly the Anglo-Saxon, scene in the moment of newly powerful anxieties of social purity and danger? Who, in the brave new world of Anglo-American civilization, will have final "say" over the conditions of its production and reproduction?

Mastery and the Theater of Conversion

Dormer's tactical attempt to change the subject of representation sets the cultural agency of fiction in opposition to the conduct of a public sphere whose base rhetoric is definitive "of the period" (*TM* 375). Linking women as a distinctly "foreign" constituency across lines of class and nation, *The Tragic Muse* represents femininity as a virulent strain of alterity within the Anglo-Saxon civic body. Usurers all, the novel's female authors and readers dominate a cultural

economy of indiscriminate production, tailored to their "ornamen-
tally vulgar," distinctly modern appetites for sentimental and sensational *frisson* (375).

As numerous readers have argued, James implicates his male
surrogates in the same cultural economy, conjoining female theatricality and male voyeuristic desire. Yet he continues to discriminate a
self-conscious form of male authorship that undermines its complicity with the ethos of usury. As fantasized by Nash, this authorial
power is the unacknowledged legislation performed by "great poets" as against "the verbiage of parliamentary speeches": "*Their
words are ideas* – their words are images, enchanting collocations
and unforgettable signs" (121). With reference to the "great structure[s]" they rear – structures of feeling, rather than "of stones and
timbers and painted glass" alone (121) – the novel distinguishes with
increasing insistence between two versions of masculine culture-
building: one that consumes female self-display and thereby sup-
ports an economy of sensational reproduction, and another that
appears to call such power into question, destabilizing the marketplace as a site for the production of narrative and cultural agency.
The distinction fails at certain crucial moments in the novel, as when
Dormer's aspirations become party to the very violence, brutality,
and usurious rhetoric they are intended to depose. But it tells dramatically in its collapse. Oscillating between ironic and romantic
stagings of its cultural aspirations, *The Tragic Muse* reinvents a meaningfully Anglo-Saxon social body at the expense of its own investment in transgressively cosmopolitan stagings of nation and race.

This protocol can be traced throughout the novel in an apparently inadvertent, extended textual wordplay. At the critical moment of Dormer's first dialogue with Julia Dallow, as they discuss
the possibility of his election to Parliament, the narrative partially
discloses its investment in their contest over the act of representing
the social body. Adverting to the life of "those great truths" that
would stem the "fine flood" of political rhetoric, which "has nothing to do with the truth or the search for it," Dormer strives to curb
the dangerous power Julia wields (75). As the commander of a
traditional "pocket boroug[h]," she virtually has the election in
hand (41); as Dormer notes, " 'It's her place' " and she will "put"
her own candidate "in" (127). Unsuccessfully resisting Julia's offer
to manage his political campaign and finance it to boot, Dormer
"still stand[s] there with his hands in his pockets" (76). Julia herself
calls attention to the figural resonance of this gesture, so common
to James's problematically passive male protagonists: " 'if you are
going into it with your hands in your pockets I'll have nothing to do

with you' " (76). In response, Dormer "instantly change[s] the position of these members." Julia, governor of political and discursive realms, has pockets in hand; the man who contests her power has his hands in his pockets. In this staged and embodied chiasmus, James registers embattlement over the containment of resources – of literary history, of sustaining myths of race and nation – that enable the project of nation-building, of "do[ing] something or other for one's country" and its ongoing "civilisation" (77).

Men standing apart, in resistance, with their hands in their pockets: throughout *The Tragic Muse*, this overdetermined pose dramatizes the Jamesian ethos of refusal, whereby conspicuously passive public men undermine the logic of possession, regulation, and sexual control that permits an economy of debased exchanges to thrive. But even as Dormer's refusal suggests the complicity of traditional masculinity with the civic failures it ostensibly defends against, his gesture also gives voice to a resonant anxiety about the status of male "members" in the newly convertible social body of James's designs. The vitally Anglo-Saxon public he imagines gives way to an audience whose difference resists his negotiation. Lady Agnes, urging Nick to remain at Harsh with Julia after his election, calls his attention to the problem. " 'Aren't you her member, and can't her member pass a day with her, and she a great proprietor?' " she asks (165). With "an odd expression," Dormer counters: " '*Her* member – am I hers?' " Finally, his disgust for the "poor torpid little borough" he " ' "represent[s]," ' " with the forceps of double quotation marks, records anxiety about the very power that Dormer seems to abjure, that of harnessing both feminine perversity and feminine gentility in the making of a productively cosmopolitan alterity (165).

James takes some pains to obscure Dormer's complicity in the sexual economy of bourgeois masculinity; he does so, ironically, by multiplying – that is, by repeating in other contexts – the symbolic gesture intended to counter the reproductive logic of usury. Discovering that Gabriel Nash has extended an insidious financial patronage to the Rooths, Sherringham is "not able to repress a certain small twinge" of competitive angst, accompanied by "the apprehension that he too would probably have to put his hand in his pocket for Mrs Rooth" (143). Having thus disposed of that member, he becomes ever more determined that "he should have his money back with interest" (157). Usurer that he ironically turns out to be, Sherringham will nonetheless not be repaid in the sexual currency he demands. In response to his proposal of marriage – or rather, his plan to "lock [Miriam] up for life under the pretence of doing her good" (472) – on the eve of her initial "magnificent" success, the object of his desire affirms her own destiny of "figuration" as the voice of the nation's identity and ideals (466). Determined to immure her in "the deepest domesticity of private life" (468) – "'Just quietly marry me,'" he proposes, "'and I'll manage you'" (465) – Sherringham issues a monitory warning, spoken with "a touch of superior sternness" that, James notes, is "meant to be tender" (471). Calling his appeal "a flood of determined sophistry," Miriam opposes to it the effect of her form of representation, which "simply stir[s] people's souls," offers them "*other* possibilities" of identification and response (466, 475). "Radiant" with "a splendid vision" of her gift, she counterproposes a "true marriage" – a "closeness of union," an "identity of interest" – that would privilege her performative power, and thus undo Sherringham's rigid hierarchy of private and public, of feminine and masculine, of the stage and the theater of "man" (475). In barely suppressed fury, Sherringham responds with "a passionate but inarticulate ejaculation." "[T]urn[ing] away from her," he "remain[s], on the edge of the window, his hands in his pockets, gazing defeatedly, doggedly, into the featureless night" (475).

This scene of proposal in turn recalls Dormer's interchange with Julia in the temple of Vesta. Here the reiterated gesture of contested masculine power becomes a form of regulation, whereby the novel stages Sherringham's deserved come-uppance. (He is, after all, the novel's foremost representative of a dubiously genteel and "genuine[ly] British mistrust of the bothersome principle" of art [476]). More importantly, the repetition of the gesture displaces the "shining confusion" shared by Dormer, the narrator, and James himself about the forms of regulation and control they forego onto Sherringham, who "dumbly and helplessly rage[s]" in a melodrama of imperial masculine governance (457, 475). In his insistence on this figure of the suitor with his hands in his pockets, James might be said to engage in an act of authorial master-baiting. Staging the demise of mastery, exposing its complicity with the usurious economy of consuming desire, the novel defends against its own prevailing ambivalence about the claims of alterity, and about the power of "transmut[ation]" that Miriam alone appears to wield (457). Left alone on the novel's center stage, Sherringham "stands" not only for the violence of masculine possessiveness, but for a sterile expense of desire – that of the international agent without constituents or a "body," speaking only for and to himself (469).

As women become increasingly powerful agents of transformation in the English body politic through transgressive performances of race, nation, and class, the novel cedes mastery with more violent overtones. In Sherringham's case, that violence is exposed as the *fonds* of his erotic desire, which reprises that of *The Bostonians'* Basil Ransom. Seeking to incarcerate Miriam in the "seiz[ure]" of his "long embrace," Sherringham will "releas[e] her only to possess her more" (415). As he awaits her arrival at the deserted house in Balaklava Place for their final confrontation, he regrets "that he himself had not gone round, not snatched Miriam bodily away, made sure of her and of what he wanted of her" (461). When she arrives, he promises that he " 'won't hurt you' " but acts to prevent her escape, "walking round to get between her and the French window, by which she apparently had a view of leaving the room" (471, 462). In response to her ultimate entreaty – " 'Let us hold our tongues like decent people and go about our business' " – Sherringham enforces the letter of the law of masculine desire: " 'I simply hold you, under pain of being convicted of the grossest prevarication, to the strict sense of what you said a quarter of an hour ago' " (477). Threatening that he will " 'com[e] back in a year to square you,' " he reveals the thrust of his "domestic . . . and colonial policy" as an urgent need to maintain rigid distinctions between public and private, theatricality and authenticity, racially pure and contaminated, so as to naturalize his own authority in bearing the white man's burden (479, 63).

The violence of Sherringham's outbursts is surely meant to distinguish his vulgar desire for possession from more productive negotiations of racial and national self-affirmation. Dormer initially appears to speak for the latter, countering the logic of possessive acquisition with a moralizing motto: "To do the most when there would be the least to be got by it was to be most in the true spirit of production" (419). Making deliberate gestures of refusal – of the political arena, of the bankrupt culture-building implied by primogeniture, of erotic mastery – he responds to the power of female narrative and to narratives of women's power with a figural mastery that partially distances him from the forms of corrupt rhetoric he abjures. Countering Julia's defense of periodical literature, he replies: " 'You say things every now and then for which I could kill you. "The article of the month," for instance: I could kill you for that' " (181). Disdaining her "horrible ambition," Dormer plays at the language of mastery; in the theater of metaphor he stages and partially transcends his own anxieties about the governance of women in the public sphere. Thematizing his own failures of "possession" and control, Dormer authenticates his refusal of "the great mission" of inherited patriarchal power that sustains the imperial and narrowly nationalist "sense of England" (63, 197).

But Dormer will finally be mastered by the same shining confusion that inaugurates Sherringham's unease. Against the theatricalized spaces governed by feminine desire and design – the *boudoir*, the *salon*, and the temple of Vesta, that "ornamental structure" erected on "artificial foundations" (182) – the novel posits another kind of cultural architecture, figured by the country house of Dormer's political mentor: Beauclere. Named in honor of "those great truths" nurtured within the ideal republic, Carteret's conspicuously "Norman" estate signifies the doubleness of the cosmopolitan design (75, 197). Adverting to the moment of the Conquest, it suggests both the productive force of longstanding racial contact and exchange and the fragility of a distinctly Anglo-Saxon character under siege.[22] Ultimately, however, Dormer's vision of the great feudal estate defends against the latter circumstance. Fleeing from the encounter in the temple of Vesta to the sanctuary of Beauclere's abbey, a "great church" with "huge Norman pillars" that resembles "the indestructible vessel of a faith" (195), Dormer and the novel recover a comforting vision of representativeness, a "grand kind of reciprocity" between the Anglo-Saxon inheritor and the forms of "achievement and endurance" that his "apprehended revelation" of his racial culture sustains (197, 195): "foundations bafflingly early, a great monastic life, wars of the Roses, with battles and blood in the streets . . . these things were connected with an emotion that arose from the green country, the rich land so infinitely lived in, and laid on him a hand that was too ghostly to press and yet somehow too urgent to be light" (197).

Unlike Julia's earlier sexual advances, the invisible hand of this historical *Geist* arouses Dormer to a desire for union, not with any mere woman but within a totalized civic body. In a "throb that he could not have spoken of, it was so deep" – a "throb," that is, too pure for mere words – Dormer imagines a form of "legisla[tion]" that would conjoin "the sentient subject" to his constituency in a "reciprocity" of broadly racial feeling, "a national affection" (197). Thus forestalling the vulgar "advertising" of the "mountebanks" in the political and theatrical arenas – a term associated alternately with Sherringham, Julia, Lady Agnes, and Miriam herself – Dormer sustains the novel's fantasy of a form of cultural reproduction true to the deepest history of a broadly racial feeling, "simply the sense of England" (197).

In order to enable Dormer to do this work, the novel must change its subjects in more extensive ways, so as to repossess the

power of less discriminating forms of alterity. James ultimately pro-
tects the possibility of productive cultural "transmutation" and
transmission by changing his principals with a vengeance – in effect by converting them, in a narrative process that underscores the
fluidity of civic identity even as it militates against specific agencies
that resist James's novelistic management. Most obvious, of course,
is the case of Miriam Rooth, transfigured by the end of the novel
from *cabotine* to "productive force" who commands "the language
of art, the richest and most universal," "testify[ing]" to the organic
life of literary and national histories (497). Heir apparent to the
English drama, Miriam becomes free to reinvent a cosmopolitan
"consciousness," "personality," and cultural idiom by virtue of the
racial alterity she has learned so resourcefully to manage.

Notably, however, the Jewishness that marks her difference and
her powers of management "disapp[ears]" in the process " 'without
a trace' " (511). "[N]o longer Miss Rooth," the *soi-disant "jeune An-
glaise*," she becomes a thoroughly English subject and genteel *bour-
geoise* (519, 46). Her greatest triumph is not "the very perfection" of
her Juliet – which "mark[s] an era in contemporary art" – but her
perfect mastery in effacing and revising her own origins (528, 522).
Manipulating the organs of English populism, nation-building, and
taste, the "newspapers with columns of irreducible copy," Miriam
"pour[s] forth . . . floods of unscrupulous romance," tells "all different tales" of her origins in "rival versions, surpassing each other in
authenticity"; she thereby exploits, even as she eradicates, the
"blankness" of her racial alterity (494). This kind of conversion is
precisely what the novel struggles, without complete success, to
regulate and exploit. Even Dormer fails to fix her character as
Tragic Muse or racial icon *à la* Rachel in the permanence of portraiture, which "know[s] nothing of death or change" (497). Like the
novel at large, he remains "troubled about his sitter's nose, which
was somehow Jewish without the convex arch," and which cannot
be made clearly to signify "irreducible" cultural origins (280).[23]

Despite that refractory organ, Miriam achieves the conversion to
which James as author of *The Tragic Muse* aspires, transforming
herself as the "unique" representative of a revitalized national culture (494). Her achievement must therefore be bounded by com-
pensatory shifts that relocate in other arenas the contestatory
power she is, as woman and Jew, so resonantly figured as commanding. The most striking of all such changes concerns Mrs. Rooth,
whose penchant for "gossiping" and banal moralizing James increasingly redacts as "underhand commercial habits" (443). As Dormer paints Miriam, the Jewishness that must be exorcised from his

subject to ensure her fitness for representation rebounds onto the
demonized mother:

> A queer old woman from whom, if you approached her in the
> right way, you could buy pots – it was in this character that she
> had originally been introduced to him. He had lost sight of it
> afterwards, but it revived again as his observant eyes, at the
> same time that they followed his active hand, became aware of
> her instinctive appraising gestures. . . . Mrs Rooth's vague, po-
> lite, disappointed bent back and head made a subject, the
> subject of a sketch, in an instant: they gave such a sudden
> pictorial glimpse of the element of race. (443–4)

Observing her movements, Dormer "f[inds] himself seeing the immemorial Jewess in her," "holding up a candle in a crammed back
shop" (444). Although it "had never occurred to him before that
she was of Hebrew strain," Dormer immediately converts Mrs.
Rooth, the indefatigable Neville-Nugent, on the spot: as she is
"flanked by such a pair" as her husband and child, he reasons,
"good Semitic reasons were surely not wanting to the mother"
(444). In the context of his own immemorial art – "the indestructible thread on which the pearls of history were strung" (498) – Mrs.
Rooth becomes the calculating "descendant of a tribe" that figures
both the richness of self-invention and the bankruptcy of commer-
cialism unredeemed (444).

By the same nation-building token, the novel must make Gabriel
Nash disappear "like a personage in a fairy-tale or a melodrama,"
precisely because his unstable alterity contests James's version of
racial theater (511). Joseph Litvak argues that Nash's exit from the
narrative represents an "extreme," if not "terroristic," instance of
James's "counterplotting," mounted against Nash's exposure of the
dangerous analogy between the transgressions of the true artist
and the sordid excesses of the "*bête*" (Litvak, 258, n. 25). But the
fate of "the indefinite and elusive" Nash is not merely an instance
of James's failed efforts to evade the contagion of theatricality; it
also performs a crucial conversion. Even as Dormer imagines Nash
"gone to India, and at the present moment . . . reclining on a bank
of flowers in the vale of Cashmere," he also imagines that Nash's
image is "gradually fading from the canvas" of his unfinished portrait, "for all the world as in some delicate Hawthorne tale" (516,
511). The disappearance of the image suggests the shifting registers of race and nation that enable Nash's cosmopolite freedom;
from Samarkand to Seville, where the "wild fig-tree grows" (123),
he "shall only *be*, more and more, with all the accumulations of

experience" (511). Yet it also suggests another "moral" (512). Writing Nash, and the pursuit of "low" forms of passing and signifying, out of the picture, James reserves Nash's power of cosmopolitan transformation and identification for his own revision of genteel cultural politics.

As *The Tragic Muse* draws to a close, it suggests with increasing unease the costs of thus sustaining investment in an Anglo-American cosmopolitanism with the capital of contemporary race thinking. Numerous readers have hastened to point out that the authentic artistry with which Dormer valiantly struggles to keep faith becomes a mere handmaiden to the vulgar class and party politics he despises. In part, however, that failure ensues from the novel's ambivalence about the forms of otherness with which it identifies. Faced with a choice between the hermetic fixity of the country house and the usurious reproductive capacities of racial and class upstarts like the Rooths, Dormer and the novel ambivalently contract to the former. In the penultimate chapter, James raises the curtain on Julia Dallow playing hostess, "magnificent entertainer" and "perfect mistress of the revels," to the Dormer family at Broadwood during the Christmas holidays, in a feast of "supremely sociable" intercourse that includes "extemporized charades" (513).

The novel stages this event not merely to reinforce the insight that even its most decorous figures are contaminated by the culture of publicity, but to insist on an ultimately failed distinction between James's form of culture-building and the narrower versions of Anglo-Saxonism with which it shares certain anxieties about the cosmopolitan imagination. Mimicking the "types" of self-invention they abhor, the Dormers ironically confirm the transformative power of social identity unmoored from the laws of empire, blood, and caste:

> There had been a moment when . . . Lady Agnes, an elderly figure being required, appeared on the point of undertaking the part of the housekeeper at a castle, who, dropping her *h*'s, showed sheeplike tourists about; but she waived the opportunity in favour of her daughter Grace. Even Grace had a great success. (513–14)

Unlike the Rooths, who add an extra "o" to their name to "smarten it up" and thus enable their genealogical revisions (47), the Dormer women drop "*h*'s," entertain and play at class transgression, in order to shore up the hierarchies of race and nation that sustain their family romance.[24] Staging the ongoing drama of patrimony in the face of class and national decline, the play announces that "[t]he Dormers" are "so much in it, as the phrase was, that after all their discomfiture their fortune seemed in an hour to have come back" (513).

Participating "in the charades and in everything," Dormer is part and parcel of this regulatory act (514). Fulfilling Nash's dire prophecies, he ends up " 'sketch[ing]' the whole company," "do[ing] all [Julia's] friends, all the bishops and ambassadors" (513, 507). Ironically, the only portrait he appears able to finish and put on display is Julia's, a fact that reveals his fundamental inability to reinvent the "insular" and narrowly "representative" Anglo-Saxon character – writ in his own "lean, strong, clear-faced" countenance, with its conspicuously "straight nose" – he exhibits from the outset (7, 9). Ceding his transgressive aspirations to narrower nation-building possibilities, Dormer ends by embracing the patriarchal cultural imperative he initially resists. He remains a "finished productio[n]" whose own finished productions can only replicate and multiply, rather than meaningfully revise, the virtually "bankrupt" social orders he inhabits (7, 376).

Yet Dormer's reproductive mode, like Miriam's, turns out to be insufficiently separable from James's cultural project. Standing wholly, in the end, on his achievement of "the noble portrait of a lady," Dormer inadvertently figures a version of James at the moment of *The Tragic Muse*, in a nostalgic allusion to an earlier text that more successfully negotiates both its intended transnational audience and its cultural resources (529). By the end of the novel, James's identifications with cosmopolitan alterity will collapse into the well-made ending, with the requisite marriages and reversals of fortune, of the distinctly English literary tradition he has attempted to redirect. At last, the inconsistent narrator reappears on the scene to impose a form of closure that registers the partiality and instability of James's revisions. Briefly reporting the "facts" of personal "destiny" taking shape "even now," the narrator closes the gap between the indeterminate present of the narrative and "contemporary history" (529). In a final theatrical gesture, that voice once again adopts the pose of the "historian" celebrated and defended in James's essay on Trollope:

> During those two days at Harsh Nick arranged with Julia Dallow the conditions, as they might be called, under which she should sit to him; and everyone will remember in how recent an exhibition general attention was attracted, as the newspapers said in describing the private view, to the noble

portrait of a lady which was the final outcome of that arrangement. (529)

But the narrator's refusal of authority to represent – his final insistence on the civic and public character of "describing" the "private" – collapses into the threatening newspaperism which the high representational mission contests, even as it wards off the "sharp sense of modernness" occasioned largely by the "remarkable career" of Basil Dashwood and "his wife" – aliens, entrepreneurs, managers, and Jews within the cultural theater of Anglo-America (529). Defending against and appropriating their representatively "modern" power, to erase, revise, and circulate fictions of origin, to breach and reconfigure the boundaries of culture, James scripts his fantasy of performative reinvention of an "Anglo-Saxon total," but does so in accordance with laws of filiation whose legitimacy and value to the novel's culture-building project he has judiciously challenged. Finally James can be said, in this fiction intimately concerned with the transgressive power of metaphor as a political resource, to disfigure his own representational designs. The racial logic he appropriates from popular contexts enables but ultimately limits the range of his performances in the cosmopolitan mode. Not until the moment of *The American Scene*, when James maps a more pointedly historicized version of whiteness onto the boundaries of postindustrial America, will he engage the full range of consequences of his own racial figures and acts of identification. In this earlier moment, the work of reinventing an international audience united under a shifting standard of the Anglo-Saxon is only achieved, in the last words of *The Tragic Muse*, by a reincorporation of orders of race, nation, and gender in which the aspiring novelist himself has "ceased to believe" (530).

5

DOCUMENTING THE ALIEN:
RACIAL THEATER IN
THE AMERICAN SCENE

Our object is not to imitate one of the older racial types, but to maintain a new American type and then secure loyalty to [it] . . . the American race.

> – Theodore Roosevelt, Speech to the New York Knights of Columbus, 1907[1]

The immigrant of to-day, be he Slav, Italian or Jew, starts upon this trail [of Americanization], with no culture, it is true, but with a virgin mind in which it may be made to grow.

> – Edward A. Steiner, *On the Trail of the Immigrant*, 1906

[The picture] speaks a language learned early in the race and in the individual.

> – Lewis Hine, "How the Camera May Help in the Social Uplift"

How are Americans to be made? In the emergent industrial nation to which Henry James returned in 1904, the "Americanizing" of "the new American" (Steiner, 292), or what James would call "the recruiting of our race" (*AS* 46), had become a definitive cultural project. As waves of predominantly Southern European immigration mingled alien "strains of blood" with those of so-called native Americans, nativists and progressivists alike struggled to reconfigure the nature of nationality and cultural filiation. Immigration, along with black migration and spreading military expansion into the haunts of a "decaden[t] . . . Latin race," put at issue the social and ideological entity of "the American" at large, in whom racial and national identity newly coalesced and coincided.[2]

In his own extensive observation of American manners, institutions, and public life in *The American Scene*, the restored Ameri-

158

can absentee records numerous scenes in which the making of Americans – of American "race," of American culture, of American civic fate – is enacted. Shortly after his arrival on the shores of Manhattan James takes an autumn drive on a public coach traversing a scenic valley in New Hampshire, where he finds himself under "the spell" not of nature, but of "the large liberty" with which "a pair of summer girls and a summer youth, from the hotel," take "all nature and all society . . . into the confidence of their personal relation": "they talked, they laughed, they sang, they shrieked, they romped, they scaled the pinnacle of publicity and perched on it flapping their wings" (*AS* 23–4). What strikes James most forcibly is their dangerously "uncorrected, unrelated state" (310), which resists the transformative work of social experience, resists "the human or social function at large" (24). In summation, James notes that "[t]he whole phenomenon was documentary; it started, for the restless analyst, innumerable questions, amid which he felt himself sink beyond his depth" (24).

For the latter-day reader of *The American Scene*, the keynotes of James's commentary sound familiarly: the failure of "continuity, responsibility, transmission" (8), the "so complete abolition of *forms*" (18), the "speculative" excitement with which James reads such tellingly named "figures in the carpet" (19, 12). Yet here James's *données* suggestively emerge under the sign of the "documentary." James employs the word in its only extant contemporaneous meaning, derived ultimately from the legal arena; the scene in question is of the nature of document or text, affording evidence as to the deeper depths of the American character. The residential neighborhoods of new Boston become "quite documentary"; they "testify with a perfection all their own to a whole vast side of American life" (176). So too the public monuments of American cities are "documentary" in granting the deeply curious observer an "enjoyed leave" to "examine" and speculate at will on the American "consecration of time" (225); so, at the Royal Pinciana in Palm Beach, "Vanity Fair in full blast" (323), the truly "national" ("in the largest sense of the term") character of the visitors' indomitable "bourgeois propriety" makes the whole spectacle "documentary" (326, 238). Throughout *The American Scene*, the documentary or evidentiary nature James ascribes to America as text specifically raises both the problem of the American race, in its cultural and national forms, and the representational protocol that will most sensitively register and redact it.

At large, I want to argue, *The American Scene* hazards – or more accurately, theorizes and performs – a notion of the documentary that purposefully engages emerging technologies and idioms for documenting the American race. The conduct of the text, with its intricate metonymies and "chains of association," vividly rehearses the complexity of racial exchanges – identification, anxiety, and desire – seen to inform virtually every site for creation of the new American type.[3] Variously described as decentering, impressionist, and mimetic, the narrative of *The American Scene* can more explicitly be said to perform, as it acutely witnesses, an emergent form of racial theater in which James's own documentary designs as observer and the designation of the American remain in fruitful dialogue. Aligning itself and competing with the emerging documentary modes of mass visual culture, James's purposively "restless" style of response explores the racial logic of America's distinctive modern idiom, through which the character of whiteness, in its "inveterate bourgeois" form, is being forged (272).

In Richmond, in one salient example, James visits various sites sacred to the mythos of the Confederacy, including the Confederate Museum full of tragically sanctified "relics" (275). The "poverty of the exhibition" from "one ugly room to another" itself makes the museum's chambers deeply "documentary"; the "unappeased visitor" is immersed "up to his neck" in "the social tone of the South that *had* been" (275, 276). Perusing its all-too-unreconstructed "sorry objects," James makes of them a pointed object lesson in American self-invention (276). The "smothered flame" of Southern *ressentiment* becomes a "reversion of the starved spirit" to a dangerous cultural mythology, over which a primitiveness of aesthetic achievement – a virtual "illiteracy" – "hover[s] like a queer smell" (277). The fetishes of Southern piety here constitute no more and no less than a "dim, dusty collection of specimens, prehistoric, paleolithic, scientific," on display for the "musing visitor," who objectively examines the evidence "of a singularly interesting 'case' " (277, 276).

James's figure of reversion, whereby he renders Southern gentility and *amour-propre* equivalent to a racial atavism commodified for the anthropologically-minded observer, gives more dramatic point to the climax of this local scene. His only fellow-visitor turns out to be a "gallant and nameless" son of the new South, who offers *in propria persona* a more "lively interest of type" (278). Exuding a "natural piety," the handsome Virginian provides a running commentary on "certain objects" on display, gathered from his father's regiment and "identical with relics preserved in his own family" (278). With "highly conversable" panache, the young man recounts a "paternal adventure," the "desperate evasion of capture, or worse, by the lucky smashing of the skull of a Union soldier." A "capital kind of Southerner," the new son declares himself " 'ready to do' " such "far-off things" " 'all over again' " (278). For James, his "cool platonic passion" makes the Virginian "so much the kind of Southerner I had wanted," one with a richly furnished historical consciousness. But the platonic passion turns out to register and take its shape from passions of quite another kind. "[T]hough he wouldn't have hurt a Northern fly," James notes in conclusion, "there were things (ah, we had touched on some of these!) that, all fair, engaging, smiling, as he stood there, he would have done to a Southern negro" (279).

Certain features of this exchange that recur throughout the text bear remarking: the encounter in the scene of auratic artifacts; the homoerotic, even "queer," identification of James with his accosted specimen; the contest of sorts between them for narrative supremacy; the apparent resolution of both the identification and the contest in James's recognition that the machinery of racial violence drives the historical imagination of the new son, who is also, tellingly, a "fine contemporary young American" (278). Yet James's masterful narrative resolution turns out to be spurious; the image of the Southern negro as mythic victim returns us to the episode inaugurating the Richmond encounter, where James, pursuing the "concrete . . . in the name of history," finds himself following a "wide, deep street" – "a place of traffic, of shops and offices" – clogged with "shabby Virginia vehicles . . . in charge of black teamsters" (271). If James's grammar leaves open the question who is in charge of America's modes of conveyance, the sight of black men laboring en masse in the public thoroughfares occasions a pointed anxiety that will recur throughout the text. For James the image itself is resonantly documentary; it "emphasized for me with every degree of violence the already-apprehended note of the negro really at home" (271).

The violence structural to the new son's self-constitution as Southerner and white American turns out, then, to echo the violence with which James "apprehends" blackness as a fact of the national life, blackness "really at home" in the American public sphere. In narrative terms James might be said to redirect the feared violence and primitivism of laboring black men onto the force of his own perception, and onto the culture of racist gentility that has produced the Virginian and his treasured relics. If this rhetorical gesture encodes James's own racial uncertainties, it nonetheless activates and sustains an extended meditation on the American racial imaginary and its cultural forms. Prompted by the sight of the teamsters to meditate

on "*his* own arts" for "fixing and saving" his gathered impressions –
the "projected light of his conscience" – James "f[inds] himself" observing the State Capitol "in course of reconstruction" (271, 272).
Musing on America's "national affirmations," he laments the bourgeois character of its architecture, its "builded forms of confidence
and energy," whose absence of a unifying spiritual or religious "sym-
bolism" figures as "a fine blank space" in "the very middle" of the
social canvas (273).

This is not, however, merely another plea for the nurturing of
the "aesthetic appetite," or even a recognition of the need for his
own "abeyance of judgment" on the ongoing formation of "values
of a new" bourgeois order (273, 274). In the wake of James's racial
unease, the "fine blank space" of his figure implicates a national
self-imagination that fails to interrogate its own logic of nation- and
culture-building. "[A]pprehensively" poised between the spectacle
of the teamsters and the display of Confederate relics, James un-
veils a collective "portrait" of America's "multitudinous People," in
which "all the accessories of the figure [are] showily painted," while
"the neat white oval of the face itself" remains "innocent of the
brush" (273).[4] What kind of face will America put on its unfolding
"history of manners and morals" (273), on its facts of racial difference and exchange, on its national mythologies of collective, assimilated American character?

Far from the pushing crowds of urban New York, the Richmond
scene nonetheless typifies James's documentary project of apprehension and response, which not only takes up the making of whiteness as an explicit theme; through metonymy and associative logic
it rehearses the complex patterns of identification, withdrawal, and
mastery that constitute that making. Rehearsing his own random
yet heavily freighted encounters with American spaces, icons, and
selves, James performatively meditates on American character and
culture-building and on the limits of his own attempts to represent
them. At large James works to create a space of cultural agency
beyond the reach of the bourgeois expertise governing the project
of Americanization, yet alive to the power of its emergent habits of
seeing and recording. In particular, his documentary project in *The
American Scene* is in dialogue and contest with the framing power of
visual, or "phantasmagoric," technologies to document race and
thus to manage the range of bourgeois America's ongoing responses to the question of how national culture and citizens are
made. James's engagement with this project helps to account more
richly for the mixed register of his own cultural politics, which

promote an ethos of openness to racial exchange even as they record vivid urges to conduct, and to resist, racial management.

In the following pages I trace that engagement in several specific sites opened up by *The American Scene* itself: documentary or "reform" photography, exemplified by the Ellis Island work of Lewis Wickes Hine; mass visual culture, consistently linked by James with racialized forms of excess and "multiplication"; and modes of conveyance, especially the Pullman train, whose spectacular rituals of racial contact are performed in the service of consolidating the culture and cultural values of white America. In these sites of exchange, James contests rival authorships for the power to inscribe new chapters in the ongoing tale of the American tribe. Working as documentary observer, he cannily represents each of these sites as a theater of nation-building, in which "alien" forces participate in the making of a distinctly American race. Documenting that activity across boundaries dividing high and low cultural formations as well as whiteness and its constituting others, James performatively explores alternative modes for naming a shifting American social body.[5]

"Human Documents": Ellis Island and The American Scene

One of *The American Scene*'s most resonantly "documentary" moments transpires as James recounts his wanderings with a "remembering mind" over the grounds of Harvard College (*AS* 43). He comments at length on the "belated delimitation of College Yard" through the erection of fences and other barriers that create a space "inaccessible . . . to the shout of the newspaper," a "place to think, apart from the crowd," in the larger "land of the 'open door'" (44, 41). This "drawing of the belt at Harvard is an admirably interesting example of the way in which the formal enclosure of objects at all interesting immediately refines upon their interest, immediately establishes values" (45).

In James's carefully chosen idiom, the architectural and psychic framing of Harvard enables the old buildings to "gro[w] a complexion," just as it promotes possibilities for intimate "analysis" of "the type of the young men coming and going in the Yard" (45). Within its newly bounded precincts James is free to mine the "treasure[s] of illustration" on display and to meditate on the "physiognomic character" of America's managerial classes in training (46). In the midst of his meditation, he notes that he has "not yet" been "out to Ellis Island," to "catch in the fact, as I was to catch later on, a couple of hours of the ceaseless process of the recruiting of our race" (46). Within the "marked . . . *milieu*" of Harvard, Ellis Island emerges as the *omphalos* of his "haunting wonder as to what might be becoming of us all, 'typically,' ethnically, and thereby physiognomically" (45, 46).

This narrative episode is documentary in a very particular sense; it suggests how powerfully the framing of social spaces allows for the representation and the production of social and national type. More specifically, it figures the work of photography as an emergent mode of documenting national culture, for framing sights and creating sites of American character. Especially telling is the entanglement of James's aesthetic critique of open spaces with the Ellis Island experience; the passage resonates with nativist anxiety about American immigration and the policy of the "open door," vented throughout Brahmin circles in monitory images of the "wild motley throng" pressing through the nation's "unguarded gates" (Aldrich, 57).[6] Yet James's image suggests a further openness of its own in its canny linking of the sons of the bourgeoisie in Cambridge, sporting the "unmitigated 'business man' face," and the "foreign matter" being transformed at Ellis Island into an industrial work force (*AS* 46). The "great 'ethnic' question" (86) becomes a synecdoche for the larger question of the American race (*"whom [will] they look like the sons of?"* [46]); both register America's "artless need to get [it]self explained" (82). At stake is "the right measure for" the ongoing "ceaseless process" of making up Americans – whether "the art of the painter of life by the concrete example, the art of the dramatist or novelist," or that of "the reporter at large" (47, 46). What cultural forms, James's documentary image asks, will frame, document, manage the making of Americans, the "recruiting" of a national body?

To these questions the social uses and the cultural work of photography are particularly relevant. By 1904 photography had already become a primary resource throughout Anglo-America, and particularly in the U.S., for reimagining the city as a psychosocial space of racial contact, definition, and exchange. James's work under the sign of literary art bears a particular relation to this culture-building politics, one perhaps most resonantly framed by the documentary photography of Lewis Wickes Hine, founder of the American project of "reform" photography.[7] Linked in various incidental ways with James's texts, Hine's famous photographs of urban immigrants, laborers, working children, and the culture of the machine literalize – or, more precisely, give historical exactitude to – forms of confrontation with otherness that inform emergent critiques of American industrial capitalism and its production of the urban reserve army. Yet his photo studies also suggest their own need to manage otherness in the service of an inclusive social body and progressive modes of culture-building. Redirecting the project of cultural mastery into the work of enlightened documentation, Hine's "human documents" give pointed context to, and suggestively render the limits of, James's analogous style of race thinking.

In the winter of 1905, at precisely the moment James visited "the terrible little Ellis Island," Hine was also wandering its precincts, where as many as 5000 immigrants a day were being "marshalled, herded, divided, subdivided, sorted, sifted, searched" and "fumigated" (60). Ellis Island not only inaugurated Hine's work as a photographer; it became the subject of a lifelong photo-study of "representative individuals of foreign extraction," in a project "document[ing] the significance, to our country," of immigrants' lives.[8] Drawn initially, like James and numerous other visitors, by a voyeurist urge to "capture and record some of the most picturesque of what many of our friends were talking about," and by the entertainment value of the Island as "a costume ball" with "multicolored, many-styled national" types, Hine increasingly tested the meaning of the American progressive enterprise and its style of nation-building against the challenges posed by the facts of racial alterity.[9] In the process he transformed the social possibilities and value of camera work. In a formulation with resonance for James's project and self-representation, he "went to Ellis Island as a school photographer" and "left it a master" (Trachtenberg 1977:123).

Hine indeed came to the Island as a school photographer, but not of an ordinary kind. In 1905 he was teaching geography at the Ethical Culture School of New York, founded by the progressive reformer Felix Adler. During 1900–1, Hine had studied educational theory at the University of Chicago under John Dewey and Ella Flagg, as well, perhaps, as the sociologist George Herbert Mead. In his introduction to *Men at Work*, the only volume of Hine's photographs published for a mass audience during his lifetime, he would take a passage from William James's "The Moral Equivalent of War" as his point of ideological departure.[10] When he took up a camera for the first time in 1904, he did so in order to promote progressivist Deweyan concerns with the efficiency and relevance of his students' education, documenting their activities for their own study so as to enable them to integrate forms of "doing" and "knowing." Ellis Island would function as a kind of laboratory for his students' assimilation of a progressive cultural politics; his pho-

tographs of immigrants were intended to inculcate "the same regard for contemporary immigrants" as "for the Pilgrims who
landed at Plymouth Rock" (D. Kaplan, xxv). Armed with a cumber-
some 5 × 7 camera, magnesium powder for light flashes, and heavy
glass plates, Hine produced nearly a thousand glass negatives between 1905 and 1908 alone, including copious negatives made at
Ellis Island, of which only a handful of prints survive (Gutman, 83;
Kaplan, xxiv–xxv; Doherty, ix). Few in number, these images are
nonetheless crucial as texts of the cultural politics and the politics of
culture in which *The American Scene* participates and intervenes.
Tentatively negotiating the felt power of individuality over and
against racial "representativeness" or "type," Hine's photo-studies,
like James's documentary mode, attempt to free themselves from
the reigning conventions and cognitive habits of the picturesque.
Yet both cultural observers employ strategies of identification with
the alien that remain linked with styles of cultural affirmation performed through the management of racial difference.

One particular "human document" usefully connects Hine's
work with James's text, an image entitled "An Immigrant Family at
Ellis Island" (1905; Figure 5.1). Employed without ascription as the
cover illustration for the most recent edition of *The American Scene*,
the image offers a performative meditation on American character
making that comments usefully on James's own. Like virtually all of
Hine's immigrant and work portraits this one exploits the uncanny
power of frontality; each of its four subjects, ignoring the conventions of both bourgeois and ethnographic portraiture, return the
camera's documentary gaze.[11] Hine's hallmark use of the middle
range creates a certain psychic distance between camera and subject, in which the irreducibly particular details of the latter's "character" and life-world – the measured uncertainty of the girl's affect, the name inscribed in careful rounded letters on the corded
bag – emerge. Paraphrasing Alan Trachtenberg, we might say that
Hine's image itself creates a scene, a social space in which otherness
can be explored in its fullness of detail and measured against the
motives and activity of its documentary observers (Trachtenberg
1977:124).

Indeed, the protocol of detail in this photograph ultimately records how knottily entangled is the impulse of identification with
otherness and technologies of social management. Hine densely
fills the frame of reference, which thus suggests the claustrophobic
experience of submission to the "prodigious process" of assimilation, yet remains laden with objects of compellingly personalized
meaning (*AS* 60). Like unabashedly typological portraits, his study

Figure 5.1 An Immigrant Family at Ellis Island – 1905: Photo-study by Lewis Hine. Source: Lewis W. Hine Collection; United States History, Local History & Genealogy Division; The New York Public Library; Astor, Lenox and Tilden Foundations.

makes much of picturesque details and the comfortingly typical "costumes" of the arrivals.[12] But the precision of his camera further suggests the social meaning of their clothing in the context of race "recruiting." The textured quality of the image calls attention to the abundance with which its subjects are dressed – caps, shirts, petticoats, vests, scarves and more – in their most valued and valuable attire. The infant girl wears a ruffled pinafore and bonnet; the older girl, an elaborately tucked and ruffled cap and dress with an embroidered collar; the boy, a suit complete with vest and neatly knotted tie. The mother wears a dress shirt adorned with distinctive decorative pipings. All three children have high quality, carefully buttoned leather shoes.

The camera's deliberate focus on such detail insists on the way the immigrants have outfitted, even armored, themselves against the shock of the new and the machinery of assimilation. Nonetheless the managerial imperative of its "intendedly 'scientific' feeding of the mill" of American culture (AS 60) is directly signified by the placard tucked into the boy's hatband, a device used by immigration officials for marking arrivals – usually men and heads of families – with control numbers to facilitate the elaborate system of examinations to follow. In Hine's documentary rendering, the placard echoes the visual effect and function of the luggage tags predominant in the background at right. The photograph thus records the felt gap between the ideology of assimilation, the work of giving human value and social place to the otherness of Americans in the making, and its local realities. Caught in a notably stiff and awkward posture, bent under the weight of his duffle bag, the boy is designated as both an object of assimilation and a future laborer in the culture of efficiency that gives birth to this very scene.

The marking of the youth in the scene of nation-building follows on the absence of a more securely patriarchal presence, an immigrant father. Hine's caption – "An Immigrant Family" – neatly calls attention to this fact, registering a certain anxiety of authority in the life-world of the immigrants and in the documentary project.[13] The need to taxonomize the group as a family is prompted not only by the logic of assimilation as a social practice, which takes the family as the bedrock unit of urban industrial production and reproduction, but also by the desire to manage racial and ethnic alterity. Hine's title reflects reformist platforms of the era that link "family" with "manhood" and "patriotism" and assert that "upon the preservation of the home depends the vitality of our Republic" (Riis, 20, 113).[14] Framed by the ideology of domesticity, the immigrants can be more easily assimilated into an American social "family" and a larger family of man.

Yet Hine's image registers a certain discomfort with the process it endorses. His study records two distinct gazes under the guise of frontality: that of the female children, focused directly at the camera, and that of the mother and youth, directed to the right of and some distance above the lens. Are the mother and son distracted by an attendant of Hine's, or by an immigration official or procedure, as their relative anxiety suggests? In any case, the double gaze registers an instability in the source of documentary authority, in effect distancing the camera from the project of Americanization through enlightened management. Hine certainly enables a sentimental reading of this gesture; it is open to us to assert, in the progressivist idiom, that the camera's deepest interest resides in the youngest of the immigrants (here, presumably future mothers and molders of native "character") who can be most effectively imbued with the nation-building values that will induct them as citizens of a newly incorporated America. But the slightly wayward gaze of mother and son forces us to confront the costs of fideism in this process. Dividing the gaze, the very expression, of otherness, Hine's photo exposes its own ambivalence about the project of managing "the great 'ethnic' question" under the rubric of Americanization (AS 86).

Hine's 1905 "human document" thus adumbrates a tension that structures his most powerful work, between a progressivist ideology and an ambivalence about the forms of identity and identification it promotes. Working under the sign of the progressive "survey," whose avowed intention is "to make the [American] town real – to itself," Hine embraces the ideal of managed meliorations of social contact and exchange, "the more conscious use of intelligence to achieve a more rational collective life."[15] The Ellis Island images, however, suggest Hine's interest in a more complex generation of the social – in what Trachtenberg, following George Herbert Mead, reads as "sociality," a capacity for self-diffusion, for provisionally internalizing the voices of others as a condition for social selfhood (Trachtenberg 1989:204). In this view, national culture and society at large consist not of an aggregate of managed relations but of "all the others with whom one interacts, imaginatively as much as materially" (Trachtenberg 1989:204).[16]

This tension bears particular weight in relation to the racial theater of Ellis Island. I have suggested that "An Immigrant Family" records the tension internally but also negotiates it in a subtle divison of labor. While the image works to "arouse sociality," or a more complex openness on the viewer's part to the claims of otherness on the evolving American character, its caption registers a certain discomfort with the necessity of racial management. In this respect, "An Immigrant Family" is representative of Hine's responses, and suggestive of James's, to the Ellis Island experience. Virtually all of Hine's immigrant photos are accompanied by a narrative of some kind, a practice that would become increasingly prominent as Hine circulated his images in collages, posters, montages, and other "Hine-o-graphs." By hand or in typewritten notes, Hine appends elaborate captions and summaries to his photostudies that function as social data. The self-consciously allusive "Mother and Child – Italian, Ellis Island" (1905), for example, is accompanied by a note identifying its site as that of "the detention cell" where "1700 immigrants were crowded into a room which was built to accommodate 600"; to the hauntingly beautiful "Jew From Russia at Ellis Island" (1905), Hine has affixed a note that remarks: "Jewish immigration from Russia dates back to the 1840s. The Russo-Japanese War in 1905, and the Pogroms kept the exodus high. Today there are supposedly 2,000,000 Russian Jews in America" (Figure 5.2).

Here in miniature is the progressive ethos of documentation *par excellence*. As Hine went on in 1908 to document shockingly abusive child labor practices, the currency of fact – of hard data at the back of each image – would accrue increasing ideological value. His photos would "set the authorities to work to see 'if such things can be possible.' They try to get around them by crying 'fake,' but therein lies the value of the data" (Hine, cited in D. Kaplan, 7). The National Child Labor Committee would call his photos "of great value in furnishing visual testimony in corroboration of evidence gathered in field investigation."[17] Value in this context equates with testimony, corroboration, documentary evidence; Hine's photos perform a social function, have social meaning, under the sign of social information and the transformative power of the fact. Of his own "straight photography" – his term for images presented without benefit of supporting textual evidence – Hine writes: "All along I had to be doubly sure that my photo-data was 100% pure – no retouching or fakery of any kind."[18]

But the project of "100% pure" visual testimony becomes troubled when purity itself – racial, national, and ethnic – is the subject in question. Hine's inscriptions on the Ellis Island photographs suggest how difficult the production of legitimate data becomes in the face of racially coded forms of otherness. For each image he

Figure 5.2 Jew From Russia at Ellis Island – 1905: Photo-study by Lewis Hine. Source: Lewis W. Hine Collection; United States History, Local History & Genealogy Division; The New York Public Library; Astor, Lenox and Tilden Foundations.

provides a statement of the subject's racial or national origins, implying the power of ethnographic taxonomies both to manage and
familiarize difference with ease. Yet careful study reveals that Hine
frequently assigned different racial types to the same subject in
different photographs, while his racial designations are themselves
notably unstable. One handwritten caption reads: "Italian at Ellis
Island – 1926 or Jewish?" Another identifies its subject as "Italian,
Ellis Island," but is accompanied by an additional caption reading
"Albanian"; a third image is labelled "Russian Jew [overstruck] (?)
Ellis Island 1926," while its caption of record reads simply "Racial
Type."[19] Hine would later lose a lawsuit to his own employers over
such a typological caption; he had labelled a print of a youth taken
in Hell's Kitchen, and published in his photo study *Boyhood and
Lawlessness*, "The Toughest Kid on the Street," and the subject was
literally an altar boy who "felt slandered" by the imputation (Doherty, 2). Reflexively resorting to the affective power of typology to
arouse curiosity and confirm the ideal of social management,
Hine's project of "100% pure" documentary is undone by its own
anxiety of purity. Face to face with the complexities of otherness,
his camera work abrogates the cultural mastery he claims: the
power to assess with confidence the character of the new America.

   In announcing his intentions for *The American Scene* in its preface, James explicitly distances himself from the cultural politics of
"information" invoked by Hine. Eschewing "matters already the
theme of prodigious reports and statistics," James advertises his
own "record" as "naked and unashamed" as to such "information"
(*AS* ix). Instead his "intimate intelligence" will concern itself with
"features of the human scene" and "properties of the social air, that
the newspapers, reports, surveys and blue-books would seem to
confess themselves powerless to 'handle' " (ix, x). If his own measure of this "expression of character" proves less than complete, it
will nonetheless document the "human subject" of America, the
question of its "character," with greater and more productive "care"
(x). James's documentary stance echoes the sociality of Hine's approach as well as its anxieties about the management of race as a
social and representational resource. But it incorporates (one is
tempted to say assimilates) both of these responses – openness to
otherness, anxiety about managing otherness – into a more sustained and performative critique of the logic of Americanization.

   That logic of incorporation is figured in James's most resonant
trope, that of appetency or consumption, to which the analogy of
Hine's project gives sharper focus. Hine's Ellis Island images suggest how voraciously assimilation in its progressivist form consumes

human potential, even as they themselves participate in bourgeois America's hungry consumption of the racial picturesque.[20] In *The American Scene* James vigorously forestalls this form of incorporation. In sought-after confrontations with America's aliens, the "restless analyst" dramatizes his own failures of appetite, of "ingestion" (59). James's figures of appetency indict the relentless American "*will to grow*" in part by implying that the incorporation of "foreign matter" jeopardizes the health of the national body (38, 46). Yet James's repudiation of the managerial ethos nonetheless enacts other, more productive kinds of management. His mode of documenting the making of Americans moves actively to confront the particular unease of Hine's documentary strategy: that of the liberal imagination forced, by the ungovernable facts of racial contact, to historicize the otherness it seeks to entertain as a precondition for American social agency.

This alternative documentary motive structures James's rendering of the "acute facts" of Ellis Island and of his own "impression" thereof (61). He frankly admits that its operations occasion "a thousand more things to think of than he can pretend to retail" (60–1). The latter phrase calls attention to the movement of James's narrative: he has just abandoned Wall Street, the ultimate province of retailing, for the ferry to the Island, confirming his distance from the "market" world of downtown with its "pushing male crowd" (60). In effect, James proleptically displaces the threat of the aliens as threatening racial hordes onto "the heaped industrial battlefield" of Wall Street, with its "welter of objects and sounds in which relief, dignity, meaning" have "perished utterly and lost all rights" (60). Inaugurating this imagistic commerce between downtown and Ellis Island, the narrative suggests that the "immense momentum" of capitalism and of the progressive ethos adopted to curtail it have alike created conditions whereby the aliens are robbed of "rights" and meaning (60). The "prodigious process" of the immigration "mill" submits the bodies of future industrial workers to manifold "grindings and grumblings," whose rote efficiency fuels capital's "universal will to move" and the culture of wage slavery into which the aliens will be inducted (60).

Throughout the Ellis Island passages, three forms of appetite contend: that of consumer America, that of the aliens, and James's own. Self-consciously risking a nexus of images that allies him with both nativist and scientist cultural politics and with unexamined ethnographic desires, James raises a crucial question: how can the "affirmed claim of the alien" to citizenship be made compatible with a coherent "idea of the country" (61, 62)? The "visible act of

ingurgitation on the part of our body politic and social" may produce a "wonder" – or unease – that the hungry analyst "couldn't
keep down" (61). But it also heralds a critical opportunity for the
reincorporation of America and the consequent redirection of our
"American fate" (61). Relocating race and cultural filiation in the
shifting site of "one's relation to one's country," James contests
progressive models of the civic in which social agency and race
consciousness are forged (61).

At Ellis Island, James differently enacts the role played by these
models in the constitution of Roosevelt's "American race," white
and bourgeois America. In the grammar of the third person, he
tests his own sense of "*dis*possession" (62, emphasis added) in the
"lurid light" of social fact (115), in the spirit of "the sensitive citizen" who "may have happened to 'look in' " on the immigration
machine; the latter "comes back from his visit not at all the same
person that he went. He has eaten of the tree of knowledge, and
the taste will be for ever in his mouth" (61). James's unease becomes
a productive symptom of the citizen's ingestion or assimilation of
"the truth . . . come home": "it shakes him – or I like at least to
imagine it shakes him – to the depths of his being"; "I positively
have to think of him, as going about ever afterwards with a new
look . . . in his face, the outward sign of the new chill in his heart"
(61). Here the mass and corporate appetency of "ingurgitation"
(61), the scientific feeding of "the great assimilative organism" (91),
give way to the sensibility of a newly self-conscious bourgeois
citizenry – one with both a heart and a face – forced to submit its
"instinct" of national and racial purity to the "free assault" and
"presumptuous interest" of the aliens (62). James himself will end
this extended meditation on Ellis Island by noting the persistence
of a "fond alternative vision" of "the luxury of" a "close and sweet
and *whole* national consciousness" such as is made possible in the
land of "the Switzer or the Scot" (62). But *this* "ideal," rather than
the assimilable alterity of the aliens, turns out to be the thing "one
couldn't keep down" (62, 61). "[B]eguiling" and "duping" his own
anxiety of dispossession – his own capacity, we might say, for racial
distaste – James relocates assimilation as a social act from the corporate to the individual body, figuring a newly American "being" in
whom the requirements of American citizenship – active incorporation of difference as the grounds of culture-building – will contend
with the "universal will" of capitalist assimilation and its "appetite at
any price" (62, 60). The metonymic commerce James opens between Wall Street and Ellis Island ultimately works to forestall "the

clamorous signs of a hungry social growth," in which no less than "the prize of the race" is "in sight" (212, 58).

James's critique of appetency, and specifically of the "avidity" of New York downtown (55), thus puts him in contention for the power to document and manage racial difference productively. In the Ellis Island and New York city passages, he does so by explicitly countering the "immense" and hungry "machine" of American culture-building with appetites of his own invention (89). Everywhere seeking sensation, the "hungriest of analysts" with his "starved stomach" and tightened "aesthetic waistband" prepares to consume "the queer feast" prepared by the "look" of America (111, 48, 105). Identifying himself as a "pilgrim" with "the sharpest appetite for explanations" (ix), he assertively explores a cultural landscape in which "the rich taste of history is forbidden" in lieu of a less discriminating appetite that has "broken out and [is] feeding itself to satiety" (81, 213). Literally embodying the question of "[w]hich is the American," of "[w]ho and what is an alien" (89), James's contestatory figures self-consciously turn on the anxiety of control they seek creatively to resist.

That anxiety resonantly recurs in "A Spring Impression," where James considers the relation of his own acts of "surrende[r]" to the urban theater of difference (83). Even as he immerses himself in the "vast hot pot" of the city, where "a little of *all* my impressions" is "reflected in any one of them," his figures evince a certain concern about ingestion of the "fusion" and its irreducible "common element" (83, 84). The "taste of each dish in the banquet recalls the taste of most of the others," from "the fish and the sweets" to "the soup and the game"; the "whole feast affects one as eaten" with "the general queer sauce of New York" (84). In Central Park, where "the fruit of the foreign tree" has been "shaken down" with "a force that smother[s] everything else," the "brooding visitor" remarks the "singleness of impression" made by the alien: "Is not the universal sauce essentially *his* sauce, and do we not feel ourselves feeding, half the time, from the ladle, as greasy as he chooses to leave it for us, that he holds out?" (84). Yet even here, as a more predictable anxiety of incorporation governs, James appears productively overwhelmed by his "almost inexpressibly intimate" relation to heterogeneity, which occasions the "need of mental adjustment to phenomena absolutely fresh" (83, 84).

The metonymic conduct of James's figures betrays neither a conflict between the raw and the cooked nor a fear of the racial primitive within mastered civilization so much as the difficulty of resisting his own anxieties of representational management. One such "fresh" phenomenon, an encounter on the Jersey shore with a group of foreign laborers constructing one of the "huge new houses" that stand for "the expensive as a power by itself," enables the staging of a pointed drama of discrimination (6, 7). "[O]n the spot" of the production of America's *nouveaux riches*, James loses not his appetite but, metonymically, his tongue, his ability to speak and thereby to represent the subject at hand (85). The "element of communication with the workers" lapses – "that element which, in a European country, would have operated, from side to side, as the play of mutual recognition, founded on old familiarities and heredities" (85). Missing in this locus of racial contact is the "instinctive," "easy sense" of "a social relation with any encountered type," upheld by a social "scale" of measurable, ethnographically confident racial distinction (85). The reality of racial exchange in what James ironically calls the "land of universal brotherhood" thoroughly displaces the returning native American: "Italians, of superlatively southern type," the "diggers and ditchers" in question resist both cosmopolitan understanding and assimilation into the conventions of the ethnographic picturesque (85, 84). "It was," James writes, "as if contact were out of the question and the sterility of the passage between us recorded, in due dryness, in our staring silence" (85).

The consequent "shock" attests to James's disenfranchisement from the culture of appetency in which both the Italian laborers and the newly rich – the moral "aliens" in this scenario – participate (85). But it also provides James a figure for documenting and confronting his own unease in the absence of self-affirming forms of racial contact. Having abandoned his overtures to the laborers, James goes on, midparagraph, to record another episode of shock so as to manage difference – or rather, resist managing it – more productively. Wandering in the New Hampshire hills, far from the money-mad crowds, James loses his way and is forced to "appea[l], for information, at a parting of the roads, to a young man, whom, at the moment of my need, I happily saw emerge from a neighbouring wood" (85). As on the Jersey shore he receives a "blank stare" in response to his inquiry. Determined to make his way home, James musters all of the cultural resources at his disposal:

> seeing that he failed to understand me and that he had a dark-eyed 'Latin' look, I jumped to the inference of his being a French Canadian. My repetition of my query in French, however, forwarded the case as little, and my trying him with Italian had no better effect. 'What *are* you then?' I wonder-

ingly asked – on which my accent loosened in him the faculty of speech. 'I'm an Armenian,' he replied, as if it were the most natural thing for a wage-earning youth in the heart of New England to be. (85)

Seeking to confirm his whereabouts, James becomes – as he will more dramatically in other allegorically American sites – a foreigner in his own land, betrayed by cosmopolitan mastery, misled by the force of ethnographic typologies that prove radically insufficient to the American real. Only in the moment when his fantasies of "brotherhood" are relinquished can James compel any kind of exchange, as his belated query "loosen[s]" the alien's "faculty" of response (85). His failures occasion yet another "shock," a "chill . . . for the heart" in "the heart of New England" that recalls the "new chill" in the heart of the sensitive citizen at Ellis Island (85, 61). No less than the bourgeois citizen whose culture he observes, James is forced to pose for himself "the question of intercourse and contact" between the American and its intimate "strangers" (87). By reverting to troubling figures of appetency, he considers the social possibilities opened up by the failure of his own confident taxonomies to take in the alien and make "profit" of the act (85). " 'What meaning,' " he dialogically asks in a moment of theatrical self-address, " 'can continue to attach to such a term as the "American" character? – what type, as the result of such a prodigious amalgam, such a hotch-potch of racial ingredients, is to be conceived as shaping itself?' " (86).

If the hugeness of these questions, and the variability of "ingredients" in "the cauldron of the 'American' character," free James from "the immediate need" of precise "conclusions," thus "multiply-[ing] the possibility" for hungry speculation, they also frame the aims of his documentary project (86, 87). What Hine's unstable captions inadvertently register, James's shifting figures openly perform, declaring their own narrative insufficiency. The hungry analyst "doesn't *know*, he can't *say*, before the facts" of difference; "the facts themselves loom, before the understanding, in too large a mass for a mere mouthful" (87). Ultimately James documents the necessity of being overwhelmed, more or less productively, by the "*il*legible" quality of racial difference, whose "fantastic" grammar "belong[s] to no known language" (87). Even as he meditates on the logic of racial management that Hine's photography exemplifies, James counters the appetite for assimilable data by embracing the very form of confusion, the cultural "baffle[ment]" (149), that Hine attempts to regulate. Transfiguring nativist racism – disgust, loss of appetite – as a loss of speech, James makes the "ingurgitation" (61) of racial alterity both a precondition of and a salient risk for his attempts to elaborate the making of the American social body, the "New York intermarriage" that is itself both "remarkable" and "unspeakable" (149).

American Scenery *vs.* The American Scene:
Phantasmagoria as Racial Theater

If the culture-building imperative of Hine's project clarifies James's documentary aims, it also lends a certain depth of field to certain gestures of positioning on James's part – in particular his response to the "New Jerusalem" of the lower East Side, staging grounds for the "Hebrew conquest of New York" (*AS* 95). Here James's productive openness is marked by a brooding ambivalence about the "intensity" of the Jew's "aspect" and "race-quality" (94). In James's recounting, the New York Jew embodies racial history as a dangerous form of "excess": animated by "the gathered past of Israel mechanically pushing through" it, Rutgers Street "swarm[s]" with the "immitigable, unmistakable" signs of "a Jewry that had burst all bounds" (94, 95). The problematic "strength of the race" predictably turns out to involve precisely the Jewish power of reproduction, the "multiplication, multiplication of everything" – of the commercial ethos no less than of the "swarming" population itself (94).

These figures of excess turn out to be inseparable from anxieties of authorship, of the narrative management of racial difference, understood as "the golden truth" of emergent industrial America (109). At stake on the site of Jewish "overflow" (94) is the power of James's documentary to resist foreclosure on its affective contact with "the swarming ambiguity and fugacity of race" (144) and "the discipline of the streets" (126). At stake, too, is the power of James's project to contest and distance itself from other, less socially productive modes of framing "the rich Rutgers Street perspective" in all its multitudinous "complexity" (95). Remarking the "portentous" quality of Jewish difference, which "reduces to inanity any marked dismay quite as much as any high elation" on the part of the native observer (95), James stages his own overmastery by the mass production of American meaning. The "portent" itself is "one of too many"; "Phantasmagoric for me, accordingly, are the interesting hours I here glance at content to remain" (95). Defeating a "neat applied machinery" for the ordering and valuation of difference, the heterogeneity of "the New York phantasmagoria" in the Jewish ghetto eludes the control of the documentary project. (Thus

James's peculiar grammar of subordination, which makes the inter-
lude in Rutgers Street itself "content to remain" disordered in the
face of his merely "glanc[ing]" attention.) In a gesture of partial
submission to that heterogeneity, James enjoins on himself a certain
restraint: "Let me speak of the remainder [of his time in the ghetto]
only as phantasmagoric too, so that I may both the more kindly
recall it and the sooner have done with it" (95).

James's insistence on the "phantasmagoric" quality of Jewish excess invites a historicizing scrutiny. While the term aptly describes
the epistemological challenges of late capitalist urban experience, it
also names and links that experience with a specific earlier technology of documentation and exposure: "phantasmagoria," the exhibition of images or optical illusions produced by the magic lantern, an
apparatus whose technology anticipates that of film and heralds the
inauguration of mass visual culture.[21] James's broadside on the phantasmagoric multiplicity of the Jewish tenements – where "race-
quality . . . push[es] through" as portentously as "the whole quality"
of the "pushing male crowd" does on "the heaped industrial battlefield" (94–5, 60) – stakes out the contestatory interest of his narrative in such alternative documentary modes as photography, the
half-tone image, and the stereograph. These phantasmagoric activities, James implies, impose both a technology and a politics of
culture-building on the alien, all too ready to submit to, and (in the
case of the Jew) all too ready to master, the project of reproducing
bourgeois America.

The logic of James's phantasmagoria, both a social and a representational strategy, is usefully recapitulated in a catalogue produced as an advertising supplement by the T. H. McAllister Optical
Company in 1892. Entitled "The Dark Side of New York," the
brochure advertises a new collection of "lantern" or stereograph
slide images for sale, "nearly 200 views illustrating the wretched
conditions under which the lower 'other half' of our dense population live and die."[22] Capitalizing on the audience created by mass-
produced photographic urban studies, principally Jacob Riis's seminal urban study, *How the Other Half Lives* (1890), McAllister rushes
"views" into print in response to "the frequent inquiries of our
customers" – both lecturers on the progressive reform circuit and
private middle-class consumers – for authentic documentation of
slum life.

These images and the stereographic technology associated with
their use assist powerfully in the transformation of middle-class
American status, identity, and identification through forms of pleasure predicated on opportunities for racial contact and control.

Perfected in midcentury by none other than Oliver Wendell Holmes, in a design that would hold sway for over eighty years, the hand-held stereograph (the original medium of Riis's slum images) provided the viewer with a more immediate, interactive exposure to hitherto "alien" subjects. Placing a double image whose distinct halves had been photographed from adjacent points of origin behind a viewing apparatus with an adjustable focal length, the stereograph viewer enjoyed the effect of a certain visual mastery, that of the three-dimensional and "instantaneous panoramic view" (Darrah, 2).

Aggressively marketed through subscription schemes, door-to-door sales, and boxed editions hawked with the slogan "A stereograph for every home" (Darrah, 3; Hales, 266), the apparatus lured middle America at the turn of the century with the promise of traffic in racial difference. Exhibiting immigrants at Ellis Island, ethnic "types," and exotic urban venues as well as other "educational" views, the stereograph occupied the busy intersection of progressive reformism and ethnographic consumerism. If, as Holmes declared in an essay published in the antebellum *Atlantic Monthly*, it served as "the card of introduction to make all mankind acquaintances" (Holmes 1859:744), it also gave white America *carte blanche* to stage controlled contact with racial others, from the Ainu of Japan and central African pygmies to black migrant laborers and Jewish pushcart peddlers. Opening up the spaces James occupies in *The American Scene* – tenements, subways, streetcars, the ghetto, and other "underworld" sites of both progressive and sensationalist interest – the avowedly documentary stereograph allowed Americans to fantasize race with unprecedented immediacy, and simultaneously to control and catalogue it with ever more progressive and "scientific" precision.[23]

Two distinctive features of the stereograph as a culture-building activity bear remarking vis-a-vis James's interests. First, the problem of reproduction or "multiplication" posed by its print technology: the sheer number of images of urban life – as many as six million still in circulation in turn-of-the-century America, just after the height of the stereograph trend – works to jeopardize the possibility of creating distinctions between sensationalized images and more self-conscious documentation of the complex attitudes occasioned by race matters. Because stereographs often went uncredited, they were copiously recirculated, with "fresh" text appended to furnish the *frisson* of up-to-the-moment contact with changing social conditions. One particularly resonant example of this cultural mobility is given by a popular image produced by the Keystone View Company as early as 1899. It records two black children picking cotton, an enormous basket in the foreground, their diminutive figures virtually engulfed by overgrown bolls; the caption reads: "We's done all dis s'mornin'" (Figure 5.3). A verso text dated 1905 notes that "Pickaninnies as young as eight years can pick cotton. A twelve-year-old child can pick 20 or 30 pounds a day." Providing the middle American with descriptions and statistics concerning the cotton harvest, the text concludes by linking the satisfactions of the picturesque with those of the progressive conscience assuaged. "The fields," it notes, "are a charming study in black and white – colored men, women and children scattered everywhere . . . The whole Negro population swarms into the cotton fields. Good wages are paid to encourage them."

By 1913, however, in a recirculated version of the same image, the site has been identified as a Mississippi plantation and the text altered to pique more explicitly reformist sympathies. Adverting to the "poverty and unhappiness" of "the 'black belt,' " this text details the conditions of unskilled labor, noting that "the more ignorant it is, the cheaper. This is why we had slavery and why we brought in the negro." It nonetheless goes on to celebrate the "wealth" produced by King Cotton – or rather, by the "hands . . . called on for picking, from Uncle Remus to the pickaninnies." Affording the viewer the dual satisfactions of liberal sympathy and nation-building, the text notes that the U.S. "produces about 80% of the whole world's crop" – "our largest export," worth over 700 million dollars. Yet another text attached to the same image identifies the site as an Arkansas farm, recounting in best chamber-of-commerce style the virtues of a state "rich in resources" and boasting "healing" hot springs and "magnificent" mountain "scenery." In eerie conjunction with the image of exhausted child labor it notes that "[a]n excellent common school system and several higher institutions of learning prove the progressiveness of the people." As a final lure, the text reverts to an explicitly ethnographic idiom: "The cotton fields, once the dread of the Virginia slave, have lost nothing of their picturesqueness with the abolition of slavery." "[N]owhere in the United States," it concludes, "can primitive negro life be better studied."

The reproducibility and mobility – what we might, following James, call the phantasmagoric quality – of the stereograph image promotes this inextricable confusion of motives and appeals: nativism, racial anxiety, curiosity, voyeurism, progressive sympathy, partial identification. The same confusion reigns even more powerfully in the vast numbers of stereographs devoted to the urban street. Here what James identifies as "multiplication" is both the

Figure 5.3 "We's done all dis s'mornin'": Stereograph, Keystone View Company. Source: Robert Dennis Collection of Stereoscopic Views; Miriam and Ira D. Wallach Division of Art, Prints and Photographs; The New York Public Library; Astor, Lenox and Tilden Foundations.

protocol of the stereograph and the favored subject of its roving and voracious eye. One late nineteenth- and early twentieth-century series documenting "alien" peddlers, the building of subways, and the swarming traffic in New York's notorious downtown was entitled *American Scenery* – a fact that speaks eloquently to the contestatory relation of the stereograph and its forms of racial theater to James's cultural project. "Along the Noted Bowery," a view circulated continuously from the 1870s through the late 1920s, clearly evidences this relation. Text appended in 1904 speaks to a markedly mixed affect of appetite or curiosity and racialized distaste, the same affect quite differently negotiated by James's images of Ellis Island and downtown. Locating the viewer physically in the stereograph's three-dimensional welter of details, the text begins with a reassuring gesture of orientation: "You are looking N.N.W. from Grand Street"; "Broadway is a third of a mile farther to the west (left) and between you and Broadway lie streets of the 'slum' district made famous . . . by the efforts made in recent years to improve them in both a sanitary and a moral sense."

Hester, Mott, and Mulberry Streets, the site of Riis's other half, teem with the anticipated alterity and decay just beyond the frame of the image; they thus put on offer the possibility of kinds of contact that both undermine and intensify the ethos of Americanism. "The Bowery itself," the text remarks, "is one of the most broadly cosmopolitan streets in the world. One finds here representations of every civilized nation and hears an inextricable confusion of languages." "[L]ined with theatres, music-halls, saloons and retail shops," the Bowery can be simultaneously advertised as a virtual laboratory for the making of new Americans and a site for exploration of pleasures "of the cheaper order." For collectors of the stereograph, the "cosmopolitan" appeal of the Bowery – the nerve center of the Tenth Ward, with its ganglia of Jewish and Italian tenements – consists in the fascination of its "picturesque crudities" as challenges to successful racial management and as opportunities for the viewer's felt liberation from the ethos of management itself: time discipline, genteel codes, and bourgeois social norms.[24]

This mixed appeal operates through the very thematics of multiplication and excess that James so conspicuously martials. A contemporaneous urban stereograph published by Underwood & Underwood, entitled "Street Peddlers' Carts on Elizabeth Street," suggests how racial difference, management, and affirmation coincide and coalesce under the sign of phantasmagoric exchange (Figure 5.4). The accompanying text, also produced in 1904, again begins by

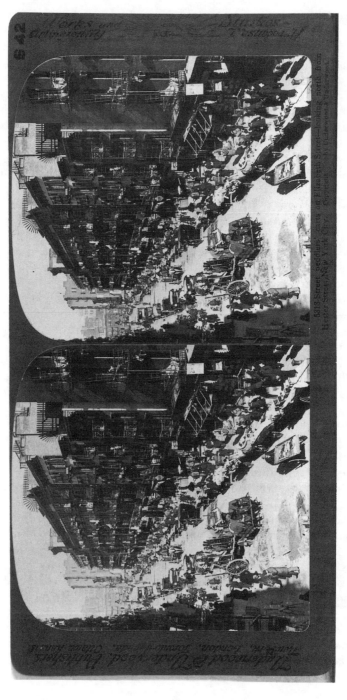

Figure 5.4 Street Peddlers' Carts on Elizabeth Street: Stereograph, Underwood and Underwood. Source: Robert Dennis Collection of Stereoscopic Views; Miriam and Ira D. Wallach Division of Art, Prints and Photographs; The New York Public Library; Astor, Lenox and Tilden Foundations.

orienting the bourgeois reader intent on a near-immersion in "the famous 'slum' district." Although the image provides a long view converging on the open sky, the text predictably urges the viewer indoors, into the shockingly claustrophobic conditions of "ground-floor rooms and basements" whose "every room from cellars to roofs" houses aliens "crowded into dirty and ill-smelling" quarters. Even the fire escapes are crammed with "bits of family wardrobe"; the whole district teems with "Italians," "Hebrews," and "others of all sorts and kinds." This racial phantasmagoria sets the stage for a certain racially inflected liberation. While the pushcarts promise access to "every imaginable sort of goods," the streets themselves offer "abundant provisions" for "drinking," relatively uncontrolled physical contact, and other forms of excess. Thus the "panoramic" long view, which muffles the shock of alterity, gives way to an invitation to the middle American to plunge vicariously into the "picturesquely dirty hives" of Elizabeth Street. "Swarm[ing]" with "all sorts" of racial exotica, advertised under the sign of excess, the stereographic slum offers bourgeois America the opportunity to manage its anxieties of racial "multiplication" while safely indulging fantasies of untethered commerce in difference, excess, and release.

Arguably what troubles James as documentary observer is not the fact of *American Scenery* but the active promotion of its form of nation-building as definitive of the new America, constitutive of "the total of American life" (*AS* 89). This cultural logic and its monitory interest for James are usefully summed up in an essay entitled "The Walk Up-Town in New York," published in the January 1901 *Scribner's* by the popular genteel writer Jesse Lynch Williams. For Williams the lure of the stereograph, with its "variety, color," and "exhilaration – almost intoxication" (Williams, 44), is mapped onto the psychic and racial geography of the city as experienced by the new American (white, male, bourgeois) on the loose.[25] Imagining the successful entrepreneur on "a walk home to be taken daily" after work, from downtown to uptown – or rather, "from the bottom of the buzzing region where money is made to the bright zone where it is spent and displayed" – Williams enjoins on his readers a model of urbanity dependent on phantasmagoric mastery (Williams, 44). As Alan Trachtenberg argues, that model is predicated on the power of the bourgeois success narrative, with its allegorical movement from "bottom" to "top"; he fails to note, however, that it is also predicated on the appeal of illicit pleasures of detour through "zones" of racial contact and exchange (Trachtenberg 1989:186).

In Williams's account, the businessman-"*flaneur*" becomes a willfully detached and mobile observer, rather than a producer, of the made city, experienced as a pleasurable array of discretely consumable scenes of almost every variety of humanity, from "modest young jackies" and "nuns, actors" and "pickpockets" to immigrants "with steerage tags" – like the one attached to Hine's subject – "still fresh"; the whole panoply making "our New York" the exemplary modern "cosmopolis" (Williams, 45, 53, 56). Of particular interest are the aliens with "bright-colored head-gear and squalling children" who populate the Pier and Castle Garden, ripe for collection in "amateur emigranting" (Williams, 45, 46). This heightened pleasure in alterity crucially assists in the binding of America's bourgeoisie into the structures of work, regulation, and mastery that it is enacted to evade, by naturalizing the viewer's alienation from the life-worlds of urban capitalism – not least the realities of racial challenge – as the grounds of an "appetizing" and "worry-dispelling" flânerie (Williams, 44). In what Trachtenberg identifies as time "stolen" both from work and domestic life, and from the cultural labor of upholding the crucial distinction between the two, the bourgeois American transforms his own alienation as a new and distinctly American form of psychic mastery. He enters the space between downtown and uptown, the space of cosmopolis, in which racial anxieties and desires can be briefly liberated from explicitly productive interest and social roles, only to consolidate the meaning of whiteness in the "bright zone" that is his ultimate destination.

Enacting this double movement of challenge and consolidation, businessmen in numerous American cities armed themselves with phantasmagoric technology for their own intervals of freedom. Producing for private "pleasure" and "adventure," such prosperous turn-of-the-century entrepreneurs as J. W. Robbins in Boston and Charles R. Clark in Chicago carried newly streamlined hand-held cameras into immigrant neighborhoods, seeking out the culture of shopfronts, alleys, bazaars and other sites of racial exchange. Their images were collected in voluminous scrapbooks, and – not unlike Hine's – captioned, apparently so as to document and renew the delights of transgressive forays across the cultural stakes dividing white and other, high and low. Such flânerie not only documents a rapidly changing urban sociology; it also records the pleasurable breaching, under the sign of privacy, leisure, and technological expertise, of a racialized cordon sanitaire (Hales, 262–4). But the very act of transgression, which gives shape to the "flaneur's" self-distancing from more narrowly bourgeois conventions, itself becomes commodified in the visual culture of "multiplication."

Phantasmagoria, as a phenomenological possibility and as a visual technology, works ultimately not as a form of liberation from bourgeois discipline but as a mode for reincorporating racial curiosity in the service of reproducing bourgeois America.

Understood as a contestatory response to the logic of *American Scenery*, James's figures of multiplication in the Jewish quarter mean more variously than his readers have suggested. On the site vigorously opened by the stereograph, the site of "overflow," "excess," and "multiplication with a vengeance" (*AS* 94), the documentary observer becomes productively overmastered: "there was too much in the vision" of Rutgers Street, James confesses, "and it has left too much the sense of a rare experience" (95). This oxymoronic formulation usefully distances James from such entrepreneurial traffickers in racial difference as the marketers of the stereograph and its forms of cultural appeal. The excess of rarity, of uniqueness, remarked in his impressions of the New Jerusalem makes virtually impossible *their* multiplication in service of undifferentiated cultural narratives about either the alien conquest of New York or the pleasures of "surrende[r]," "especially intimate surrender," to racial exotica (83, 90). Implicitly opposing his performative documentary politics to those of phantasmagoric mass culture, James warns that "the city of redemption" – of self-making, of mercantile and civic brokering, of phantasmagoric possibility – is "least to be taken for anything less than it was," with all its troublingly uncontainable energies (96). In the shock of the "native" American's staged exposure to "the everywhere insistent, defiant, unhumorous, exotic face" of the Jew, another form of production and reproduction can tentatively take shape (97). Where the so-called "lower" human "values," those "most subject to multiplication," can be imagined to increase or "rise, in the American air," a "wealth of meaning," a multiplicity of culture-building possibilities, ensues, "pour[ing] into the value and function of the country at large" (97).

This particular passage makes unexpected and productive use of the Jew as a figure for multiplication; in so doing, it mimes the performative possibilities of Jewish excess, of "the genius of Israel" for material "redemption" (97, 96). Yet it does so by sustaining the commerce James has initiated between the Jew in the ghetto and American modernity at large, "with its pockets full of money and its conscience full of virtue" (111). Troped as usurious getter and spender in the racial imaginary of progressive white America, which the hungriest of analysts only partially probes, the Jew on the

American scene poses an overdetermined danger for his documentary project. Uniquely linked with phantasmagoric excess, the Jew wields a historically emergent power of reproduction with which James remains in contest: that of *American Scenery* to manage the construction of the new American, to give shape to the experience of that very modernity. James's recognition of the plenitude of possibilities that the Jew opens for the reinvention of both American character and "Anglo-Saxon" tradition is tempered by anxiety about forms of cultural excess that would render his own "intimate intelligence" irrelevant (ix).

Consequently, even as the "thick growth" of James's responsiveness "reflect[s] the rich talk" animating the "Yiddish world" and its "rich Rutgers Street perspective," the latter forms of wealth afford troubling spectacles (93, 98, 95). The "rich climax" of his own sojourn on the lower East Side turns out to be a visit to the ghetto's " 'characteristic' place[s] of public entertainment," whose notable "plenitude and prosperity" bespeak the "number and variety" of their social "connotation[s]" (96, 98). In these beer-houses and cafes that constitute the "jewel" of Jewish life, James experiences a particular species of dismay concerning the fate of "English" as a language, a literary tradition, and a coherent culture specific to "the United States," where the literary artist has "his own difficulties to face" (98–9). In a remarkable series of images, the "incurable man of letters" imagines these public spaces of leisure, contact, and exchange as "torture-rooms of the living idiom" where the "future ravage" of "our language as literature has hitherto known it" has begun (98, 99). The "brooding critic" identifies with "the proper spirit of St. George," defending his "honour" in "the consecrated English tradition" by tilting at "the dragon most rousing, over the land" – the "immensity" of the "alien presence" – and listens for "the faint groan" of "the shade of Guy Fawkes," "stretched on a rack" in another "terrible modernized and civilized" space of torture (99). The incoherence of this metonymic chain voices James's " 'lettered' anguish" in response to his own prescient mapping of phantasmagoric culture as the dominant site for the making of "English" in the American future (98). Notably, the turn from the figure of Anglo-Saxon knighthood to that of failed sabotage is accomplished by another turn, "the turn of one's eye from face to face for some betrayal of a prehensile hook" – other, presumably, than that of the hook-nose – "for the linguistic tradition as one had known it" (99).

James's "exasperati[on]" within these "haunts of comparative civility" records the depth of his contestatory interest in the "agency" of American documentation (99, 98). Locally, it gives way to a kind of jeremiad against the phantasmagoric interloper – "all there for race" and with "the celestial serenity of multiplication" (94, 95) – whose "redempt[ive]" power he seeks to appropriate (96). Converting the excess of his own felt response to Jewish civic life into a figural resource, he imagines his climactic experience in that "vast" world as "a pious rosary of which I should like to tell each bead" (98). Rather than "telling," however, James is reduced – and more than once – to silence, breathlessness, a mere "piteous gasp" (99), in which the American reader mindful of "civic piety" is intermittently invited to join (66). Consistently, the Jew stands for that "portentous" too much, "too many," to which the "brooding critic" always "come[s] back" with the "gasp" of refused or controverted mastery (95, 99). Commanding the "Accent of the Future," the Jew embodies the logic of a mass reproduction whose power to forge a new America "make[s] the observer gasp with the sense of isolation" (99, 90).[26]

Self-consciously "piteous" and involuntary (99), this reiterated or multiplied response apparently distinguishes James from the linked types of the Jew as climber and the self-made bourgeois who, rather than "gasp," mechanically "gras[p]" (201) and even "*grope*" (117) at "more or less greasy greenbacks" (15), contriving "the national life" (245) as cultivation of "the expensive as a power by itself" (7). But James's gesture of distinction undoes itself as such, as he makes it clear that the "genius of Israel" for phantasmagoric reproduction is hardly an extrinsic threat to purer American character, but rather the "heavier expression" of its futurity (97, x). Emblematic in the racial code of excess of the new America's will to grow, its "appetite at any price," the immigrant Jew is made to bear the burden of phantasmagoria as an incipient cultural logic (60).

Yet even as the Jew embodies James's anxieties of mass production, that figure also enables the staging of James's concerted efforts to avoid mastering them. Taking up the rich Rutgers Street perspective, James mimics the phantasmagoric protocol of the stereograph, only to foreclose in his openly staged anxieties on the confident satisfactions of its ethnographic designs. Favored subject of *American Scenery*, putative master of its ethos of multiplication, the Jew ultimately stands in James's text for both the infinite reproducibility of phantasmagoric culture and the challenge it creates for the documentary project: that of sustaining an openness to overmastery and its "saving complexity" (7), in and through which other cultural uses of difference can be experienced and "retail[ed]" (61).

"Training for Freedom": The Pullman and the
Spectacle of America

If urban phantasmagoria yields a "rich climax" in the "drama" of
James's return, another "strongest impression" ensues on the occasion of a visit to a theater in the Bowery (*AS* 96, 139). In James's
youth, he recalls, the Bowery had served as home to an "Anglo-
Saxon" drama whose "instincts" were "nursed in the English intellectual cradle" (142, 140); it has since become a stage for "the richer
exoticism" of "the aspirant to American conditions" (140, 141).
Traveling from the life-world of uptown to that of the Bowery,
James "submits himself" to the "awful hug" of the modern electric
car (64):

> I electrically travelled through a strange, a sinister over-roofed
> clangorous darkness, a wide thoroughfare beset, for all its
> width, with sound and fury, and bristling, amid the traffic, with
> posts and piles that were as the supporting columns of a vast
> cold, yet also uncannily-animated, sepulchre. It was like mov-
> ing the length of an interminable cage, beyond the remoter of
> whose bars lighted shops, struggling dimly under other pent-
> house effects, offered their Hebrew faces and Hebrew names
> to a human movement that affected one even then as a break-
> ing of waves that had rolled . . . from the other side of the
> globe. I was on my way to enjoy, no doubt, some peculiarly
> 'American' form of the theatric mystery, but my way led me,
> apparently, through depths of the Orient, and I should clearly
> take my place with an Oriental public. (139–40)

The space of the electric car, a favorite subject of stereographic
and photographic study, induces a phantasmagoria whose uncanny
dynamism transforms the known landscape of James's past in images of loss and death. Ironically, the effect of movement through
the lurid and illegible "blaze" of the "Hebrew" world is an
encagement that aligns James with the Jews he observes in Rutgers
Street (97, 95), whose tenement fire-escapes he has likened to "the
spaciously organized cage for the nimbler class of animals in some
great zoological garden" (96). What James "enjoys," with a certain
dubiety, is a "peculiarly 'American' form" of surrender, not only to
the instability of the past but to the psychic dislocations of the
present (140). To make his "way" in America's public space and
civic life is to be "led . . . through depths of the Orient," to "take
[one's] place" with "an Oriental" – that is, a racially overdetermined, phantasmagorized – American "public" (140).

James's readers have tended to focus on the scene that follows this moment of conveyance, in which he comments on the character of the "so exotic audience" of the East-side theater and its appetite for the luxury of candy (142). But the logic of metonymy, which links "the monstrous chain" of the trolley itself with his experience in the theater (64), suggests that the electric car in the Bowery is already a theatrical site, a cultural space in which "domestic drama[s]" of identity are acted out and on (142). Both a trope for the documentary project of conveying social reality and a historically charged arena for the transaction of racial "apprehension" (58), the electric car – along with the Elevated, the subway, and the Pullman train – provides a stage for James's exploration of the making of the American race. As passenger on the car and as spectator in the Windsor Theatre, James witnesses the same drama: the " 'production' " of an American public, as a "houseful of foreigners, physiognomically branded as such," confronts "our pale poetic" and proffers in return the "pervasive facial mystery" of its alterity, viewed "as in the white light" of an "ineradicable Anglo-Saxon" past (140, 142, 143).

Aligned in its phantasmagoric spectacle with visual culture, the space of the public conveyance offers a crucial site for the production of America and Americans. On its "large impersonal stage" (53), "especially intimate surrender" to contact and exchange is performed and "shocks of surprise" by otherness are entertained (90, 28). In James's account, the public conveyance throughout America, and particularly the "great moving proscenium of the Pullman" (312), with its highly charged cultural history, becomes a site of and a metonymy for the nation-building energies he engages and resists. From the very outset, as the restored absentee undergoes "instant vibrations" that "f[all] into a train of associations" (1), as he pursues "differences of angle" in social perspective that "gathe[r] into their train a hundred happy variations" (19), as he "lay[s] down . . . every inch of the train of association with the human, the social" (157), James stakes out a contestatory interest in the "constructive" energies of American conveyance, entangling his own train of thought and "critical spirit" of response with the Pullman's form of "commerce" with its cultural moment (130, 106). Simultaneously, the Pullman and other modes of conveyance, "the supreme social expression" of American identity (292), pose a particular "challenge" to James's intimate "curiosity" (24): the challenge of " 'Authority' " to promote civically and imaginatively richer American selves (101). At stake in the spectacles acted out within and by the Pullman is nothing less than the making of civic consciousness, through what James trenchantly calls "training for freedom" (249).

For the documentary analyst, such training promotes an increasing awareness of his own investment in American conveyance as a "democratic institutio[n]," one that "determine[s] and qualif[ies] manners, feelings, communications, modes of contact" (39). Initially the train serves as a predictable figure for anxieties of "merciless multiplication" (54). Observing "the chain" of newly built villas along the New Jersey shore, "where the shadows of the waning afternoon could lengthen at their will and the chariots of Israel . . . could advance," James imagines the "huge new houses" (which exhibit "a certain familiar prominence in their profiles") confessing to their own "extreme expensiveness" no less than to the indelible race character of their occupants: "German Jewry – wasn't it conceivable?" (7, 6). Figuring an absence of character, an excess unredeemed by saving complexity or self-consciousness, bourgeois New York "in *villegiatura*" resembles "a train covering ground at maximum speed and pushing on, at present, into regions unmeasurable" (6, 7). Here the "bullying railway" embodies the "*will to grow*" (32, 38), that "great religion" of multiplication practiced by bourgeoisified Jews (133), heralding the "push[ing]" and crowding of native Americans into the shrinking "margin" of the democratic state (134, 39); it thus figures "the herded and driven state" of the Anglo-Saxon subject "pushed and pressed in" to the bewilderingly phantasmagoric spaces of the Elevated, the Elevator, the electric car (134).

Yet within the "foreign carful" itself, the isolated observer registers how just such anxiety of otherness structures the "great assimilative organism" of productive America (89, 91). In "densely-packed East-side street-cars," where the "foreign" are intensely "*at home*" (90), a "portentous" process of racial transfiguration ensues (318). In the "crepuscular, tunnel-like avenues that the 'Elevated' overarches," "figure after figure and face after face . . . betra[y] the common consequence and action of their whereabouts" (90). All "so visibly on the new, the lifted level," the foreign riders of the El are "glazed . . . over as with some mixture of indescribable hue and consistency," a "wholesale varnish of consecration" applied "out of a bottomless receptacle, by a huge white-washing brush" (90, 91). Rehearsing on the El his role as "oncoming citizen," the immigrant proves his " 'American' value" as he allows himself to be, "infallibly, penetrated" by progressive attempts to reforge his filiation and " 'manners' " (91). Sitting "there in the street-car," he ineluctably "go[es] about his business," that of submitting himself to the making of new Americans for a "colourless" bourgeois state (91).

James's shifting responses to the phantasmagoric quality of the "promiscuous American car" (26) concern more than the "beguilement of the artless traveller" by the "extent, the ease, the energy" of the new conveyances, in which "nature and science . . . joyously rom[p] together" with a "particular type of dauntless power" (52, 54). Increasingly, the conveyance – and especially the Pullman train – affords an "impersonal stage" for James's productive rehearsal of this beguilement as a critical resource for "a new kind of civic consciousness" (53, 255). Although "disconcert[ed] . . . to have to owe [his] perception, in part, to the great straddling, bellowing railway" (20), James chooses that "false position" as a crucial role in the American "comedy and tragedy of manners" (106, 314). Exploiting the "restless" freedom its energy promulgates (18), James performatively contests its leading role in the making of American cultural meaning and history.

The force of James's performance depends in large part on his precise recognition of the "dauntless power" of the Pullman as both a cultural icon and an agent in the consolidation of the American bourgeoisie (54). The Pullman Palace Car Company built its first passenger car in 1864 to carry the body of Abraham Lincoln from Chicago to Springfield; its very origins index its agency in the literal and psychic work of nation-building.[27] By 1905, at the moment of James's travels, Pullman had become a watchword for progressive efficiency – the "merciless" application of scientism (54) – and ruthless monopolization. Taking over its last competitor in the leisure travel industry in 1899, the Pullman cartel blanketed the country within two decades with as many as 9,800 cars on track that would have girdled the earth five times over, inaugurating continuous American transcontinental travel (Malken, 8). As James notes, the "direct connection between the snow-banks and the orange-groves" of the North American continent is crucial to the creation of America as dynamic geopolitical space, a "grand territorial unity" traversable "all without 'losing touch' of the Pullman" and its mastery (218, 52). No less aggressive in its corporate expansion, Pullman boasted a cash surplus so large at the turn of the century that it paid a 50 percent stock dividend, followed by an additional 36 percent dividend in 1906. Between 1900 and 1910, the traffic on Pullman tripled and its assets doubled; net profits peaked at the end of that decade with a return of over nineteen million dollars (White, 261). Conjoined with the American hotel to stand for "the

richest form of existence," the Pullman is the "supreme social expression" of American character, both a figure and a vehicle for "*all
the facts of American life*" (292).

As James cannily recognizes, the culture of "richness" crucially
assists in the consolidation of America's bourgeoisie through an ultimately racialized commodification of leisure. By 1904, Pullman had
successfully begun to remake American travel under the sign of
"taste, fashion, and publicity" (White, 249). Preaching "the merits of
luxury" to the newly moneyed, Pullman promised "to put the pre-
mium hotel on wheels," advertising its facilities for training America's entrepreneurial classes for their destined social mastery (White,
250). Trading on the appeal of Americanized modes of refinement,
Pullman implicitly contracted to refashion the managerial classes in
that image, offering such on-board services as personal valets, bar-
bers, manicurists, and private secretaries, along with parlor cars
complete with libraries of "classics" and sumptuously served and
prepared fare. A typical menu of 1900 underscores the kind of
training Pullman provides; the menu includes Halibut Vin Blanc,
Capon Financière, Apple Fritters Glacé au Kirsch, and Punch
Crème de Menthe, all at the price of a dollar (McKissack and
McKissack, 18). As stage settings for the rehearsal of this cultural
accession, the Pullman cars themselves were no less imposing (Figures 5.5, 5.6, 5.7). Their interiors were panelled in conspicuously
rare imported woods (mahogany, amaranth, ebony); the seats uphol-
stered in velvet and velour; the fixtures fashioned of crystal and
windows of full leaded glass. The overall effect, as one Pullman
conductor noted in 1901, was to transform "plain Mr. Smith" from
"the thriving little metropolis of Squawkerville" into "a grand seigneur" and allow the "ladies" of the newly bourgeois class to "sweep
with . . . a disdainful mien into a parlor car as if the very carpet ought
to feel highly honored by their tread" (Holderness, 49–50).[28]

Despite his own vigorous skepticism about the cultural agency of
"the dominant American train," James partially indulges the fantasy of conveyance and uplift it stages (*AS* 20). Under the "beguiling
and predisposing influence" of the Pennsylvania Railroad and its
interurban lines, he grants this "institution" the power of "a style
and *allure*" of its own – one not presumably unlike the "*allure*" of
the male crowd in Wall Street, whose mutually reinforcing entrepreneurial and leisure interests the railway accommodates (197, 60).
Ironically, however, James fantasizes the Pennsylvania train as a
space of respite from these very energies of multiplication and "the
vulgar assault of the street" (72). After "a little frequentation" of
the Pennsylvania line, he imagines it "almost as supplying one with

Figure 5.5 Interior View, Pullman Sleeping Car, *Merlin,* c. 1893. Source: Courtesy of the Smithsonian Institution, National Museum of American History/Transportation; Pullman Collection, Neg. #2137.

Figure 5.6 Pullman Observation Car, *Isabella*, 1893. Source: Courtesy of the Smithsonian Institution, National Museum of American History/ Transportation; Pullman Collection, Neg. #3671.

Figure 5.7 Interior View, Pullman Parlor Car, *Santa Maria,* 1893: Like the *Isabella,* the *Santa Maria* was specially built by Pullman as a show-piece for the Colombian Exposition – extremely effective advertising for Pullman's signature training in culture style. Source: Courtesy of the Smithsonian Institution, National Museum of American History/Transportation; Pullman Collection, Neg. #2270.

a mode of life intrinsically superior . . . – as if indeed, should one persistently keep one's seat, not getting out anywhere," the Pullman "would in the end carry one" to some "ideal city" (197). "[U]nder this extravagant spell," he "fancie[s] the train, disvulgarized of passengers, steaming away . . . to some terminus too noble" to appear in the official "schedules" (197–8). The "consciousness" of this idealized conveyance, James concludes, "would have been thus like that of living, all sublimely, up in a balloon" (198).

This figure recalls a more widely remarked moment from James's preface to *The American*, where he defines the art of literary romance. The latter genre, James argues, treats experience "disengaged, disembroiled, disencumbered," liberated by the novelist, who "cut[s] the cable" that fastens the "balloon of experience" and its "commodious car of the imagination" to "the globe" itself (*AN* 33–4). In the space of the Pullman, however, James subjects this fantasy of consciousness untethered "from the conditions that we usually know to attach to it" to pointed scrutiny (*AN* 33). His own "sublime" experience of conveyance beyond the prosaic confines of Jersey City to some "nobler" terminus turns out to mime the enterprise of the Pullman itself: that of "disvulgarizing" the American bourgeoisie, providing training in the power of "style," assisting in the transformation of the *arriviste* "over the land" (*AS* 197–8, 99).

James's self-correcting gesture testifies to the kinds of contact staged by and within the Pullman. The train and its eternal "car-window" provide a literal and psychic frame of reference; its interior space is "a positive temple of the drama" of American culture-building, acted out "under its" magesterial "dome" (314). Sweeping across the nation, the Pullman offers the "boards of its theatric stage" to "modes of contact and conceptions of life" that will train Americans for a certain version of freedom (39). Finally the Pullman is "only another," if paradigmatic, tool for the great "*democratic assimilation*" (258) – "only another case of the painting with a big brush, a brush steeped in crude universal white, and of the colossal size this implement [is] capable of assuming" (219). Opposing its driving energy of conveyance, James conducts the most remarkable metonomy of *The American Scene*, a dialogue with the Pullman extended over its final forty pages. Miming the fluidity of nation-building contact occasioned in the space of the train, he records a series of encounters that productively contest the Pullman's power to frame and manage the value of whiteness, of the "American" as national and racial entity. In this context, James's documentary style itself becomes a vehicle of training for freedom, putting America's phantasmagoric possibilities to more richly productive use.

The section in question begins in the Charleston chapter, as James takes up the cultural politics of "publicity" in a linked critique of the Pullman and the American hotel. Struggling against his overpowering "sense of the degree in which the American scene is lighted . . . by the testimony" of these institutions, he adapts his own documentary mode to record and counter the "supreme social expression" of "the hotel and of the hotel-like chain of Pullman cars" (291, 292). In a dialogic address to "the American sensibility" animating this "grimly formidable" scene (241, 287), James imagines the Pullman as a rival text for "represent[ing] the stages and forms" of America's "evolution": "it would be terrible not to be able to suppose that you are as yet but an instalment, a current number, like that of the morning paper, a specimen of a type in course of serialization – like the hero of the magazine novel, by the highly-successful author, the climax of which is still far off" (293). Underscoring his contestatory interest in American futurity, James remarks that these "perpetually provisional" American sites, "the Pullmans that are like rushing hotels and the hotels that are like stationary Pullmans," offer testamentary "evidence" on the making of American character as if "in course of being pressed out . . . by the turn of a screw" (293).

James responds to this implied representational challenge with a remarkable train of thought that constitutes both a documentary examination of the Pullman's forms of racial theater and a performative revision of them. Against the "chain of Pullman cars" mastering America he counterposes a linked series of his own "American memories and impressions" (292, 304), which "have so hung together" in a continuous "history" as to be virtually inseparable (304):

> When I think of Florida, for instance, I think of twenty matters involved in the start and the approach; I think of the moist, the slightly harsh, Sunday morning under the portico of the Charleston Hotel; I think of the inauspicious drizzle about the yellow omnibus, archaic and 'provincial,' that awaited the departing guests – remembering how these antique vehicles, repudiated, rickety 'stages' of the age ignorant of trolleys, affected me . . . as the quaintest, most immemorial of American things, the persistent use of which surely represented the very superstition of the past. (304)

The apparently random character of this "chain of relations" (224), however, conveys a pointed "act of selection" (304), as James's casual meditation itself becomes a vehicle for testing the powers of the documentary enterprise:

I think of the gentleman, in the watchful knot, who, while our luggage emerged, was moved to say to me, for some reason, 'I guess we manage our travelling here better than in *your* country!' – whereby he so easily triumphed, blank as I had to remain as to the country he imputed to me. (304–5)

Emblematic of the salubrious shocks of recognition and discovery James elsewhere entertains, the "lively surprise" of this misrecognition initiates an intricate series of racial exchanges (305). Documenting his role as alien in the Pullman world, illegible as "native" or male American in his watchful passivity, James stages an ambivalent act of identification that both emphasizes and defends against his "blank[ness]":

I think of the inimitable detachment with which, at the very moment [the gentleman] spoke, the negro porter engaged at the door of the conveyance put straight down into the mud of the road the dressing-bag I was obliged, a few minutes later, in our close-pressed company, to nurse on my knees; and I go so far, even, as almost to lose myself in the sense of other occasions evoked by that reminiscence; this marked anomaly, the apparently deep-seated inaptitude of the negro race at large for any alertness of personal service, having been throughout a lively surprise. (305)

Himself emerging theatrically at "the very moment" of James's psychic need, the "negro porter" is pressed into heavy psychic labor.[29] The latter's "detachment" neatly figures James's liberation from the norms of American "manage[ment]" and pushing masculinity (305), as signally instanced inside the cultural space of the Pullman by the "extraordinarily base" and "ravenous" drummers and bagmen he encounters "in completely unchallenged possession" of the "dining-car" (306). But it also instances the problematic pressure of racial management for the analyst seeking to represent the new America to and for itself. As he lays his own cultural "dispossession" at the feet of the porter, James takes refuge in a banefully rueful nostalgia (62). Fantasizing a return to "the old Southern tradition" of "the house alive with the scramble of young darkies for the honour of fetching and carrying," he instead confronts the porter and the "negro waiter" in the Pullman world, who "len[d]" themselves not to bourgeois desires but to "the rough, gregarious bustle of crowded feeding-places" and "conveyance[s]" (305). If the Negro porter unceremoniously dumps James's baggage into the mud, the Negro waiter is by contrast painfully "zealous" – "so zealous to break for you two or three eggs into a tumbler, or to drop for you three or four lumps of sugar into a coffee-cup, that he scarce waits, in either case, for your leave" (305). "Fall[ing] below" the fantasized service commanded by "the old planters" and "the cotton gentry," figuring the very extremes of overmastery and efficiency, the Negro in the Pullman stands for the "almost completely unservanted state" in which the hungry observer finds himself (305, 288): "I had succeeded in artlessly becoming a perfectly isolated traveller, with nobody to warn or comfort me, with nobody even to command" (288).

For the latter-day reader, this unsettling on-board romance of return to "the old Southern tradition" strikes a doubly false note (305); James has, after all, just meditated at intricate length and with uneasy acuity on the "character" of an American South haunted by precisely such fantasies. Too, in resonant earlier passages in his self-representation, he has expressed the desire to attain to the very statelessness he dramatizes here. It might be argued that James, on this site of racial conveyance, tentatively probes his discomfort with the very "blankness" he has embraced. But his train of American associations conveys more than vulgar racism writ in anxieties of authorship or filiation. Engaging phantasmagoric culture, James uncomfortably appropriates the highly overdetermined *dramatis persona* of the porter – the figure who, on the minstrel circuit, had tellingly been nicknamed "Willie Servus." He thereby documents the deep roots in slavery of the making of whiteness on the Pullman even as he dramatizes his *own* "deep-seated inaptitude" for Americanization under the sign of bourgeois "richness" (305). Yet James himself notably fails to recognize in the porter – a figure whose dumping of the bag might well be taken as another trenchant critique of the project of Anglo-Saxon embourgeoisement – a mirror image of or counterpart to his own. In resisting the Pullman's forms of mastery, James ultimately builds on an unreconstructed divide between black and white, through which his productive ambivalence and documentary openness to the "alien," the "human and 'sectional,'" can be sustained (305).

Like his fantasy of conveyance untethered, James's racial romance goes to the heart of Pullman's nation-building logic, the commodity of black labor put on offer in the training of white America. By 1867, Pullman had created a work force drawn exclusively from the ranks of former slaves whose job would be "total personal attention to the passenger" (Santino, 7). Having tried women and conductors in this role, George Pullman himself quickly realized the advantages of hiring African-American men,

who could be forced to accept lower pay for work equal in difficulty and kind and whose service would affirm the social mastery
of his white clients.[30] Aboard the train, Pullman revived the social
relations of white supremacy; "smiling" Negro porters responded
with professional alacrity to the appetites of passengers who indis-
criminately addressed them, in the tradition of slave naming, as
"George's boys" or merely "George."[31]

Yet the ensuing exchanges, and the racial and cultural affirmation they promoted, remained fragile and unstable, a social fact
that James's plantation fantasy unevenly explores. In particular,
that fantasy stages the anxiety occasioned in the America of managed expertise by the spectacle of the free Negro refusing his assigned place in the industrial order; the latter's dangerously untethered energy is then reconstructed, in popular iconography and
phantasmagoric logic, as a "natural" unfitness for productive
work.[32]

This challenge to American nation-building is, as James's observations on the Pullman world suggest, particularly powerful within
and around American modes of conveyance. From the turn of the
century until the first World War, the Pullman Company – headed,
in an irony not lost on black workers, by Robert Todd Lincoln, son
of the late President – increased its force of black laborers and
service workers so rapidly that it became the largest employer of
black labor in America.[33] The railway industry consequently
formed a double arena for racial theater, enacted both in racial
contests over labor and hiring practices and in the highly managed
contact between service workers and the newly middle-class pa-
trons whose cultural status they affirmed.[34]

White workers throughout the railway industry make defensive
claims about the universal "carelessness, indifference, ignorance
and incompetence of the 'Burr-head' " (Whittaker, cited in Foner
and Lewis, 248) – or what James genteelly redacts as "the apparently
deep-seated inaptitude of the negro race" (305). But the Pullman
porter, virtually synonymous, in this period, with blackness, elicits
the most trenchant anxieties of racial purity and social mastery. A
uniquely powerful figure in the American imaginary and in the
great "*democratic assimilation*" (258), the porter embodies physical
and social mobility, a freedom of movement between the alternative
styles of the rural and the urban, the agrarian and the industrial, the
southern and the northern, the white and the other. Training white
America aboard the dining cars, parlors, saloon cars and sleepers of
the Pullman in the freedoms of managerial and social mastery, the
porter simultaneously inducts black America into the ethos of bourgeois self-making (Figures 5.8 and 5.9).[35] In a social figuration with

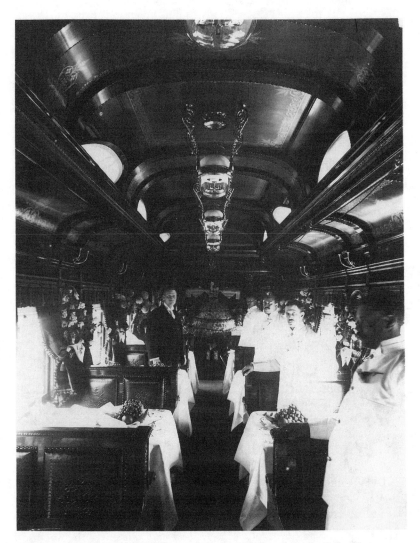

Figure 5.8 Dining Car, B&O, c. 1895: A rare interior view of a dining car and its highly trained staff in service on the B&O line. Source: Courtesy of the Smithsonian Institution, National Museum of American History/ Transportation, Neg. #48372.

particular implications for James's project, the "negro porter" with his "inimitable detachment" (305), traveling between every major city in the United States from "Maine to California" and "the Great Lakes to the Gulf of Mexico," is said to be America's first genuine "cosmopolit[e]" (DesVerney, 33; Harris, 78).[36]

Figure 5.9 Lounge Car, B&O, c. 1920. Source: Courtesy of the Smithsonian Institution, National Museum of American History/Transportation, Neg. #50741.

James's "lively surprise" (*AS* 305), itself a recognizably vaudevillian effect, registers the perceived threat posed by the cosmopolite porter to upward mobility as a form of white cultural mastery; it self-consciously echoes the logic of more urgently racist icons of the porter's "inaptitude." One such source, an early American feature produced by Biograph Films and entitled "The Hold-

Up of the Rocky Mountain Express" (1906), deliberately plays the paradigm of productive individualism against the shiftlessness of black workers, unfit for a productive social role in the drama of westward expansion.[37] The very title of the film suggests the embeddedness of mirroring relations and exchanges within the ongoing creation of Roosevelt's American "race." Anticipating a romantic tale of western outlawry in the tradition of the dime novel and popular film, the viewer begins by witnessing a "hold-up" of another kind: obstruction to the masterful efficiency embodied in the Pullman, occasioned by incompetent black porters whose antics delay the progress of westward expansion and the train.[38] In reality, by the early decades of the century there were not unreasonably held to be "more blacks carrying bags in the Pennsylvania Station with PhDs than . . . teaching school all over the South" (McLaurin, BSCP). When Pullman porter Theodore Selden later died in a wreck, authorities were able to identify his disfigured body only by his Dartmouth Phi Beta Kappa key (Harris, 78). Yet popular narratives of "capers" and hold-ups proliferate, precisely because they make possible the deeper narrative of American enterprise, confirming white fitness to manage the resources of the American continent and beyond.

James's train of thought on board the Pullman begins to probe the logic of this investment in "the limit" of the black worker's "accomplishment" (305). More specifically, it exposes the fear of cultural displacement, evinced as James's own "blank[ness]" of national filiation, roused by the spectacle of the black worker freely disposing of the "baggage" of white supremacy (305). Yet James's performative exploration of the making of whiteness obviously turns on anxieties of whiteness he means in part to forestall. The figure of the native son "nurs[ing] on his knees" the "dressing-bag" he has retrieved from the porter's *insouciance* and "the mud of the road" (305) effactually distances James from the ethos of the pushing hotel world and its species of American character. This effect, however, depends in part on a far more fraught mythos of emasculation: the fantasized threat of black male sexuality to white mastery and to the purity of the American social body.

James's local resistance to the design of bourgeois masculinity partially turns on such fantasies, staged on the site of the Pullman in particularly pressing forms. In the *Railroad Trainmen's Journal* of June 1900, for example, one white manual laborer raises the specter of the "lawlessness" of the "educated negro" in service in the cars: "They walk all over the white ladies' dresses and shove them and their children about because they can" (Foner and Lewis, 260).

This euphemism for rape is itself a signal instance of the weighty anxieties being "nursed" by white America; it voices insecurity about the physical intimacy between white and other Americans in the space of the Pullman, an intimacy that threatens even as it enables the project of cultural mastery. In *The American Scene* and on the American scene, the power of the porter to confirm whiteness – dramatically staged in James's arrival at the Charleston Hotel, as James himself is both disserved and dispossessed – is read back as a form of violation of whiteness. Asa Philip Randolph, later organizing the highly successful Brotherhood of Sleeping Car Porters, would shrewdly marshal this perceived power under the sign of the New Negro movement, calling for the recognition among porters that black "manhood," the founding resource of the Pullman empire, was being used to transform workers into "silent, sleeping . . . slave[s]" on their own cars (Randolph, 1, 3).

James's studiedly inappropriate figures for black labor engage these linked phantasmagoric fantasies of the porter's "inaptitude" and insolent power of "dispossession." Their most salient documentary value is partially inadvertent; it resides in the *conveying* not of James's arrival in a newly bourgeoisified Florida, but of the way that popular forms of race thinking condense and invert the real conditions of American racial exchange. The same inept porters and over-eager waiters of James's staging in fact depended heavily on tipping; aboard the Pullman, porters received their full wages only after logging four hundred hours of service per month, and they remained on call twenty-four hours a day, responsible for a broader array of safety, service, and operational procedures than any other railroad laborer.[39] In all their numerous duties, porters were subject to famously stringent surveillance, conducted by efficiency experts – "spotters" – checking for infractions of Pullman standards. The latter habitually examined sleeping and dining cars in white gloves; as one porter noted, they "would run their finger along the windowsill and write you up for dust" (Santino, 27). Commissary regulations required particularly careful study; an early edition of the Pullman handbook devotes five pages to the proper serving of a bottle of beer (Malken, 10–11). All services were to be performed with adroit dispatch and "zeal" by the same workers familiarly known as "Georges" or "Burr-heads"; Pullman itself boasted that a skilled porter could assemble both the upper and lower berths of a sleeping compartment in three minutes or less (White, 278).[40] James's version of labor aboard the Pullman ultimately documents, with partial self-consciousness, the narrative practices by which racial hierarchies are sustained: his tales of the Pullman, reiterating phantasmagoric images with a vengeance, invert working conditions that enforce exhausting standards of "productivity" for black workers, even as they enable a nation-building mythos of black unfitness for Americanization.

If James's use of the Pullman as a richly productive site for documenting American styles of racial management and affirmation implicates him intermittently in their logic, it also occasions hard scrutiny of his role in American racial theater. Musing on the "intellectual economy" of the South as his narrative of travel in the Pullman begins, James recalls "some ten minutes spent . . . in consideration of an African type or two encountered in Washington" at "the railway-station" (*AS* 267, 269). Awaiting "the delivery of my luggage after my arrival" (presumably by a recalcitrant porter), he observes "a group of tatterdemalion darkies loung[ing] and sunn[ing] themselves within range" (269). To attend to these figures – whose conspicuous leisure, on the site of conveyance, links the Pullman porter inside the train with the teamsters James has earlier observed in Richmond – is "to feel one's self introduced at a bound to the formidable question, which rose suddenly like some beast that had sprung from the jungle" (269).

James's syntax leaves it unclear whether the formidable question, in "the intimate presence of the negro," is of his "own . . . ease of contemplation" or of the uniquely American subject of race (269). This ambiguity, like the springing on the reader of James's master figure for his own work, has social and performative designs that transcend James's authorial self-consciousness. Both strategies render the documentary mode inseparable from the racial practices and gestures of identification it records. Collapsing his own role as passive observer (potentially self-deluded, à la John Marcher) onto a trope of primitive "negro" sexuality, James "discompose[s]" the "thumping legacy" of slavery on its "native scene" (269). If the "Southern black," "all portentous and 'in possession of his rights as a man,' " poses a formidable challenge to the documentary project, that figure nonetheless enables richer understanding of the making and consolidation of American cultural mastery.

Throughout *The American Scene*, porters and other black laborers productively hold up James's train of thought, allowing for local detours into resonant questions about the dependence on race thinking of white America's imaginary and of the documentary project probing it. Taking up the Pullman as icon of the will to grow, as arena of luxury and ease, James ultimately challenges the whole "mission" of its enterprise, its "general pretension" of serving nation-building "American ideals" (317). Miserably attended aboard the "run" from Jacksonville to Palm Beach (313), in the very precincts of pleasure and "refreshment" (326), he notes that the "buffet-car" and the hotel buffet alike make "a sordid mockery of" the larger desire they create (315). As he contemplates "going supperless to bed," his meditation reaches its own "hungry climax" (315, 317): an awareness of the "art" with which the Pullman and the "hotel-spirit" "practis[e] upon" the American desire for self-affirmation, "convert[ing]" it "into extraordinary appetites" (316, 317). As price of admission to its theater of luxury, the Pullman "exact[s]" a costly "compromise" of the bourgeois self whose social identity it consolidates (318): the exchange of taste for consumption, of "energy" for "force," of "curiosity" for "preoccupation" (320). This ongoing process of " 'refine[ment]' " makes troubling capital of "the American character" (320, 324), yet it already "portentously" defines "the native consciousness" at large (318).

Miming the mixed gestures of identification and anxiety afforded by the Pullman, James's documentary mode ultimately counterposes against that "driving force" its own conspicuously delicate acts of "discriminat[ion]" (327), whose vigilance attends a public "so placidly uncritical that the whitest thread of the deceptive stitch" in its own self-fashioning "never makes it blink" (330). The contest remains necessarily unequal, and nowhere more interestingly than in the final stages in James's train of thought. By way of concluding *The American Scene*, he self-consciously "settle[s], at the eternal car window," to contemplation of "the general conquest of nature and space" mounted in "the general pretension of the Pullman" (332, 333). What comes into view is no longer the spectacular scenery of James's earlier journeys but his own documentary form of response, his performative embattlement with the "making" of national character (333). Addressing the "missionary Pullman" from within its conquering precincts (335), James gives final voice to his contestatory interest in racial and national fate with "the eloquence of . . . exasperation":

'I see what you are *not* making, oh, what you are ever so vividly not; and how can I help it if I am subject to that lucidity? . . . If I were one of the painted savages you have dispossessed, or even some tough reactionary trying to emulate him, what you are making would doubtless impress me more than what you are leaving undone; for in that case it wouldn't be to *you* I should be looking in any degree for beauty or for charm. Beauty and charm would be for me in the solitude you have ravaged, and I should owe you my grudge for every disfigurement and every violence, for every wound with which you have caused the face of the land to bleed.' (333–4)

The imagined condition of the noble savage frames more dangerous forms of savagery – "crudities," "invalidities," "monstro[sities]" – perpetrated by the Pullman and its "pretended message of civilization" (334). "[C]onverting" the "large and noble sanities" that are America's founding physical and psychic resource, the Pullman leaves a trail of spoilage in its wake, "as some monstrous unnatural mother might leave a family of unfathered infants on doorsteps or in waiting-rooms" (334). In displacing the "beautiful red man with a tomahawk" (334–5), the missionary Pullman itself becomes a "great symbolic agent" of adulteration, of an "irresponsibility" that forecloses on more "finely human" and "successfully social" modes of America as Republic and as social entity (335).

But the "devil's dance" led by the Pullman rehearses James's own delicate gestures of filiation and turns of phrase (335). Refusing to sustain his identification with the red man, James instead emphasizes the "same criminal continuity" of his own metonymic mode, not unlike that evidenced in the Pullman's "caper" and spread across the American continent (335). In a characteristically Jamesian effect of "association," the scene of partial identification with the painted savage sends the reader back in James's train of thought to an earlier moment, when the restored absentee, not yet self-consciously at work beside the Pullman's "great square of plate-glass" (335), surveys the view from the Capitol building in Washington, the "ark of the American covenant" (258). There, as he lingers "quite [by] myself" on the Capitol grounds, James encounters "a trio of Indian braves" (260). Unlike the master of those democratic vistas confidently "possessed" of a vision of "the great Federal future," the Indians are all-too-obviously "dispossessed of forest and prairie," "as free of the builded labyrinth as they had ever been of these" (260). In their faces, "at its highest polish," James sees "the brazen face of history"; "there, all about one, immaculate, the printless pavements of the State" (261).

Taken as a starting point for James's excursus on the Pullman's training for freedom, this local image measures the distance he has traveled as a documentary observer of America and Americanization. Beginning to resist the dubious freedoms fostered in a national life that puts its founding acts of self-invention under erasure, James paradoxically records his own enlightenment under the sign of the phantasmagoric. "[P]roject[ing] as in a flash an image" of time "foreshortened and simplified" (261), the braves have been remade in the image of the new America, with "neat pot hats, shoddy suits and light overcoats" whose pockets are, the wary James is sure, "full of photographs and cigarettes" (260). The latter

"cert[itude]" is, in retrospect, chilling: perhaps the braves have purchased stereographs of tourist Washington, offering the same "admirable standpoints" and "dominating command" of "the American scene" that James himself has just been enjoying (260); perhaps
they carry ethnographic views of native America, of the type produced by *American Scenery*, for sale to viewers with nativist designs.
In any case they are prime "specimens" of the "State" of Americanization (261), in which products of authentic racial history (tobacco,
tribal dress) are reproduced as phantasmagoric commodities for
the cultural training of the new American race.

For the restored absentee still enjoying a visual command of the
American scene from the heights of the Capitol, the trio of braves
occasions an immediate phantasmagoric shock, jolting a fatuously
romantic "mind fed betimes on the Leatherstocking Tales" and fantasies of westering with the image of "brazen" nation-building. By
the final passages, the differently staged figure of the native marks
how actively James has given himself over to America's theater of
culture-building; the "beautiful red man with a tomahawk" whom
the Pullman displaces is exempt from Americanization and from
the forms of phantasmagoria in which that cultural process is enacted, James implies, only at the cost of becoming extinct (333–4).
Documenting the perils, the "disfigurement" and "violence" (334),
of its "boundless" spreading of the American gospel of uplift, James
nonetheless remains "seated by the great square of plate-glass"
aboard "the missionary Pullman" (335), bracing himself for the
"awful modern privilege" it affords, of a "detached yet concentrated stare," a "monstrous" spectatorship that "den[ies] to so many
groups of one's fellow creatures any claim to a 'personality' " (286).
It is the culminating achievement of his master text – whose project
has been the embrace of overmastery – thus to renew the urge to
document the Pullman's "constructive" cultural will, laid down in
managed forms of racial contact and exchange (120). Himself converted, as an agent of the phantasmagoric vision he has so urgently
resisted, James ends by taking up a posture of intensified contest for
the power of producing the "next instalment" (293), the "very next
'big' impression" (335), in the unfinished narrative of America's
cultural design. Still witnessing and adjusting in the scene of conveyance, the restored absentee, deeply aware of his own "equivocal
embodiments of the right complexion" (286), concludes by coming
full circle, positioning himself, armed only with memory, "impressions," and an articulate sense of the "finely human" (335), so as to
conduct an alternative training for freedom.

AFTERWORD

The art of representation bristles with questions the very terms of which are difficult to apply and to appreciate; but whatever makes it arduous makes it, for our refreshment, infinite, causes the practice of it, with experience, to spread round us in a widening, not in a narrowing circle.

— James, Preface to *Roderick Hudson*

In his concluding preface to the New York Edition, James considers the difficulties of revision, conceived as following in "the very footprints" of his earlier work. The exercise turns out to be strenuously "active," "thanks to the so frequent lapse of harmony between" his "present mode of motion and that to which the existing footprints were due." Pursuing "the clear matter" of his intention across "a shining expanse of snow," the reviser with "exploring tread" discovers that he has "quite unlearned the old pace" and finds himself "naturally falling into another, which might sometimes more or less agree with the original tracks," but most often "break[s] the surface in other places." Tracking one's own signifiers becomes, James suggests, a kind of performance, an "infinitely interesting and amusing *act*" that turns out to be both "high[ly] spontane[ous]" and governed by "immediate and perfect necessity" (*AN* 336).

Rereading my own pages, I am keenly aware of the kinds of "excess" and "deficiency" James describes (*AN* 336). In fact, this book began as a very different project. Shaped in its originating moment by the disciplinary cross-currents of post-structuralism and the (then) new American studies, it took for its central object of concern questions of authority, mastery, difference and self-difference, as resonantly raised by and within James's texts and

211

style – wickedly delicate, profoundly ambivalent, strenuously exact by turns. His productions appeared at the time to be especially well accommodated by such treatment. Indeed, in the American academy of the 1980s, the James canon provided as animate a body of texts on which were performed pioneering and broadly post-structuralist operations as the texts of the Romantics and the postmoderns. Meanwhile, within the precincts of American Studies, James was proving a rich if often negative resource for canon and disciplinary revisions; his texts were being variously marshalled by critics as disparate as Myra Jehlen, Carolyn Porter, Philip Fisher, and Eric Sundquist in the mounting of strong challenges to standing paradigms of the novel vs. the romance, of ideology and literature, of art and cultural power.

My initial aim, as I reconstruct it, was to consider the ways in which James's language, rhetorical strategies, and narrative structures worked, over and against their own claims to cultural authority; to plot the ideological and literary historical grounds on which those claims were staked and revised. But James's texts proved increasingly resistant to, excessive of, this project in quite specific and instructive ways. My own terms simply – or rather, complexly – failed to account for what came to interest me more and more: the fluid sociality of James's art, evidenced, in part, in frequent and frequently aggressive gestures of cultural positioning between and within the American, the Anglo-American, the English; the European and the Continental; the genteel, the vulgar, the queer. While a deconstructed Jamesian master was elaborating on the thematics of representation, of the consciousness seeking to construct experience as readerly narrative, the James of American studies strove largely, once again, to "transcen[d] both class and history," or to drown out "the loud and discordant appeals of a commodity culture" in the making (Jehlen, 136; Agnew, 76). Meanwhile, I found myself increasingly engaging another James: one who trafficked in history, with a subtlety worthy of his own *brocanteurs*, pawnbrokers, and *ficelles*, at the busy intersection of cultural objects and social identities; who recorded and thought deeply about the white noise of said commodity culture – the unattended-to contexts of cultural articulation and naming (including the fictive) through which claims to cultural identity, including those of whiteness itself, were being forged.

Trained, in a post-deconstructive, "new" historicist climate, to practice a hermeneutics of suspicion, to be most vigilant in the face of distinctly literary claims to cultural power, I found my work attuned more and more to James's fluid understanding of the pow-

ers of culture, as staged and staked in richly variegated forms –
literary, ethnographic, popular, visual – of appeal. More and more,
as James himself might theatrically say, his texts served to open an
expansive view onto the ways in which canonical literature, in contest and contrast with other expressive practices, "*makes*" interest,
"*makes*" desire, makes most acutely conditions for the performance
of cultural identity and identification in changing cultural moments (*AN* 62). It would be impossible to locate a precisely pivotal
moment in these shifting concerns, conditioned by theory wars,
canon debates, and disciplinary shifts as much as by the pleasures
and challenges of the Jamesian text. But what interests me here is
the unexpected utility of such "deviations and differences," as
James so knowingly describes them (*AN* 336).

If certain traces or tracks of a readerly ethos of suspicion remain
visible, "break the surface" of my own readings, they turn out to be
themselves accommodated and repaid by James's texts – especially
with regard to the emergent terms of my study – in surprisingly
productive ways. Indeed, the conditions of revision have enabled
me usefully to go "behind," and to perform, the most Jamesian
logic of all: that of suspension and suspense. Everywhere in James's
texts forms of suspense govern, linger, seduce; former lovers and
informants hang fire; *ficelles* with baited breath await the effects of
their conversational strategems; experience becomes a spiderweb
suspended ever so lightly from the corners of inhabited rooms;
sentences themselves echo the shape of bewilderment, plunging us
into the heart of "mysteries abysmal" (*AN* 78). Suspended between
critical stances and idioms, between a certain skepticism about
James's investment in the category of the aesthetic and a powerful
interest in the expansive gestures it enabled, my ongoing work has
tried to follow more closely, to trace more accurately, the protean
lineaments of James's cultural performances, and of the discursive
and social vehicles they employ.

If the effect, chapter by chapter or even line by line, is notably
other than uniform, my hope is that I have thereby held in abeyance the impulses both of theory-baiting and of hagiography; that I
have achieved a certain suspension of critical judgement with respect to the implications and value of James's chosen modes of
culture-building – and by extension, with respect to the richly saturated, complex idioms in which they are hazarded and performed.
Such gestures of suspension as James's texts enact and invite may
be of special moment in this, our fin-de-siècle moment, governed
by its own distinctive reordinations of cultural value and practices
of cultural affirmation and exclusion. Over and against narrower,

NOTES

Notes to Introduction

1. As a general rule, I have followed current conventions (typographical and other) in scholarship on race with respect to racial naming and designation. My larger aim is to call attention both to the use of racial terminology in particular contexts and to the instability and cultural force of all such naming. On the specific practice of reading "whiteness" as a cultural subjectivity, marked by gender and class and constituted in and by discursive repertoires, see Frankenberg, 11–16 and Roediger, "On Autobiography and Theory," 3–17.

2. Most prominently, Posnock and Boelhower have focused attention on issues of ethnicity, taste, and the construction of alternative forms of American identity. Sedgwick's reading of Jamesian psychosexuality in "The Beast in the Closet," *Epistemology of the Closet*, 182–212, and Kaplan's revisionary biography have persuasively argued that James's texts contest cultural constructions of both homosexuality and masculinity. Other texts that have influentially revaluated the cultural work done by James's texts in their moment and in literary critical paradigms include Rowe's *The Theoretical Dimensions of Henry James*, Freedman's *Professions of Taste*, Banta's *Imaging American Women*, and (albeit to negative effect) Seltzer's *Henry James and the Art of Power*.

3. Relevant accounts of the cultural studies movement and of the implications of its emphasis on popular and mass culture, particularly as practiced and theorized by scholars aligned with the University of Birmingham Center for Contemporary Cultural Studies, include: Stuart Hall, "Recent Developments in the Theories of Language and Ideology," in Hall et al., 157–62; Lawrence Grossberg, "Cultural Studies Revisited and Revised," in Mander, 39–70; Mukerji and Schudson, "Rethinking Popular Culture," 8–18; During, "Introduction" to *The Cultural Studies Reader*, 16–25; and, with a salutary attention to the limitations of both high formalist and hagiographic models for reading mass culture, Dana Polan, "Brief Encounters," 167–87. Of particular relevance within the larger field have been founding attempts to elaborate on the

215

production of subordinate groups or subjects within late capitalist culture, especially Dick Hebdige's *Hiding in the Light*, Paul Gilroy's *"There Ain't No Black in the Union Jack,"* and Gilroy et al., *The Empire Strikes Back.*

4. For a critical overview of the pioneering work of Raymond Williams on dominant and alternative cultures, and of E. P. Thompson on the role of culture in mobilizing class identification, see Mukerji and Schudson, 39–41. The *locus classicus* of the problem of high vs. low for readers after the Frankfurt School has been Horkheimer and Adorno's "The Culture Industry: Enlightenment as Mass Deception"; in another succinct formulation, Adorno attacks forms of cultural production that "are advertisements for themselves, bearing the commodity character like a mark of Cain on their foreheads" in "preview of" a form of fulfillment they "promis[e] and will never deliver" (Adorno, "Transparencies on Film," 205). The standard recent account of Adorno's reading of the culture industry – one that has controversially perpetuated certain of the oppositions it addresses – is Andreas Huyssen's "Adorno in Reverse: From Hollywood to Richard Wagner," in *After the Great Divide*, 16–43.

5. Mohanty, 326; Spurr, 3; Bongie, 4–5. On the problem of "high" art as a site of complex contests and allegiances of class, taste, and cultural power, and of training for a middle-class public, particularly across national lines, see Freedman, xxiii–xxiv and 101–32; on James's strategies for appealing to the emergent tastes of middlebrow audiences, particularly in the context of the theater, see Jacobson, "Responses to Failure," 81–99 and Anesko, 19–24.

6. During, in Bhabha 1990, 138; he responds in part to Edward Said's observation, in *The World, The Text, and The Critic*, 169, that contemporary critical discourse has provided little to enable discussion of the "actualities" of literature as an emanation of concepts of nation and race.

7. In this linking of James's projects with the popular, I depart strongly from other readings – including Alfred Habegger's *Henry James and the 'Woman Business'* as well as William Veeder's more generous *Henry James – The Lessons of the Master*, with its interest in the educative intention of James's fiction, and Thomas Strychacz's argument, epitomized in "Fiction from a Newspaperized World," 45–61 – that in effect take James to task for an anxiety of mastery that consists in mining popular or mass culture and then concealing his dependence on its forms and formations, exposing but nervously transuming "secret liaisons between mass cultural and modernist writing practices" (Strychacz, 8).

8. I extrapolate here from Bhabha's discussions, in "The Other Question" and "Of Mimicry and Man," of the racial stereotype as a mode of ambivalence – the primary point of "subjectification" for both colonizer and colonized, in which fantasies and defenses of originality are staged – and of mimicry as a strategy of "reform, regulation and discipline" that appropriates alterity so as to allow for the "visualization" of colonial power.

Several of the essays included in *Nation and Narration* extend Bhabha's work so as to consider the socially performative dimensions of distinctly literary texts in varied national and nation-building contexts. Most relevantly, David Simpson's "Destiny Made Manifest" reads Walt Whitman's poetry and its reception as exemplary texts for reframing "the relation between formal expression and political content, between narrative and nationality"; Gillian Beer's "The Island and the Aeroplane: The Case of Virginia Woolf" approaches Woolf's novels as "appropriations of the island story" through which English nationality and cultural identity are configured. In his introduction to *Literature and Imperialism*, a volume that follows quite differently in the tradition of British cultural studies, Robert Giddings unwittingly suggests the complexity of literary patterns of enunciation and address; he concludes by recuperating Kipling and Hardy as authentic voices of "the hired labourer of British imperialism" and "the failure of diplomacy to avert war" and concludes that "The whole chilling subject cried out for the irony and detachment of Joseph Conrad and E. M. Forster" (Giddings, 20–1).

9. Turner distinguishes actively between the liminal mode of ritual, in which participants act out "statelessness" by taking on special roles, often parodic or inversive of normative social roles, and the "liminoid" character of rituals enacted through the leisure activities of industrial societies; in his formulation, the liminoid experience enables the participant to stand apart from constitutive roles and norms but is not necessarily productive of cultural or psychic transformation – and is hence available for reincorporation into, and reification of, existing social orders.

10. Bowlby's *Just Looking*; Halttunen's *Confidence Men and Painted Women*; Amy Kaplan's *The Social Construction of American Realism*; Jennifer Wicke's *Advertising Fictions*. Of most immediate interest is Litvak's *Caught in the Act*, which superbly details the harnessing of theatrical energies within the developing paradigms of novelistic narrative; at large, he articulates a more nuanced and open-ended version of theatricality, conceiving "subjectivity as performance" and "denaturaliz[ing] – read[ing] as a *scene* – the whole encompassing space in which that subjectivity gets constituted" (xi–xii).

11. Leavis, 9–23; Edel, Introduction to *Partial Portraits*, xvii; Massingham, *The Great Victorian*; Brodhead, 105.

12. Marianne Moore, "James as a Characteristic American"; Anderson, *The American Henry James*; Buitenhuis, *The Grasping Imagination*; Fussell, *The French Side of Henry James*; Hutchinson, *Henry James: An American as Modernist*; Tintner, *The Cosmopolitan World of Henry James*. Genealogically inflected studies include: Long, *The Great Succession*; Brodhead; Leavis; and perhaps most influentially F. O. Matthiessen, famously coining the received truth that James "started where Hawthorne left off" (*American Renaissance*, 301).

13. Banton, *Racial Theories* and *The Idea of Race*, particularly "The Racializing of the West," 13–25; Williams, *Keywords*, 248–9, 213–15. On anthropological, biological, and cultural models of race with which class, nation, ethnicity, genus, and other typological formations con-

tinue to be entangled, see Omi and Winant, 58–69; Wallerstein, in Balibar and Wallerstein, 71–85; Goldberg, especially "The Masks of Race," 61–89. Studies of the emergence of "nation" as an organizing category of political experience, of nationalism, and of the nation-state are legion; originating formulations include Hobsbawm's *Nations and Nationalism Since 1780* (in which "The Transformation of National-ism, 1870–1918," 101–30, is especially relevant) and Benedict Ander-son, "The Origins of National Consciousness," in *Imagined Communi-ties*, 37–46.

14. Also apposite is Hobsbawm's notion, in Hobsbawm and Ranger, 1–4, of cultural formation as the invention of traditions – "practices, nor-mally governed by overtly or tacitly accepted rules and of a ritual or symbolic nature, which seek to inculcate certain values and norms of behaviour by repetition, which automatically implies continuity with the past" (1).

15. Influential versions of the argument to performance from the incep-tion of James's canonization include: Joseph Warren Beach, *The Method of Henry James* (1918); Percy Lubbock, *The Craft of Fiction* (1957); Dorothea Krook, *The Ordeal of Consciousness in Henry James* (1962); Richard Poirier, *The Comic Sense of Henry James* (1967); Laurence Hol-land, *The Expense of Vision: Essays on the Craft of Henry James* (1964; reprinted in 1982).

16. Freedman, "The Poetics of Cultural Decline," argues elegantly for the larger relevance of James's strategies in the quintessential master text to reordinations of Anglo-American cultural capital and identity at the turn of the century.

Notes to Chapter One

1. See Fussell, 49, for a different treatment of this passage; he too takes up the problem of cultural difference and acquisition, but largely in order to address the issue of translation as a literary formalist or narratological problem.

2. For discussion of the evolving disciplinary and popular terms of this debate, see Haller, 60–8, 203–10; Gould, "Measuring Bodies," 113–45; Eiseley, 264; Stocking, "Victorian Cultural Ideology and the Image of Savagery (1780–1870)," 186–237; Gossett, "Nineteenth-Century Anthropology," 54–83. Lynn Wardley alternatively reads the ethno-graphic imaginary in James's internationalist fiction as instancing his more direct participation in anxieties of the social and textual body.

3. These texts of the early and mid-1870s included: "[William Dean How-ells's] *Italian Journeys*"; "Taine's Italy"; "Saint-Beuve's Portraits"; "Haw-thorne's French and Italian Journals"; "Taine's Notes on England"; "Taine's English Literature"; "Sainte-Beuve's First Articles"; "Sainte-Beuve's English Portraits"; "The French at Home"; "Nadal's Impres-sions of England"; "Charles de Mazade on French Literature and the Empire"; "[Julian Hawthorne's] Saxon Studies"; "Renan's Dialogues

and Philosophic Fragments." Among James's later and more widely read essays entertaining ethnographic designs are "Sainte-Beuve" (1880) and "The Reminiscences of Ernest Renan" (1883).

4. "Taine's Italy" (1868), reprinted in James, *LC2* 826; "Taine's Notes on England" (1872), reprinted in *LC2* 832.

5. Haller 88–9, 138–60, Gould 85–6, and Stocking 238–73, discuss in detail the competing disciplinary sources and formations of ethnography or ethnology and anthropology, as well as their differently inflected interests in Britain and America. Despite important differences in the styles and projects of ethnologists vs. anthropologists, Stocking concludes that "so many of the assumptions of the prior 'ethnological' orientation persist beyond the 1860s (even into the twentieth century) that the idea of revolutionary paradigmatic succession" from ethnographic to anthropological, or physical scientific, models "becomes . . . debatable" (239). My underlying interest is in the psychic economy common to both groups, although more pronounced in the latter: that of a "cultural marginality and psychological dualism" that shore up and breach the race politics of "gentility" (Stocking, 253).

6. And in the formation of public policy; Haller, 204 ff., discusses the ways Livingstone's *Missionary Travels and Researches in South Africa* (1858) was invoked to support late nineteenth-century and early twentieth-century immigration and citizenship restrictions.

7. Pratt discusses in detail the complementarity of scientific and sentimental travel writing as specifically bourgeois forms of culture-building that displace older narrative traditions. See in particular chapter 5, "Eros and Abolition," 86–107, in which she details strategies for transfiguring colonial activity in and as forms of individualist romance.

8. Nott and Gliddon, vii, xii; Charles Kingsley (1863), cited in Stocking, 147.

9. Gould, *Mismeasure* 82, points out that craniometric evidence not only governed popular discussions of race history and character, but that it "embarked on a life of [its] own," as improper primary documentation "endlessly copied from secondary source to secondary source" became codified as unassailable evidence.

10. American editor Henry Holt wrote that " 'no philosopher ever had such a vogue as Spencer' " from 1870 to 1890; cited in Haller, 128.

11. Beer, 30, argues for Darwin's indebtedness to the poetics of expedition and the accessibility of Darwinian science for a wide audience of middle-class readers.

12. See in particular Stocking's discussion in "Travelers and Savages: The Data of Victorian Ethnology (1830–1858)," 79–83, of the uses made by earlier ethnologists of memoirs, diaries, and notes of travelers, explorers, naturalists, missionaries, and other practitioners of excursion.

13. Galton's publications included *The Narrative of an Explorer in Tropical South Africa* (1853); *The Art of Travel; or Shifts and Contrivances Available in Wild Countries* (1855); "Hereditary Talent and Character" (*Macmillan's*, 1865); and *Hereditary Genius: An Inquiry into Its Laws and Conse-*

quences (1869), as well as numerous works on Browning and other literary figures.

14. Haller, 140, 154. Haller makes painstakingly clear the ways in which the doctrine of social evolutionary progress – the tenet of modification of race character or traits through social activity – became laden with essentialist or hereditarian baggage as soon as race analysis turned to the study of "primitive" or non-Aryan peoples.

15. For a useful contemporaneous catalogue of such related terms in the context of attempts to theorize race difference and white supremacy in post-evolutionary terms, see Brinton, 100–101. On paradigms of racial measurement, elaborated in the pursuit of more exact distinction between and within related "tribes," "stocks," and "groups," see especially Handlin, who points out that such systems for classification vacillated hugely between varying principles or criteria of difference, including color, nationality, religion, and language; he notes, 90, "in the case of the Negro it was color that was the distinguishing feature, in the case of the Jew religion, and the case of the [Teuton], language" on which race "character" was founded.

In the context of contemporary race theory, Goldberg, 70–89, traces the interchangeability of race as signifier with those of class, ethnicity, culture, and nation in evolving racial ontologies, with attention to what he calls the "illocutionary" force of racial idiom and typology in this historical "phase" of elaborating racial expertise.

16. For more focused discussion of the ways that "Anglo-Saxon" as racial signifier undergoes specific connotative shifts throughout the century, from its initial notation of linguistic identity to a racial designation structured by exchanges between the "savage" or alien and Anglo-American civilization, see Stocking, 62; Gossett, 310–38; and chapter four below.

17. Of his own writings on excursion in the *Nation*, James privately declares that they "tend . . . to over-refinement"; *Letters* 1:300.

18. Once again, James's local gestures suggest both investment in and distancing from the presumptions of African travelers. In a somewhat mysterious parting shot, he writes: "Mr. Southworth is, we regret to say, Secretary of the American Geographical Society." Does James's "regret" concern the scientific interest of Southworth's text in "figures," quantitative notation of the prominence of flora and fauna, as one that obscures the romantic and erotic *frisson* of Africa as text? Or might his "regret" concern the sacrifice of such erotic interests to the stifling gentlemanliness of official scientific culture? Even in a relatively inconsequential review of this kind, the complexities of reading ethnographic interests, and James's engagement with them, resonate.

19. It is worth recalling in this context that Livingstone crosses the desert with "Mr. Oswell and Mr. Murray" – the latter being the "noted travelle[r]" who provides James, and countless other Anglo-American leisure tourists, with travel-guide protocols for observation and cultural response; Chambliss, 68.

20. Torgovnick, 29–30, renders the meeting of Livingstone and Stanley in telling detail, and offers a brief but suggestive reading of its importance as an icon of racial affirmation and homosociality in evolving Western (largely Anglo-American) protocols of modernity and postmodernity.

21. This rendering echoes the structure of feeling that dominates deathbed scenes connected with African travel, a virtual subgenre within the field. Typically such narrative moments conduce to the affirmation of homosocial bonds, effected via racial heroism, and of Anglo-Saxon race character; see for example, Kingston and Low's accounts of the death of Clapperton, tended by his aide, 117–19, and of the feared death of Stanley, 477.

22. This illustration, entitled "The Massacre of the Manyuema Women," is quite unself-consciously reprinted as the leading image for Thomas Pakenham's *The Scramble for Africa*, xxv. Its implicit claims for the character of whiteness, writ as mastery of a moral power to discipline the darker races, tend to stand in eerie tension with Pakenham's project, a fluent popular account of the state-building motives and designs of European colonizers.

23. This kind of rhetoric issued both from the left and the right in the distinctive cultural politics of Britain and America; Weeks, 133, points out that Sidney Webb warned of a dire need to avert the decline of the birth rate among Anglo-Saxons, lest the English nation be taken over and overtaken by the Irish and the Jews; and Pick, 194, notes that Thomas Carlyle agitated in a post-Darwinian rhetoric against the Irish as figures of "squalid apehood," who "must either be improved or else exterminated." James gestures toward the same particularly Anglo-American vision of "darker" races at home and abroad in *The American*, 73, as the Tristrams comment on Newman's announced project of taking a wife. When Mrs. Tristram asks if he has " 'any objections to a foreigner,' " Newman asserts that he " 'ha[s] no prejudices' " even as Tom Tristram jovially declares, " 'No Irish need apply.' "

24. Lears, 258–60, argues that the orientalizing antimodernists in question were indeed "at the forefront of cultural change" in America, assisting in the transition from an older ego-ideal to a new and dominant therapeutic mode. But if they collectively revitalize and transform the "achievement" ethos of the high bourgeoisie, they do so precisely through a posture of ambivalent withdrawal from its most obvious activities of cultural production. Thus, Lears notes, their orientalizing activities have long been misread by cultural historians (in part because of the work of antimodernists themselves) in ethnographic terms of belatedness, as the nostalgic gestures of a " 'dying race,' " rather than as forms of accommodation that forged the basis for the cultural hegemony of an emerging managerial class.

A similar interest in the "Oedipal structure" of Western travel and travel writing governs Dennis Porter's *Haunted Journeys*; he constitutes a wide-ranging tradition of travelogue – including Darwin's *The Voyage of the Beagle* – centrally "focused on reconciling the call to pleasure" of the foreign "with the demands of duty emanating from home" (17, 10).

25. William Sturgis Bigelow, *Buddhism and Immortality* (1908); cited in Lears, 232.

26. Buzard too connects James's "sensitive 'traveller,'" and the discourse of the picturesque in which James intervenes, with an ongoing ethnographic pursuit of self-authentication; the latter, he argues, is intended to achieve "the integrated wholeness" figured as the property of "genuine cultures" (194). But Buzard's James in effect fetishizes such authenticity; in my reading, James's texts evidence awareness of the constructedness of authenticity itself, as an effect mobilized in support of notions of the American, the Anglo-Saxon, and their varying cultural properties.

27. Of "The Impressions of a Cousin," Buitenhuis, 130, interestingly suggests that the "appearance of such a character [as the Caliph] in James's fiction is almost unaccountable in the light of his own repeated references to the monotony of type among the Americans of the commercial class." If the tale indeed represents the "artistic nadir" of James's internationalism (133), it nonetheless suggests the ready availability of orientalist (and antisemitic) tropes, in and through which what Buitenhuis describes as the archetypal innocence and racial purity of the American woman can be upheld.

28. In "Italy Revisited" (1877), James assaults Ruskin as an "insufferable," "precious," "pedantic," comically "pedagogic" cultural critic (*IH* 128–9), figuring him as both chief justice of "a sort of assize court in perpetual session" and a frustrated schoolmarm who "pushes and pulls his unhappy pupils about, jerking their hands toward this, rapping their knuckles for that, sending them to stand in corners and giving them Scripture texts to copy." Against this alternately "Draconian" and effeminate form of authority, James urges a style of response steeped in pleasure, "spontaneous, joyous, irresponsible" (*IH* 129–30). On the originality of James's responses to Ruskin vis-a-vis canonical and current art criticism, see Viola Hopkins Winner, 19–22.

29. At full length, the 1886 edition of *Baedeker's Northern Italy* (Leipsic: K. Baedeker, 1886), 239, notes that "Vasari calls [Tintoretto] '*il più terrìbile cervèllo, che abbia avieto mài la pittura*'" and describes Tintoretto as the "prominent master . . . who squandered his eminent abilities on superficial works . . . and in his eagerness for effect threw away the rich golden tints which formed a distinctive characteristic of his school." While James celebrates the intense complexity of Tintoretto's scenography, *Baedeker's*, 253, finds him annoyingly "perplexing" and prefers Titian's "glowing rapture" and "jubilant delight."

Notes to Chapter Two

1. Gould, 69; Nott, cited in Stanton, 183. Horsman, 135, notes that *Types of Mankind* sold 3,500 copies in the first four months of its publication and that, by 1871, it was selling in its tenth edition.

2. Brodhead argues that James adopts realism without regard for its usual legitimations, in service of producing a "new system of properties" for the novel (115). In his version of James's drama of "self-renovation," however, realism turns out to be an unequivocally bad investment.

At large, there is very little agreement as to which of James's texts can productively be understood as generically realist (rather than naturalist, melodramatic, or romantic), and what ends their realist intentions serve. William Stowe treats the full range of James's texts – *The American*, *The Princess Casamassima*, *The Wings of the Dove* – as realist, insofar as they systematically work to "mak[e] experience intelligible" by teaching readers "alternate ways of understanding" social reality (19). Elissa Greenwald is interested, following Fredric Jameson, in the use of romance strategies to inform realism, in a generic intermarriage that "dramatizes the struggle of meaning to realize itself" (6); she consequently identifies James's relevantly realist texts as *The Portrait of a Lady*, *The Bostonians*, *Wings of the Dove*, and *The Golden Bowl*. Fred See marks off James's work of the 1890s, and particularly *The Spoils of Poynton*, as his most powerfully realist work, concerning "the struggle of the sign to transform itself according to the new mode of signifying called realism" while "working free of the ornate allure of mystifying attitudes and texts" (123–4). Michael Davitt Bell defines James's realism as "a distinct phase" occurring in the mid-1880s, after the *Portrait*, beginning with "The Art of Fiction" and most fully instanced in *The Bostonians* and *The Princess*; in thus characteristically circumscribing James's realism, however, Bell argues that it is virtually unconnected with American literary and cultural movements altogether. Seltzer, "Physical Capital: *The American* and the Realist Body," argues that *The American* is paradigmatic of the realist novel's definitive "anxieties about what counts as a person or subject," and of the way living property and the "recurrent scene (of representation) are inextricably linked in the realist text" (136). Habegger, *Gender, Fantasy, and Realism*, redefines realism so as to make James negatively central to a canon of texts that "giv[e] individual features" to "standard character-types" drawn from American women's fiction (x); ultimately, Habegger argues for the failure of James's texts to do so convincingly. He further argues, 289–302, that James's American mastery qua realist writer was virtually created by such critics as Philip Rahv and Lionel Trilling, in and through their critical designs on *The Bostonians*.

3. I am indebted throughout to Rowe's rich discussion, 58–83, of James's "Victorian Anxiety of Influence"; his argument to James's "bid for *authority*" via a critical construction of Trollope suggestively explores "the power and authority of English aristocracy" as the grounds for that construction, although his proximate concern is the fate of distinctly literary modes and gestures. Peter Brooks, 198–206, has famously (if perhaps somewhat schematically) argued for a definitive nineteenth-century distinction between a centered, melodramatic but

epistemologically realist world view, associated with Balzac and James, in which "things" have "meanings" and interpretation is a revelatory activity, and a decentered, Flaubertian paradigm, in which each order of "things" refers only to other such orders, in an endless, inescapable parody of the act of interpretation; he thereby assimilates James wholly into a Continental philosophical order. Warren, 8–23, argues ambivalently for the placement of James in an American cultural context, claiming that the latter's contributions to discussions of race and cultural value are themselves "ambivalent at best" (22). Michael Bell, 71, in effect concludes from the outset of his reading of James that the latter can only be accommodated as realist under the heading of Continental influences; "what he made of their example had almost nothing in common with Howells's idea of the realist as socially responsible moral instructor."

4. Both Rowe, 61–2, and Vivien Jones suggest that this movement beyond realism at the center of "Anthony Trollope" crucially involves American literary nationality, a self-consciousness about "making room for the American synthesis" that constitutes James's emerging modernism. Yet their readings ultimately, if differently, subsume its gestures of nation-building in the transnational mode, and its uses of the language of race, to the elaboration of narrower genealogies – most prominently, a family romance of literary "transumption," succession, and "sublimat[ion]" of the national literatures or resources represented by such figures as Trollope.

5. The latter text, it should be noted, typifies the journal's linked concerns with the literary critical problem of regionalism and the political problem of post-Reconstruction racial feeling; the ongoing adventures of Brer Rabbit and Mr. Man ultimately serve to render both "comical" and "venerable" the "appearance" on the American scene of the free "darkey," who liberally allegorizes the "mighty quare gwines on" in the contest of racial natures as a comic battle of species difference. Harris, 340, 346.

6. Sanborn's published works include biographies and critical evaluations of the lives and works of Thoreau (1882), Brown (1885), Bronson Alcott, and Hawthorne; he held editorial posts at the Boston *Commonwealth* and the Springfield *Republican*.

7. Taney, *Dred Scott v. John A. Sandford*, 19 U.S. Howard (1857), 403; Fehrenbacher, 340. Sundquist, *To Wake the Nations*, 236, notes that Taney's opinion "[v]irtually spell[s] out the artifice of which racially discriminatory laws were made" and that it is "not, strictly speaking," biologist but rather "blur[s] the biological into the constitutional in an even more unsettling and philosophically rigid way."

8. Jones, 121–2, for example, argues that James's responses to Trollope form part of his specific appeals to "English readers"; Leon Edel, *Middle Years* 124, remarks of "The Art of Fiction" that "never had the case for realism in fiction, and for the novel as social history, been put in the English world with such force."

9. James revised "Trollope" for republication in *Partial Portraits* in 1888. Although his emendations are local, at the level of individual words and phrases, they occasionally resonate with different or more pointed force. In such instances, I have cited dual or variant versions of the text.

10. Rowe, 69, notes that the exhaustion of Victorian conventions, in indiscriminate repetition and production, "is not merely a literary one for James," but emblematic of "a culture secretly in ruins"; he goes on, however, to describe the "English conventionality" James undertakes to redress as a matter of " 'system, . . . doctrine, . . . form.' "

11. On similar panics on the political left about the decline in birth rates among "Anglo-Saxons" and the consequences for racial and cultural survival, see Weeks, 133.

12. *Spectator* 66 (1891), 376–7; cited in Pick, 222. Pick traces the relation of degeneration as a cultural discourse to complex processes of political reordination in different sites of European, French, and British culture. See especially his "Centres of Decay," 189–203.

13. Brodhead, 123–5, documents in some detail James's importation of an evolutionary scheme into his self-representation as a strategy for periodizing, evaluating, and privileging his own body of work. In particular, Brodhead identifies this strategy as consistently at work in James's treatments of that other precursor, Nathaniel Hawthorne. "[B]y locating Hawthorne at a less highly evolved cultural moment," Brodhead argues, "James relegates him to a conspicuously inferior, an almost unbelievably primitive evolutionary epoch. . . . Through his elaborate feats of stylistic self-display [James] makes it clear that he, for one, is of a much later and more complicated type than Hawthorne, as fully a man of the world as Hawthorne was little one" (137–8). In this context of influence, the tropes of evolution and race history serve to distance James from the "vanished race" of Americans of that "earlier and simpler type" rather than to enable his performative claims for the continuity of English and American "characters."

14. In his essay on Alphonse Daudet, also published in 1883, James declares an affinity for the intelligence of the French realist mode, scripted as a moral awareness of the changing conditions of modern subjectivity. The "new sense" foremost in "the Parisian race" – which is a "partly physical, partly moral" sense – "sees the connection between feelings and external conditions" and "expresses such relations as they have been expressed hitherto" (*PP* 206). This version of French naturalism, far from sensationalist reportage of dubious conditions and states of existence, traces the "associations awakened by things . . . into the most unlighted corners of our being, into the most devious paths of experience." This differently nuanced reading of French canons, steeped in "the vocabulary of French literary criticism" and in the "peculiarly modern" practices of French realists (*PP* 204, 207), evidences the strategic intention with which James constructs the contrast between Trollope and Zola in "Anthony Trollope," enabling his own mobility in picking and choosing cultural resources.

Notes to Chapter Three

1. Richard Chase's highly influential study describes naturalism as realism with a "necessitarian ideology." Donald Pizer advances a more synthetic version of naturalism, evolutionary doctrine, and determinism, although he ultimately argues that Chase's notion of the genre as determinist fails to account for its definitive formalization of ambiguity and ambivalence. Other critics who depart more radically from Chase's formula nonetheless register the centrality of the racial thinking that underlies naturalist types and typologies. Philip Fisher, 171, identifies the plot of decline, implicitly linked with racial anxieties and taxonomies, as definitive of naturalism; June Howard expands on this gesture, tracing the intersection of a thematics of racial, national, and characterological decline with melodramatic and sentimental formulas and documentary strategies. Eric Sundquist's "The Country of the Blue," 13, distinguishes naturalism from realism at large with recourse to instances of "the extraordinary, the excessive, and the grotesque," categories saturated with racial meaning along with "gothic" or generic significance. Even Lee Clark Mitchell, 11, who argues that the logic of naturalism is to be found in its stylistic enactment of a felt immersion in the realm of moral luck, notes that it depends on a notion of typology he relocates in the realm of "linguistic determination."

2. Reviews of the novel suggest that James's initial readers were highly skeptical at best about the novel's performance under the sign of naturalism. Julia Wedgwood, writer on religious subjects, author of a life of John Wesley, and the niece of Charles Darwin, suggests in the *Contemporary Review* that *The Princess Casamassima* is linked to avant-garde realism only in its absence of a moral center: "the frivolous reader . . . may peruse [the novel] from beginning to end without perceiving a glimmer of a conviction or a moral standard." The *Critic*'s reviewer responded even more trenchantly: "Here is a genuine romance, with conspirators, and harlots, and stabbings and jails . . . I cannot congratulate the author too heartily on his escape into fiction." Even in the *Nation*, James fared little better; its reviewer comments that the novel "fits an empirical yet generally accepted definition of realistic fiction about as neatly as does 'Aladdin and the Wonderful Lamp,' " exhibiting "a parallel of improbability." If James is "a 'realist' in the only significant . . . sense of the word," he nonetheless compromises by studying exceptions rather than types; "we are carried far away from the average man and his motives."

3. Showalter gives a detailed account of this nostalgia; see especially 76–104.

4. James thus interestingly anticipates such recent critiques of dominant models of the public sphere that employ more fully fledged versions of this associationist mode. Foremost among them is Seyla Benhabib's work on the constitution of public spheres; see "Models of Public

Space: Hannah Arendt, the Liberal Tradition and Jurgen Habermas," in *Situating the Self*, 89–120.

5. He also occludes the high degree of difficulty that beset the production of the novel, a "long-winded" and "beastly" affair, "which I hear panting at my heels" (*Letters* 3:97, 100). Well into the serialization of the novel, James privately notes that its "future evolution" is far from "clear to myself"; "I have never yet become engaged in a novel in which, after I had begun to write and send off my MS., the details had remained so vague" (*Notebooks* 31).

6. Brodhead, 158, notes that *The Princess Casamassima* makes "who and what one's parents were the first fact of one's being"; in this world, he argues, "to know oneself as someone's child is a form of political consciousness." His rich reading, however, ultimately collapses the relation in the novel between descent and dissent by relocating the latter altogether in the realm of James's relations with his own progenitor, Nathaniel Hawthorne.

7. Millicent Bell, 154–7, 174–5, shrewdly remarks on this discrepancy; ultimately, however, her interest lies in a perceived tension between naturalist and impressionist models of vision as challenges to the epistemology of the realist subject.

8. This scene recalls Alfred Habegger's argument, in *Gender, Fantasy, and Realism*, 65, that naturalism evolves in James's practice as a quite specific defense of masculinity against the established tradition of Anglo-American women's sentimental writing. But James more interestingly destabilizes the gendered terms that intermittently govern Hyacinth's self-declarations, with the effect that the traditional masculinity of Habegger's argument – and in particular its racial panic – is acutely deflected. In the moment of Hyacinth's ejaculation, "A trial of personal prowess between him and Mr Delancey was proposed, but somehow it didn't take place"; instead, the collected body of revolutionaries "emptie[s] itself" into the street (295). The romance of filiation Habegger claims to be central to James's naturalism already appears deeply misguided, inseparable from the very sentimentality it seeks to depose.

9. Accounts of the engagement of the realist enterprise at large with what Sundquist, "Country of the Blue," 15, calls "the community of the marketplace" include Fisher, 150–76; Agnew; Wilson; Trachtenberg, *Incorporation of America*, 120–5; and Strychacz.

10. James, writing to Grace Norton, 4 March 1885, *Letters* 3: 76, declares that *The Bostonians* is "something like Balzac!!! But the *Princess* will be even better."

11. Litvak, "Making a Scene: Henry James's Theater of Embarrassment," in *Caught in the Act*, 195–234. Litvak's richly worked argument, which turns on the "*inherence* of embarrassment in the Jamesian 'theater' " of gender and identity, concerns the "queerness" of James and his relations to his hero; it focuses here on the complexity of James's authorial

power, the ways it "gets a charge" out of "mak[ing] a spectacle of itself" and thus preserving the inexhaustability of the unconscious as a cultural and political resource (200, 198, 206). I will have occasion to take up Litvak's argument in more detail in Chapter 4.

12. Altick, 391–6, documents similar increases in late nineteenth-century British periodical and newspaper circulation.

13. On the entanglement of the realist literary enterprise with the new journalism and its developing promotional and managerial techniques, see Borus, 27–64; Amy Kaplan, 25–31, 97, 111–17; Wilson, "The Rhetoric of Consumption: Mass-Market Magazines and the Demise of the Gentle Reader, 1880–1920," in Fox and Lears, 40–64; Ziff, 146–65.

14. Cook, *Daily News*, 1901, cited in Lee, 161. The *Pall Mall Gazette* owed its success largely to then-editor William Thomas Stead's "Maiden Tribute" crusade, a campaign to promote raising the legal age of consent for women from thirteen to sixteen – one that allowed the journal to indulge sensational sexual fantasies under cover of bourgeois propriety. For a thick narrative of the class anxieties mapped by the *Gazette*, see Walkowitz, 81–120.

15. In fact, this linkage is forged in the novel's opening scene. When the formidable Mrs. Bowerbank descends on Lomax Place, the young Hyacinth is imagined to be "planted" in front of a "little sweet-shop" proffering "periodical literature" along with "toffy and hard lollipops," eagerly perusing "the romances in the *Family Herald* and the *London Journal*" and the "obligatory illustration[s] in which the noble characters (. . . always of the highest birth) were presented to the carnal eye" (54).

16. Showalter, 111–12, discusses the importance of this idiom of authorship, masturbation, craft, and sexual force in the dalliance of genteel literary culture with working-class men, eroticized as the ideal objects of gay desire.

17. R. H. Hutton, unsigned review in the *Spectator*, January 1887, 60:14–16; reprinted in Gard, 177.

18. As I have suggested, James's texts have been employed to legitimate queer cultural politics whose readings sometimes replicate the kind of literalism they ostensibly seek to undermine. Wendy Graham does a productively historicized reading of *The Princess Casamassima* as a text hazarding a queer sensibility; she argues that the language of racial typology in the novel intermittently mobilizes a certain kind of queerness associated with the French, the revolutionary heritage, and the "*main parisienne*" in order to "join the chorus of voices . . . vying to define homosexuality at this time."

19. Their epistolary relationship begins with Stevenson's published response to "The Art of Fiction" (1884), entitled "A Humble Remonstrance." In the ensuing exchange, Stevenson interestingly replicates the plot of *The Princess Casamassima*, booking himself as "a very rude, left-handed countryman; not fit to be read, far less complimented, by

a man so accomplished, so adroit, so craftsmanlike as you." Although "[e]ach man among us prefers his own aim, and I prefer mine . . . when we come to speak of performance, I recognise myself, compared with you, to be a lout and slouch of the first water" (cited in Maixner, 144–5). Having framed his relation to the master in such typological terms, Stevenson takes issue with James's sexual politics; of *The Portrait of a Lady* he objects "I can't stand your having written it . . . Infra, sir: Below you; I can't help it" (cited in *Letters* 3:207, n. 2).

20. Hart, 191, notes that *She* sold a thousand copies per week in England in the first years after its release, and was pirated in America in editions running into the hundred thousands.

21. Crawford, nephew to Julia Ward Howe and "spiritual heir to Ouida" (Hart, 191), had just published another romance, entitled *To Leeward*, targeted for the women's audience during the Christmas trade of 1883.

22. His theatricalized account of the failure of his realist work to win mass acclaim reads in full as follows: "I am still staggering a good deal under the mysterious and (to me) inexplicable injury wrought – apparently – upon my situation by my two last novels, the *Bostonians* and the *Princess*, from which I expected so much and derived so little. They have reduced the desire, and the demand, for my productions to zero . . . I am condemned apparently to eternal silence."

23. In the Penguin edition of *The Princess*, Derek Brewer notes that the *Family Herald* advertised itself as a "Domestic Magazine of Useful Information and Amusement" in the sentimental moral register (*Princess*, 592, n. 7). In a contemporaneous autobiographical novel entitled *A Struggle for Fortune*, Charlotte Riddel records the woman writer's anxieties about the relation between high and mass culture by invoking the same ubiquitous organ: "Where, for example, George Eliot counted her thousands, the *Family Herald* counted its tens of thousands" (cited in Showalter, 61).

24. The novel's own "polyglot mastery," we might note, is deeply bound up with the "International" character and filiations of the Princess. In Brewer's notes to the Penguin edition, fully 143 of 292 end notes are simple "translations" alone of phrases from the French, Italian, German, and Spanish, the majority of these preferred by or in conversation with the Princess.

25. The *Congregationalist*, 1884; cited in Gossett, 297.

26. In his preface to the novel, James represents the Princess's passions and energies as the facts of a character or "nature" that exceeds his authorial design, thus confirming the novel's tendency to naturalize his interventions in the politics of culture and the imagination of an Anglo-American civic identity. The Princess herself gives testimony to his historianship; she "testif[ies] that she had not been – for what she was – completely recorded" in her earlier incarnation in *Roderick Hudson*: "To continue in evidence, that had struck me from far back as her natural passion" – "in evidence at any price." Staking "her

claim" on James's "veracious history," the Princess is "in character – that was what she naturally *would* have done." Once again bound within the fiction of James's "historianship," his naturalism, the Princess can be intermittently granted a form of agency that mediates James's own.

Notes to Chapter Four

1. Gilman, 119–27, discusses the linking of the Jewish body in the Western imagination with syphilis, castration, disease, and "degraded" morality at large. Like the prostitute he stalks, the Ripper articulates ominous " 'dangers' to the economy, both fiscal and sexual, of the state" (120).

2. On patterns of immigration and demography and their immediate effects on competition for cultural and political resources, see Feldman, 167–72. With respect to the social figuration of production and reproduction, Catherine Gallagher notes the "growing hostility" in fin-de-siècle culture "toward groups that seem to represent a realm of exchange divorced from production" – "costermongers in works like Mayhew's *London Labour and the London Poor*, prostitutes in the works of Mayhew, Acton, W. R. Greg and others, and Jews in the works of almost everybody" (43). Gallagher is ultimately interested in Eliot's gendered maneuvers within this cultural mythology, and specifically her self-identification with the marketplace, which enables her to promote a moral economy that supersedes the literary economy whose "unnaturalness" she "relentlessly" exposes (47). James's performance in *The Tragic Muse* is not only structured by such manuevers; it also considers the consequences of reanimating "moral" possibilities from within a newly negotiated, and newly self-interrogating, national-cum-racial imaginary.

3. The terms for defining this alliance were very much in question. For example, Charles Walston's address to the Imperial Institute of July 7, 1898, entitled "The English-Speaking Brotherhood," employs the notion of a biocultural Anglo-Saxon alliance in order to negotiate the racial politics and nationalism of John Hay and Charles Eliot Norton. More broadly, Stuart Anderson's account of the rise of Anglo-Saxonism as a political doctrine at the fin de siècle suggests the cultural consequences of the "larger patriotism of race" throughout Anglo-America; see particularly "The Cult of Anglo-Saxonism," 17–25. Likewise, Gossett, 320–5, details the expediency of such a political alliance in the face of expansionist challenges by Germany and Russia. Simmons, in "The Conquest Reversed: King Alfred and Queen Victoria," 175–202, traces the shifting cultural work done by narratives of the Norman conquest and by the racial idiom of Anglo-Saxonism in recreating the idea of England, as well as an imperial mandate for Anglo-America or "the English-speaking race." She cites, for example, Alfred Bowker's description of Alfred the Great as "the typical man of

our race at his best and noblest," "call him Anglo-Saxon, call him American, call him Englishman, call him Australian" (189).

4. Gilman, 124, notes that "the Jew becomes the representative of the deviant genitalia, the genitalia not under control of the moral, rational conscience." At larger issue, however, are the unities of nation and race, and the forms of nation-building, understood in the era of Anglo-Saxonism to be made possible by that conscience, everywhere linked with the character and energies of the Anglo-Saxon race, a people of "action, of energy, strong will, and tenacity of purpose" (S. Anderson, 20). The deviant sexuality of the Jew in the moment of the Ripper thus threatens the political body as a distinctly racialized and nationalized entity.

5. *Poilishe Yidl* 11 (30 October 1884); cited in Fishman, 91–2. These anxieties would receive resonant expression in the writings of Joseph Banister on Jews, syphilis, and other genetically heritable diseases, in the revealingly titled *England Under the Jews* (1901): "If the gentle reader desires to know what kind of blood it is that flows in the Chosen People's veins, he cannot do better than take a gentle stroll through Hatton Garden, Maida Vale, Petticoat Lane, or any other London 'nosery.' I do not hesitate to say that in the course of an hour's peregrinations he will see more cases of lupus, trachoma, favus, eczema, and scurvy than he would come across in a week's wanderings in any quarter of the Metropolis" (cited in Gilman, 126).

6. In an anecdote circulating within the Jewish community replicated by Feldman, 174, the designs of antisemitism and the facts of assimilation coincide: a Whitechapel landlord, upbraided by a co-religionist for his oppression of a tenant, also a poor man and a Jew, is said to reply, "When I go to synagogue . . . I am a Jew, when I come for my rent, I am a *goy*."

In a later letter to Paul Bourget (*Letters* 4:90), James suggests his distance from the latter's active antisemitism by commenting on the attendance of the Prince of Wales at Ferdinand de Rothschild's funeral, and the "difference marked between French and English nerves by the fact that the Crown Prince . . . assisted yesterday, with every demonstration of sympathy . . . And no one here grudges the Synagogue a single of its amusements – great as is the place which it and they occupy."

7. The Detroit *Jewish American*, 1891; Dr. J. Silverman, Temple Emanu-El; cited in Sachar, 156. Within the American Jewish community, assimilation could also be marked by the publication in 1885 of the Pittsburgh Platform, the official platform of Reform Judaism, in which the "central duty" of American Jews is deemed to be "participat[ion] in the great task of modern times," managed resolution of "the problems presented by the contrast and evils of the present organization of society" (Hertzberg, 148).

8. Hart, 180–3, notes that a large number of American organizations for ancestor-worship – including the Sons of the American Revolution,

the D.A.R., and the Colonial Dames of America, all founded in 1890 – came into prominence in the century's last decades, as genteel Americans reorganized competing claims to caste and heredity.

9. Foremost among them is Robert Weimann, who argues that the kinds of "gaps and links" created by James's narrative register a "new perspective" on the "diminishing social representativeness of art," so that finally the novel records not the possibility of a "representative man" but the fragility of representativeness itself (439–40). In my own reading, James's sense of that fragility is itself finally social and instrumental, party to a complex set of responses, not to the diminishing returns of gentility but rather to fluctuations in the economy of culture itself. In differently motivated terms, Seltzer and Jameson also conflate the novel's uneasy hierarchy of forms of representation with commitment to class or other social hierarchies; Seltzer, 155, in effect dismisses *The Tragic Muse* as "an inventory of aesthetic and political modes of representation, and their entanglement," while Jameson, 231, characteristically reads the so-called dramatic analogy – the "metaphor and ideal of theatrical representation" that "organizes Jamesian point of view" – as yet another mode of conservative mystification.

Litvak's reading is closest to my own; he argues that "[t]he monstrosity transmitted from [Miriam's] 'form' to the 'form' of the novel as a whole keeps drifting toward the 'form' of Henry James, who would play the role of external author–subject to Miriam's 'absolutely objective' character, but who repeatedly finds himself imperiled by the baseness and arbitrariness embodied in his own inescapably theatrical metaphors." Unlike Litvak, however, I focus on James's authorial will with regard to the racializing power of figures of "baseness" and "arbitrariness."

10. Litvak, who is particularly concerned with the theatrical and queer self-inventions made possible by metaphor, confines his attention to the relation between metaphor and a figurally racialized usury to a local observation on Miriam's linkage with Bernhardt, James's " 'muse of the newspaper.' " Barish, 464–9, treats in passing the powerful linking of actresses, prostitutes, and Jews in nineteenth-century culture at large, although without specific interest in the racial politics of *The Tragic Muse*.

11. Weimann, 440–1, describes this act as the "secur[ing] of a new freedom from representativeness." His reading, however, fails to account for the novel's representational motives in a larger political context – namely that of the very "national or class origins" from which *The Tragic Muse* ostensibly achieves "independence."

12. Tintner suggestively considers the cosmopolitan ideologies and styles that James productively engages and transforms, with attention to complexly linked impulses of internationalism and antisemitism that emerge most powerfully at the moment of the Dreyfuss affair. See in particular "The 'Inquiet Chercheur' and the 'Restless Analyst': Bourget and James," 159–232.

13. Gordon and Stokes suggest in detail how closely the novel's questions about "being" vs. "doing," about "life" and "conduct," find "form" in the contrast between Paris and London as material arenas for artistic production and as the expression of national or racial psyches (102, 117). But their larger argument about the topicality of the novel to the development of the theater depends in large part on their discussion of the national, cultural, broadly racialized differences between "Paris" and the "*Théâtre français*," with its "special conception of the artist," and London, with its "wholly different conception of the artist and her role" (126).

14. Freedman, 180–92, argues that *The Tragic Muse*'s engagements with the English national theater turn crucially on an opposition throughout James's apposite writings on "barbarism" or vulgarity and "freedom"; the "contagion" inherent to the cosmopolitan version of the latter itself metonymically links up not only with the Jew, but with related figures – decadents, anarchists, homosexuals. On the confluence of "strangers outside the tribe" – artists, foreigners, criminals, "perverts" and Jews – as figures used to reenforce nation-building ideals of bourgeois manliness, see Mosse, 25–47.

15. Numerous readers of *The Tragic Muse* attempt to account for the "problem" of the narrator in the formalist – and ultimately misleading – terms James retrospectively provides in his preface. Funston, 347–8, argues both that the narrator "is hardly distinguishable from other nineteenth-century narrators" or Jamesian centers of consciousness, and that this figure "call[s] attention" to the shifting modes of his narrative, thereby "destroy[ing] any allusion of life" vs. " 'art.' " Sundahl, like MacNaughton, takes measure of the novel in the realist, omniscient narrative terms – notably those of James's "indispensable centre" – that it ultimately appears to reject; "for all James's incomparable power to make the English language do what he willed," Sundahl writes, he fails to create "an organizing center in the novel proper" (215). As I have suggested, James's own terms may be less useful in reading the narrator as figure, character, or performance than the terms he both enables and partially obscures, which are productively engaged with popular race thinking.

16. Gilman, 176–7, discusses the entangled notions in the late nineteenth century of the immutability of Jewish difference or baseness and the malleability or, in biocultural terms, adaptive potential *par excellence* of the Jews as a surviving and competitive "race."

17. Brownstein reads Rachel's Jewishness as a shifting and crucial resource in her negotiation of theatrical, national, iconic, and dramatic conventions. Her brief reading of *The Tragic Muse*, 248–58, is highly suggestive, if schematic, especially in subordinating concerns about female sexuality to anxieties about the "star-making process" and the nature of public identity.

18. Later in the novel, after Sherringham has been "converted" from mentor to suitor, Miriam will appropriate a related idiom of unconvertible

racial difference to represent his proposals to Dormer: " 'He knows we haven't a common ground – that a grasshopper can't mate with a fish' " (450).

19. James's formulation recalls Ralph Waldo Emerson's private description, 10:269, of Rachel's bearing and affect on the stage; her smile, he noted in his journal, radiated "a kind of universal intelligence."

20. The *pharmakon*, simultaneous disease and cure, is a figure associated powerfully with Jack the Ripper – the diseased, perverse Jew whose likeness to the prostitutes he stalked enabled him to expunge their deviance from the suffering public body. Gilman, 111, notes that the paradigm for the relationship between this Judaized Jack and prostitutes "can be taken from the popular medical discourse of the period," and in particular from Anglo-European homeopathy, whose governing philosophy was expressed in the motto, "*Similia similibus curantur*" (like cures like). In the same logic, Miriam's racialized discursive power can be imagined to "cure" the cultural condition of usury or excess desire in which it so palpably participates.

21. Sue's popular antisemitic novel of 1844, *Le Juif Errant*, was said to be inspired by Jacques Félix, father of the actress Rachel. For discussion of the entanglement of Rachel with antisemitism, and of the confluence of Gay, theatricality, popular narrative, and cultural identity, see Brownstein, 75, 169.

22. It thus participates in a more general, and fraught, Anglo-American revaluation of the Saxon heritage as a shared racial past; see Simmons, 189–90, on the revived argument to the Anglo-Saxon as the only race capable of true "civilisation," uniquely formed for brotherhood and sacrifice and thus for authentic statecraft.

23. Miriam's conversion arguably participates in a general transfiguration of Jews in the service of legitimating contemporary institutions. The cover of the Penguin edition of *The Tragic Muse*, for example, reproduces William Etty's portrait, "Mlle Rachel" – despite the prominence, as Brownstein notes, of Gérôme's portrait of Rachel in the crucial scenes set in the Théâtre Français. Etty's portrait, in contrast with other distinctly racialized versions of Rachel, notably departs from the iconography of Jewishness to render its historical subject; her definitively straightened, Roman nose, is heavily pronounced through the use of contrast, brush stroke, and texture of pigment, as if to eradicate the stigma or signifier of Jewishness in the service of claims for the actress's powers of representation and representativeness.

24. In the New York Edition text of *The Tragic Muse*, James alters the concluding sentence of this passage to read: "Even Grace had a great success; Grace dropped her *h*'s as with the crash of empires" (*NYE* 2:416). His rather heavy-handed revision arguably tends to shift the "imperial" designs of class and racial mastery onto the thoroughly dislegitimated daughters of empire, where the original more ambivalently stages its own continuities with such nation-building performances.

Notes to Chapter Five

1. Roosevelt, *Works of Theodore Roosevelt*, ed. Hermann Hagedorn, National Ed. (N.Y.: 1926–7), 28:402; cited in Gossett, 319.

2. Franklin H. Giddings, *Democracy and Empire, with Studies of their Psychological, Economic, and Moral Foundations* (N.Y.: 1900), 243; cited in Gossett, 312. Giddings, professor of sociology at Columbia, formulates the distinction between the national and cultural destinies of the "Anglo-Saxon" and "Latin world" in an idiom to which James's self-representations can be understood as powerful responses: "A people that idly sips its cognac on the boulevards as it lightly takes a trifling part in the *comedie humaine* can only go down in the struggle for existence with men who have learned that happiness, in distinction from idle pleasure, is the satisfaction that comes only with the tingling of the blood, when we surmount the physical and moral obstacles of life" (cited in Gossett, 312–13).

3. The earliest and still deeply resonant study of the cultural implications of Jamesian style in *The American Scene* is Laurence Holland's *The Expense of Vision*. More recent revaluations have been made by Schueller, "Democratic Capitalism and the Role of Culture: The Identity of Multiple Observers in *The American Scene*," in *The Politics of Voice*, 47–65, which concerns the interdependence of James's "play of voices" and progressive ideologies, fashioned so as to expose the lack of potential for "dialogic interaction" in democratic America; Boelhower, who argues that James's text participates in inaugurating a distinctly American semiotics of ethnic difference; and Posnock, particularly "Introduction: Master and Worm; Anarchist and Idiot," 3–24, and "Abolishing the Logic of Identity: Contexts and Consequences," 105–38, which elaborate on the cultural consequences and implications for cultural criticism of James's mimetic strategies.

4. This image of the brush poised to give "colour" to American democracy participates in an active network of figures that links racial experience and American self-invention, including those of the "big brush . . . steeped in crude universal white" (219), the "biggest, freest brush" that "dissimulat[es]" the "impertinence" and "ugliness" of American public life (239), the "terrible tank" that "washe[s] out of the new subjects" of immigration their racial " 'Colour' " (92), and "the huge democratic broom . . . brandished" as a monitory sign of "the monstrous form of Democracy" in "the empty [American] sky" (39).

5. Allan Sekula meticulously documents the invention of a "more extensive" bourgeois social body in late nineteenth-century Anglo-America through the new and linked projects of photography and criminal sociology and their definition of a new object, the criminal body. Of particular interest for my concerns is Sekula's notion of the archive as a social terrain in which photography operates by "weld[ing] . . . honorific and repressive functions together," sustaining not only a social and

moral hierarchy of class identification but the imagination of mobility within it, thus interpellating bourgeois subjects as such through identification with their "betters" as well as through anxiety about the lower, criminal element (10).

6. The latter phrase was the title of a much-remarked poem by the genteel nativist Thomas Bailey Aldrich, published in the *Atlantic* of July 1892, whose opening stanza reads:

> Wide open and unguarded stand our gates,
> And through them presses a wild motley throng –
> Men from the Volga and the Tartar steppes,
> Featureless figures of the Hoana-Ho,
> Malayan, Scythian, Teuton, Kelt, and Slav,
> Flying the Old World's poverty and scorn;
> These bringing with them unknown gods and rites,
> Those, tiger passions, here to stretch their claws.
> In street and alley what strange tongues are loud,
> Accents of menace alien to our air,
> Voices that once the Tower of Babel knew!

7. Alan Trachtenberg, in "Camera Work/Social Work," *Reading American Photographs*, 164–230, argues in detail for the insufficiency of standard notions of "documentary" photography to encompass the cultural and political aspirations of Hine's work. Maren Stange, "The Pittsburgh Survey: Lewis Hine and the Establishment of Documentary Style," 47–82, alternatively reconstructs the history of documentary photography after Hine in terms of the social uses made of its "indexical" value via the project of the photographic survey.

8. Hine, "Plans for work," Guggenheim application, October 1940; cited in Rosenblum and Rosenblum, 118.

9. Hine, "Notes on Early Influence," cited in Trachtenberg 1977: 122; Hine, caption, "An Albanian Woman from Italy at Ellis Island," 1905.

10. Hine's letters of 1910, the year William James's essay appeared in *Everybody's*, include notations on the idiom of "moral strength"; see D. Kaplan, 5–6.

11. Trachtenberg 1977: 124, discusses in detail the iconographic and social consequences of Hine's abandonment of the reigning conventions of bourgeois and ethnographic portraiture, which typically deployed rigid poses and artificial studio settings, and avoid camera-subject contact "as if it were a plague."

12. On the ethnographic style of portraiture and cultural politics from which Hine diverges, see Hales, "Photography and the Dynamic City," 221–76, who discusses in depth such earlier studies as Sigmund Krausz's *Street Types of Chicago* (1891), Helen Campbell's *Darkness and Daylight* (1897), the urban work of Alice Austen (published by the Albertype company in 1896), and other imitators and adaptors of Riis's style; and Street, who documents the entanglement of generic portraiture techniques with conventional anthropological devices for

recording and naming racial type, in service of "the 'romantic' ideology in which contradictory feelings towards other cultures are resolved by 'transforming them into aesthetic phenomena' " (123). Contemporaneous immigrant portraits that give useful context to Hine's photo-studies are included in Steiner; see especially "At the Gate," from an Underwood & Underwood stereograph, 1904, and "The Sheep and the Goats."

13. Numerous of Hine's Ellis Island and ghetto images productively experiment with "family" groupings and kinship structures and their social import; among the most interesting are "Joys and Sorrows at Ellis Island" (1905), a portrait of no fewer than 17 subjects, including a baby "salut[ing] his new home," who comprise "quite a family group"; "Living Rooms of a Tenement Family near Hull House, Chicago" (1910) and "Slavic Family Living in a Shack in Cannery Community in Western New York" (1912).

14. Martha Banta's impeccable study of Taylorism and emergent modes of social control suggests how effectively family structure and the family romance are commandeered by the "all-pervasive systems" of "good management" (10); not only do progressive reformers conceptualize their melodramas of disorder in domestic terms, but captains of industry and managers of efficiency theorize the relations of capitalist to laborer as those of paternalists to impressionable children. For discussion of "foreigners" and assimilation into work practices conducted through photographic and other visual artifacts, see Banta's "House Lives," 205–29.

15. Paul Kellogg, "Field Work of the Pittsburgh Survey," *The Pittsburgh District* (N.Y., 1914), 493, cited in Trachtenberg 1989:196; Trachtenberg 1989:192.

16. Posnock, 135–7, focuses differently on Mead's readings of the social, arguing for their instrumentality within various modes of cultural theory to evolving notions of the mimetic and of an emergent logic of nonidentity.

17. National Child Labor Committee Annual Report, 1909; cited in Trachtenberg 1989:201.

18. Hine, "Notes on Early Influence," cited in Trachtenberg 1977:119.

19. For further documentation of the "narrative" element of Hine's self-named interpretive images, see Doherty, 2. He notes that numerous of the Ellis Island photographs were actually captioned years after their printing, whose dates are frequently difficult to determine.

20. Typically, Hine's images have appeared in numerous contexts – often ones that eerily controvert his avowed project – without attribution or credit, as on the cover of the St. Martin's Press edition of *The American Scene*. During the first two decades of this century, large quantities of his photos were "placed" with such "picture agencies" as Black Starr, Hiram Meyer, and Brown Brothers for commercial distribution as stereograms or advertising images; during the 1930s, *Life* bought images of Hine's that had been in continuous circulation (Gutman 1974:

35). More recently, his work portraits have been used to illustrate such disparate artifacts as commercial calendars of photography and arguments on free trade in the *New York Times*. For discussion of the commercial appropriation of Hine's images, see Doherty, viii–xi. Both commercial and cultural uses of his photo-studies suggest how powerfully phantasmagoric technology absorbs and redirects visual artifacts, even those pointedly critical of its technological and social power.

21. Miriam Hansen has written extensively and influentially on the transition from a wide range of consumption-oriented spectacles, including Worlds Fairs and dioramas, amusement parks and trick films, to the iconography and nation-building protocols of early Hollywood. In "Film-Viewer Relations before Hollywood," 22–59, she discusses in detail the representation of popular participation itself in vernacular visual iconography, documenting the instability of early film-viewer relations and of the "phantasmagoric" force of visual culture at large.

22. February 1892 Supplement to *McAllister Optical Company Catalogue*, N.Y. 1892; cited in Hales, 221.

23. On early scientizing claims for stereography, see Holmes, "Sun-Painting and Sun-Sculpture," 13–29, and Darrah, 5–6.

24. These phantasmagoric motives prevail throughout the culture of mainstream journalism, which increasingly relies on phantasmagoric visual objects for its form of appeal. The *New York Times*, for example, regularly indulges its middle-class readers' curiosity about the teeming Tenth Ward at the turn of the century, promising that "It is quite unnecessary to go to Europe in order to see a genuine Jewish ghetto." Curious readers need merely "Step off a Third Avenue car at the corner of Hester Street and the Bowery some Friday morning" for such highly "worthwhile" sights as pushcart peddlers, highly colorful denizens, the merchant "shrieking at the top of his voice: 'Gutes frucht! Gutes frucht! Metziehs! [bargains]. Drei pennies die whole lot!' " *Times*, November 1898, cited in Sachar, 154.

25. Trachtenberg 1989:184–90, provides a comprehensive survey of popular visual technology as well as a deft reading of Williams on which my own argument draws. Crucial to Trachtenberg's treatment of technologies of vision is the phenomenon of the bourgeois reader's "transfiguration" in the affect of *flânerie*, both the subject of popular writing on photography in such journals as *Scribner's* and the grounds of its relations to the middle-class reader.

26. Posnock, 276–8, argues by contrast for the Jewish nose in James as a signifier of originality, "concentration," and "hoarding of subjectivity" countering the forces of identity logic and mass reproduction.

27. Detailed accounts of the origins of Pullman are given in White's monumental study, particularly 202–85; Malken, 8–9; Santino, "The Historic Setting," 6–32.

28. Holderness details the "types of passengers" to be found on the "human kaleidoscope" of the Pullman, including "The Young Hebrew Commercial Traveler" and "The Emigrant Family"; his account at

large suggests class as well as racial panic about the kind of social mobility promoted by the technology of mobility. Clearly the culture of leisure travel was orchestrated in part as a mode of managing this panic. Another skeptical turn-of-the-century traveler called the overall effect that of "barbaric splendor" (White, 443). Whatever its aesthetic merit, the ethos of taste governing the Pullman participates in a much larger project of training entrepreneurial America in its manifest, and broadly racial, social destiny. During the period of James's travels, both Grand Central Station and Pennsylvania Station in New York, termini for the most deluxe of Pullman's lines, were being rebuilt on an unprecedented scale. The latter would open in 1910, covering two square city blocks of midtown New York and unabashedly modelled on the imperial Baths of Caracalla and the Basilica of Constantine in Rome. Grand Central opened three years later, its highly controversial Beaux Arts interior advertised as a city unto itself complete with theaters, art galleries, dressing-rooms, shops, the infamous Oyster Bar and direct underground access from the Pullman lines to the city's most ostentatious luxury hotels (Malken, 33–5). Educating the "taste," indulging the financial power, of "the ubiquitous business man," the Pullman enterprise shapes a theater of American self-invention in the "footlights of publicity" and public self-display (292).

29. Kenneth Warren, 122–4, argues that the effect of James's troubling figures of black service workers – part of a larger "compositional" as well as "sociological" pattern of setting black against white, "text against margin" – is to emblematize "the vulgarity" of American public life at large; "figures in black became for James one of the symbols of America's failure to develop any real critical or aesthetic sense" (123). His reading of racial figures in The American Scene (and particularly his observation that James's readings of the South are "all but indistinguishable from plantation romances or minstrel shows," 120) have provided a resonant challenge for my own reading; here, however, it can be argued that the failed "critical sense" in question is, at least in part, James's own, with respect to the energies of emergent mass culture. I address more fully the larger questions posed by Warren's reading of James as a figure who takes "refuge" in high culture in "Writing Culture and Henry James," forthcoming in Henry James Review.

30. Santino, "Popular Images and Stereotypes," 116–17, discusses Pullman's manipulation of racial propaganda in the service of narratives of gentility. See also Harris, 59–60, on urban labor and the burden of slave psychology.

31. Santino, 125–6, notes that A. Philip Randolph, campaigning for better working conditions for porters, began by mounting a campaign to require the placement of porters' name cards in every Pullman car they served. On porters and slave naming and rhetoric, see Randolph, "Brotherhood and Our Struggle Today," 1; on the institutionalization of slave relations and white supremacy in the tipping system, see The Pullman Porter, 12.

32. On the evolving mythology of black workers in relation to alternatively sentimental, paternalistic, and vulgarly ethnographic fantasies of blackness in contact with white America, see Frederickson, 268–72, 287–97.

33. Harris, 249–50, notes that by the end of the nineteenth century, "the word 'porter' soon became synonymous with 'black.' "

34. Within the industry, white railroaders would increasingly protest the movement of black workers outside service and into engineering jobs by reviving notions, clearly disproven by the history of blacks in railroad service, that "the negro" is "naturally vicious, slothful, filthy and indolent," "unfit for such service" and unable to "*be fitted either by birth, education or otherwise*" (Whittaker, cited in Foner and Lewis, 256). At stake in these contests, as Robin Kelley argues, is not merely the fate of desirable jobs in the rapidly expanding Pullman industry but the value of whiteness itself, given cultural substance and experiential value over and against the continued category of what Kelley calls "nigger work" (101).

35. This is the thrust of James Weldon Johnson's version, in *The Autobiography of an Ex-Coloured Man*, of the cultural figure of the Pullman porter: it is the latter who inducts the narrator into the rituals and habits of both black America – embodied in a "lower class" speaking "Negro dialect" in "all of its fullness and freedom" (Johnson, 55, 56) – *and* the white bourgeoisie, as the narrator belatedly realizes when he discovers the porter has stolen his favorite tie and his life's savings. Crucially, the porter's social role is to assist in the literalization of the narrator's double consciousness, enabling "the miracle of my transition from one world into another," both in and beyond "the freemasonry of the race" (Johnson, 20, 74).

36. Resonant personal accounts of the mobility afforded Pullman porters, particularly in the first generations after Reconstruction, are given by Benjamin McLaurin and Paul Johnson in The Brotherhood of Sleeping Car Porters Oral History Project.

37. *The Hold-Up of the Rocky Mountain Express* is catalogued in the Library of Congress Motion Picture Division as #FAA 3958. For extensive documentation of popular images of the Pullman porter, as well as a reading of the film that privileges its investments in racism, see Santino, 115–30.

38. In yet another instance of the mirroring effect of racial realities in American labor history and popular or phantasmagoric racial images, the icon of the black worker holding up the progress of the train obscures the very real threats to efficiency posed by the continued practice of railroad management in the South and West, who insisted on hiring part-time and less skilled white conductors and engineers rather than experienced black laborers during peak periods. Spero and Harns, 286, recapitulate this logic: "Not a few of those hired have been men who had lost their places on northern roads because their efficiency was below par, while another large group has been made up of so-called 'boomers' who come to one place for the cotton rush and

then go to the next for the wheat rush. Though the public has suffered in quality of service the companies have seemed satisfied. They were able to weaken trade unionism on their lines and to keep wages down."

39. Their official duties included preparing berths, kitchens, sleepers, and service cars several hours before departure (for which time they were uniformly unpaid), attending to coal fires, carrying and stowing baggage, delivering meals, running errands, forwarding telegrams, providing wake-up service, ensuring that passengers detrained at the appropriate stations, and – during their few "free" hours overnight – shining shoes for passengers gratis, with equipment purchased entirely out of their own pockets (Malken, 11).

On the economic hardships induced by the tipping system, see C. F. Anderson, 20–2, who points out that porters were themselves de facto required to tip their white co-workers – "linen men," trainmen, and other service workers – to ensure that short counts of equipment not be tallied against them, and that they received edible rations. According to his accounting, a large percentage of porters actually accrued higher incidental and living expenses than salary.

40. Such buried passages in the invention of the American race attest to the self-serving force of the myth of inept labor. So too the conditions of racial contact in the sleeping cars give ironic point to the insistence, reiterated by James, on the figure of the black worker asleep on the job. In fierce struggles to maintain the color line, and thus their own highly paid jobs, white firemen on the Georgia Railroad claim in union publications and propaganda that the black railroader at large is "constantly liable to fall asleep," lying before the furnace on cold days and "crawl[ing] into the shade" on hot ones. "[N]ot as a general rule to be trusted," the latter is booked as incapable of reading or understanding railroad orders and signals – notwithstanding the continuing performance of black firemen, brakemen, and service workers on the "better runs" of the Georgia line (Spero and Harns, 290).

Before the advent of the union, porters in particular were allowed only two hours of sleep a night on cross-country runs; they were often in practice denied even this concession, since the only spaces available to them for rest were typically the smoking car or the men's washroom, which might be in use by passengers. On the rare occasions on which porters were allowed to sleep in untenanted berths, they were forced to replace passenger linen with specially designated "black" blankets and required afterwards to "fumigate" the facilities (Johnson, BSCP Oral History). In addition, Benjamin McLaurin (BSCP Oral History) notes that porters' salaries were routinely docked for all shortages of linen, towels, glasses, matches, blankets, and even cuspidors, typically the result of passenger theft.

WORKS CITED

Frequently cited texts are listed in the Abbreviations.

Adams, Henry. *The Education of Henry Adams.* New York: Houghton Mifflin Company, 1918.

Adorno, Theodor. "Transparencies on Film." Translated by Thomas Y. Levin. *New German Critique* 24–5 (1982): 199–205. See also Horkheimer.

Agnew, Jean-Christophe. "The Consuming Vision of Henry James." In Fox and Lears, 65–100.

Aldrich, Thomas Bailey. "Unguarded Gates." *Atlantic Monthly* 20 (July 1892): 57.

Allen, Robert C. *Horrible Prettiness: Burlesque and American Culture.* Chapel Hill: University of North Carolina Press, 1991.

Altick, Richard. *The English Common Reader: A Social History of the Mass Reading Public 1800–1900.* Chicago: University of Chicago Press, 1957.

Anderson, Benedict. *Imagined Communities: Reflections on the Origins and Spread of Nationalism.* London: Verso, 1983.

Anderson, C. F. "Freemen Yet Slaves under 'Abe' Lincoln's Son, or Service and Wages of Pullman Porters." N.p., 1904.

Anderson, Quentin. *The American Henry James.* New Brunswick, N.J.: Rutgers University Press, 1957.

Anderson, Robert. "The Lighter Side of My Official Life." *Blackwood's Magazine* 187 (1910): 356–67.

Anderson, Stuart. *Race and Rapprochement: Anglo-Saxonism and Anglo-American Relations, 1895–1904.* Rutherford, N.J.: Fairleigh Dickinson University Press, 1981.

Anesko, Michael. *"Friction with the Market": Henry James and the Profession of Authorship.* New York: Oxford University Press, 1986.

Babcock, Barbara A. *The Reversible World: Symbolic Inversion in Art and Society.* Ithaca, N.Y.: Cornell University Press, 1978.

Baedeker's Northern Italy. Leipzig: K. Baedeker, 1886.

Banta, Martha. *Taylored Lives: Narrative Productions in the Age of Taylor, Veblen, and Ford.* Chicago: University of Chicago Press, 1993.
———. *Imaging American Women: Idea and Ideals in Cultural History.* New York: Columbia University Press, 1987.
———. ed. *New Essays on "The American."* Cambridge University Press, 1987.
Banton, Michael. *The Idea of Race.* London: Tavistock, 1977.
———. *Racial Theories.* Cambridge University Press, 1987.
Barish, Jonas. *The Antitheatrical Prejudice.* Berkeley and Los Angeles: University of California Press, 1981.
Beer, Gillian. "The Island and the Aeroplane: The Case of Virginia Woolf." In Bhabha, 260–90.
Bell, Michael Davitt. *The Problem of American Realism: Studies in the Cultural History of a Literary Idea.* Chicago: University of Chicago Press, 1993.
Bell, Millicent. *Meaning in Henry James.* Cambridge, Mass.: Harvard University Press, 1991.
Benhabib, Seyla. *Situating the Self: Gender, Community and Postmodernism in Contemporary Ethics.* New York: Routledge, 1992.
Bercovitch, Sacvan, and Myra Jehlen, eds. *Ideology and Classic American Literature.* Cambridge University Press, 1986.
Besant, Walter. "The Future of the Anglo-Saxon Race." *North American Review* 163 (August 1896): 129–43.
Bhabha, Homi. "The Other Question: Stereotype, Discrimination and the Discourse of Colonialism" and "Of Mimicry and Man: The Ambivalence of Colonial Discourse." In *The Location of Culture.* New York: Routledge, 1994, 66–83 and 85–92.
———. ed. *Nation and Narration.* New York: Routledge, 1990.
Boelhower, William. *Through a Glass Darkly: Literature and Ethnic Semiosis.* New York: Oxford University Press, 1987.
Bongie, Chris. *Exotic Memories: Literature, Colonialism, and the Fin de Siècle.* Stanford, Calif.: Stanford University Press, 1991.
Borus, Daniel. *Writing Realism: Howells, James, and Norris in the Mass Market.* Chapel Hill: University of North Carolina Press, 1989.
Boteler, Alexander R. "Recollections of the John Brown Raid by a Virginian who Witnessed the Fight." *Century* 26 (July 1883) 3:399–411.
Bowlby, Rachel. *Just Looking: Consumer Culture in Dreiser, Gissing, and Zola.* New York: Methuen, 1985.
Bradford, Phillips Verner, and Harvey Blume. *Ota Benga: The Pygmy in the Zoo.* New York: St. Martin's Press, 1992.
Brinton, Daniel. *Races and Peoples: Lectures on the Science of Ethnography.* New York: N. D. C. Hodges, 1890.
Brodhead, Richard. *The School of Hawthorne.* New York: Oxford University Press, 1986.
Brooks, Peter. *The Melodramatic Imagination: Balzac, Henry James, Melodrama, and the Mode of Excess.* New Haven, Conn.: Yale University Press, 1976.
Brooks, Van Wyck. *The Pilgrimage of Henry James.* Reprint. New York: Octagon Books, 1972.

Brownstein, Rachel. *Tragic Muse: Rachel of the Comédie-Française*. New York: Alfred A. Knopf, 1993.

Buitenhuis, Peter. *The Grasping Imagination: The American Writings of Henry James*. Buffalo, N.Y.: University of Toronto Press, 1970.

Buzard, James. *The Beaten Track: European Tourism, Literature and the Ways to Culture, 1800–1918*. New York: Oxford University Press, 1993.

Chambliss, J. E. *The Life and Labors of Livingstone: His Last Mile*. Philadelphia: Hubbard Brothers, 1875.

Chase, Richard. *The American Novel and Its Tradition*. Garden City, N.Y.: Doubleday and Company, 1957.

Curzon, George, Marquess of Kedleston. *Tales of Travel*. London: Century Press, 1983.

Darrah, William C. *The World of Stereographs*. Gettysburg, Penn.: William C. Darrah, 1977.

DesVerney, W. H. "Reminiscences of a Pullman Porter." *The Pullman Porter's Review*, n.d.

Doherty, Jonathan L., ed. *Lewis Wickes Hine's Interpretive Photography: The Six Early Projects*. Chicago: University of Chicago Press, 1978.

During, Simon. "Literature – Nationalism's Other? The Case for Revision." In Bhabha, 138–53.

ed. *The Cultural Studies Reader*. New York: Routledge, 1993.

Edel, Leon. *Henry James*. 5 vols. New York: Avon, 1978.

"Introduction" to *Partial Portraits. See* James.

Edwards, Elizabeth, ed. *Anthropology and Photography 1860–1920*. New Haven, Conn.: Yale University Press, 1992.

Eiseley, Loren. *Darwin's Century: Evolution and the Men Who Discovered It*. New York: Doubleday, 1958.

Emerson, Ralph Waldo. *The Journals and Miscellaneous Notebooks of Ralph Waldo Emerson*. Edited by Merton M. Sealts, Jr. Cambridge University Press, 1973.

Fehrenbacher, Don. *The Dred Scott Case, Its Significance in American Law and Politics*. New York: Oxford University Press, 1978.

Feldman, David. *Englishmen and Jews: Social Relations and Political Culture 1840–1914*. New Haven, Conn.: Yale University Press, 1994.

Fisher, Philip. *Hard Facts: Setting and Form in the American Novel*. New York: Oxford University Press, 1985.

Fishman, William J. *East End Jewish Radicals 1875–1914*. London: Duckworth, 1975.

Foner, Philip S., and Ronald Lewis, eds. *Black Workers: A Documentary History from Colonial Times to the Present*. Philadelphia: Temple University Press, 1989.

Fox, Richard Wrightman, and T. J. Jackson Lears, eds. *The Culture of Consumption: Critical Essays in American History, 1880–1980*. New York: Pantheon Books, 1983.

Frankenberg, Ruth. *White Women, Race Matters: The Social Construction of Whiteness*. Minneapolis: University of Minnesota Press, 1993.

Frayling, Christopher. "The House That Jack Built: Some Stereotypes of the Rapist in the History of Popular Culture." In Tomaselli and Porter.

Frederickson, George. *The Black Image in the White Mind: The Debate on Afro-American Character and Destiny, 1817–1914.* Hanover, N.H.: Wesleyan University Press, 1971.

Freedman, Jonathan. "The Poetics of Cultural Decline: Degeneration, Assimilation, and Henry James's The Golden Bowl." *American Literary History* 7 (Fall 1995) 3: 477–99.

Professions of Taste: Henry James, British Aestheticism, and Commodity Culture. Stanford, Calif.: Stanford University Press, 1990.

Funston, Judith E. " 'All Art Is One': Narrative Techniques in Henry James's Tragic Muse." *Studies in the Novel* 15 (Winter 1983) 4: 4–55.

Fussell, Edwin Sill. *The French Side of Henry James.* New York: Columbia University Press, 1990.

Gallagher, Catherine. "George Eliot and Daniel Deronda: The Prostitute and the Jewish Question." In Yeazell, 39–62.

Galton, Francis. *Hereditary Genius: An Inquiry into Its Laws and Consequences.* New York: Appleton, 1869.

Gard, Roger. *Henry James: The Critical Heritage.* New York: Routledge and Kegan Paul, 1968.

Giddings, Robert, ed. *Literature and Imperialism.* New York: St. Martin's Press, 1991.

Gilder, Richard Watson. *Letters of Richard Watson Gilder.* Ed. Rosamond Gilder. New York: Houghton Mifflin Co., 1916.

Gilman, Sander. *The Jew's Body.* New York: Routledge, 1991.

Gilroy, Paul, *'There Ain't No Black in the Union Jack': The Cultural Politics of Race and Nation.* London: Hutchinson, 1987.

Gilroy, Paul, et al., eds. *The Empire Strikes Back: Race and Racism in 70s Britain.* London: Hutchinson, in association with the Centre for Contemporary Cultural Studies, University of Birmingham, 1983.

Goldberg, David Theo. *Racist Culture: Philosophy and the Politics of Meaning.* Cambridge: Blackwell, 1993.

Goode, John, ed. *The Air of Reality: New Essays on Henry James.* London: Methuen, 1972.

Gordon, D. J., and John Stokes. "The Reference of The Tragic Muse." In Goode, 81–167.

Gossett, Thomas F. *Race: The History of an Idea in America.* Dallas, Tex.: Southern Methodist University Press, 1963.

Gould, Stephen Jay. *The Mismeasure of Man.* New York: W. W. Norton and Co., 1981.

Graham, Wendy. "Henry James's Subterranean Blues: A Rereading of *The Princess Casamassima.*" *Modern Fiction Studies* 40 (Spring 1994): 51–84.

Green, Martin. *Dreams of Adventure, Deeds of Empire.* New York: Basic Books, Inc., 1979.

Greenwald, Elissa. *Realism and the Romance: Nathaniel Hawthorne, Henry James and American Fiction.* Ann Arbor, Mich.: UMI Research Press, 1989.

Gutman, Judith Mara. *Lewis Hine: Two Perspectives.* New York: Gross Publishers (Viking), 1974.

Habegger, Alfred. *Gender, Fantasy, and Realism in American Literature.* New York: Columbia University Press, 1982.

Henry James and the 'Woman Business'. Cambridge University Press, 1989.

Hales, Peter B. *Silver Cities: The Photography of American Urbanization.* Philadelphia: Temple University Press, 1984.

Hall, Stuart, et al., eds. *Culture, Media, Language: Working Papers in Cultural Studies, 1972–79.* West Midlands, England: Centre for Contemporary Cultural Studies, University of Birmingham, 1980.

"New Ethnicities." In Mercer, 27–31.

Haller, John S., Jr. *Outcasts from Evolution: Scientific Attitudes of Racial Inferiority, 1859–1900.* Chicago: University of Illinois Press, 1971.

Halttunen, Karen. *Confidence Men and Painted Women: A Study of Middle-Class Culture in America, 1830–1870.* New Haven, Conn.: Yale University Press, 1982.

Handlin, Oscar. *Race and Nationality in American Life.* Boston: Little, Brown, 1957.

Hansen, Miriam. *Babel and Babylon: Spectatorship in American Silent Film.* Cambridge, Mass.: Harvard University Press, 1991.

Harris, Joel Chandler. "Nights with Uncle Remus." *Century* 26 (July 1883) 3:340–9.

Harris, William H. *The Harder We Run: Black Workers Since the Civil War.* New York: Oxford University Press, 1982.

Hart, James D. *The Popular Book: A History of America's Literary Taste.* New York: Oxford University Press, 1950.

Hebdige, Dick. *Hiding in the Light: On Images and Things.* New York: Routledge, 1988.

Hertzberg, Arthur. *The Jews in America.* New York: Simon and Schuster, 1989.

Hine, Lewis. *Lewis Wickes Hine's Interpretive Photography: The Six Early Projects.* Edited by Jonathan L. Doherty. International Museum of Photography at George Eastman House. Chicago: University of Chicago Press, 1978.

Men at Work. New York: Macmillan and Company, 1939.

Hobsbawm, Eric. *Nations and Nationalism Since 1780: Programme, Myth, Reality.* Cambridge University Press, 1990.

and Terence Ranger, eds. *The Invention of Tradition.* Cambridge University Press, 1983.

Holderness, Herbert O. *The Reminiscences of a Pullman Conductor, or Character Sketches of Life in a Pullman Car.* Chicago: n.p., 1901.

Holland, Laurence. *The Expense of Vision: Essays on the Craft of Henry James.* Baltimore: Johns Hopkins University Press, 1982.

Holmes, Oliver Wendell. "The Stereoscope and the Stereograph." *Atlantic Monthly* 3 (June 1859): 738–48.

"Sun-Painting and Sun-Sculpture." *Atlantic Monthly* 8 (July 1861): 13–29.

Horkheimer, Max, and Theodor Adorno. "The Culture Industry: Enlightenment as Mass Deception." In *Dialectic of Enlightenment*, translated by John Cumming, 120–67. New York: Continuum, 1993.

Horsman, Reginald. *Race and Manifest Destiny: The Origins of American Racial Anglo-Saxonism.* Cambridge, Mass.: Harvard University Press, 1981.

Howard, June. *Form and History in American Literary Naturalism.* Chapel Hill: University of North Carolina Press, 1985.

Howells, William Dean. *Criticism and Fiction.* New York: Harper and Brothers, 1891.

"Henry James, Jr." *Century* 25 (November 1882): 25–9.

[Hutton, R. H.] Review of *The Princess Casamassima. Spectator* 60 (January 1887): 14–16.

Huyssen, Andreas. *After the Great Divide: Modernism, Mass Culture, Postmodernism.* Bloomington: Indiana University Press, 1986.

Jacobson, Marcia. *Henry James and the Mass Market.* University: University of Alabama Press, 1983.

Jameson, Fredric. *The Political Unconscious: Narrative As a Socially Symbolic Act.* Ithaca, N.Y.: Cornell University Press, 1981.

Jehlen, Myra. "The Novel and the Middle Class in America." In Bercovitch and Jehlen, 125–44.

Johnson, James Weldon. *The Autobiography of an Ex-Coloured Man.* New York: Vintage, 1989.

Jones, Vivien. *James the Critic.* London: Macmillan, 1985.

Juergens, George. *Joseph Pulitzer and the New York World.* Princeton, N.J.: Princeton University Press, 1961.

Kaplan, Amy. *The Social Construction of American Realism.* Chicago: University of Chicago Press, 1988.

Kaplan, Fred. *Henry James: The Imagination of Genius.* New York: William Morrow and Company, 1992.

Kaplan, Daile. *Photo Story: Selected Letters and Photographs of Lewis W. Hine.* Washington, D.C.: Smithsonian Institution Press, 1992.

Kelley, Alexander, and Colin Wilson. *Jack the Ripper: A Bibliography and Review of the Literature.* London: Association of Assistant Librarians, 1973.

Kelley, Robin D. G. "'We Are Not What We Seem': Rethinking Black Working-Class Opposition in the Jim Crow South." *Journal of American History* 80 (June 1993) 1:75–112.

King, Peter. "Introduction." In Curzon, i–xvii.

Kingston, William H. G., and Charles Rathbone Low. *Great African Travellers: From Bruce and Mungo Park to Livingstone and Stanley.* London: George Routledge and Sons, 1890.

Krook, Dorothea. *The Ordeal of Consciousness in Henry James.* Cambridge University Press, 1962.

LaCapra, Dominick, ed. *The Bounds of Race: Perspectives on Hegemony and Resistance.* Ithaca, N.Y.: Cornell University Press, 1991.

Lankester, Edwin Ray. "Zoology." In *Encyclopaedia Britannica*, 11th ed. (1910–11), 28:1022–39.

Lears, Jackson. *No Place of Grace: Antimodernism and the Transformation of American Culture, 1880–1920.* New York: Pantheon Books, 1981.

Leavis, F. R. *The Great Tradition.* New York: Penguin, 1983.

Lee, Alan J. *The Origins of the Popular Press in England 1885–1914.* London: Croom Helm, 1976.

Lewis, R. W. B. *The American Adam.* Chicago: University of Chicago Press, 1956.

Litvak, Joseph. *Caught in the Act: Theatricality in the Nineteenth-Century Novel.* Berkeley and Los Angeles: University of California Press, 1992.

Lott, Eric. *Love and Theft: Blackface Minstrelsy and the American Working Class.* New York: Oxford University Press, 1993.

Lubbock, Percy. *The Craft of Fiction.* New York: Viking, 1957.

MacDougall, Hugh A. *Racial Myth in English History: Trojans, Teutons, and Anglo-Saxons.* Hanover: University Press of New England, 1982.

MacNaughton, William R. "In Defense of James's The Tragic Muse." *Henry James Review* 7 (Fall 1985): 5–12.

Magee's Illustrated Guide of Philadelphia [and] the Centennial Exhibition 1876. Philadelphia: Magee and Son, 1876.

Maixner, Paul, ed. *Robert Louis Stevenson: The Critical Heritage.* London: Routledge and Kegan Paul, 1981.

Malken, Peter T. *Night Trains: The Pullman System in the Golden Years of American Rail Travel.* Chicago: Lanike Press, 1989.

Massingham, Harold John. *The Great Victorians.* London: Ivor Nicholson & Watson Ltd., 1932.

Matthiessen, F. O. *American Renaissance.* New York: Oxford University Press, 1941.

McKissack, Pamela, and Frederick McKissack. *A Long Hard Journey: The Story of the Pullman Porter.* New York: Walker and Company, 1989.

Mercer, Kobena, ed. *Black Film/British Cinema.* London: ICA, 1988.

Mitchell, Lee Clark. *Determined Fictions: American Literary Naturalism.* New York: Columbia University Press, 1989.

Modleski, Tania. *Studies in Entertainment: Critical Approaches to Mass Culture.* Bloomington: Indiana University Press, 1986.

Mohanty, Satya P. "Drawing the Color Line: Kipling and the Culture of Colonial Rule." In LaCapra, 311–43.

Moore, Marianne. "Henry James as Characteristic American." *Hound and Horn* 7 (April 1934) 3: 363–72.

Mosse, George L. *Nationalism and Sexuality: Middle-Class Morality and Sexual Norms in Modern Europe.* Madison: University of Wisconsin Press, 1985.

Mukerji, Chandra, and Michael Schudson, eds. *Rethinking Popular Culture: Contemporary Perspectives in Cultural Studies.* Berkeley and Los Angeles: University of California Press, 1991.

Nagel, Paul C. *This Sacred Trust: American Nationality 1798–1898.* New York: Oxford University Press, 1971.

Nott, Josiah C., and George R. Gliddon. *Types of Mankind, or, Ethnological Researches, Based upon the Ancient Monuments, Paintings, Sculptures, and Crania of Races.* Philadelphia: Lippincott, 1857.

Omi, Michael, and Howard Winant. *Racial Formation in the United States*. New York: Routledge, 1986.

Pakenham, Thomas. *The Scramble for Africa: White Man's Conquest of the Dark Continent from 1876 to 1912*. New York: Random House, 1986.

Perry, Thomas Sergeant. *A History of Greek Literature*. New York: H. Holt and Company, 1890.

Pick, Daniel. *Faces of Degeneration*. Cambridge University Press, 1989.

Pizer, Donald. *Realism and Naturalism in Nineteenth-Century American Literature*. 1st. ed. Carbondale: Southern Illinois University Press, 1966.

Poirier, Richard. *The Comic Sense of Henry James: A Study of the Early Novels*. New York: Oxford University Press, 1967.

Polan, Dana. "Brief Encounters: Mass Culture and the Evacuation of Sense." In Modleski, 167–87.

Porter, Dennis. *Haunted Journeys: Desire and Transgression in European Travel Writing*. Princeton, N.J.: Princeton University Press, 1991.

Posnock, Ross. *The Trial of Curiosity: Henry James, William James, and the Challenge of Modernity*. New York: Oxford University Press, 1991.

Pratt, Mary Louise. *Imperial Eyes: Travel Writing and Transculturation*. New York: Routledge, 1992.

Rahv, Philip. "Paleface and Redskin." Reprinted in *Essays on Literature and Politics 1932–1972*. Boston: Houghton Mifflin Co., 1978.

Randolph, Asa Philip. "Brotherhood and Our Struggle Today." *Black Worker* 1 (November 15, 1929) 1: 1–3.

Renan, Ernest. "What is a Nation?" translated by Martin Thom. In Bhabha, 8–22.

Riis, Jacob A. *The Perils and Preservation of the Home*. Philadelphia: George W. Jacobs and Company, 1903.

Roediger, David. *The Wages of Whiteness: Race and the Making of the American Working Class*. New York: Verso, 1991.

Rosenblum, Walter, and Naomi Rosenblum. *America and Lewis Hine*. Millerton, N.Y.: Aperture, 1977.

Rowe, John Carlos. *The Theoretical Dimensions of Henry James*. Madison: University of Wisconsin Press, 1984.

Rydell, Robert W. *All the World's a Fair: Visions of Empire at American International Expositions, 1876–1916*. Chicago: University of Chicago Press, 1984.

Sachar, Howard. *A History of Jews in America*. New York: Knopf, 1992.

Said, Edward. *The World, The Text, and The Critic*. London: Faber, 1982.

Sanborn, F. B. "Comment by a Radical Abolitionist." *Century* 26:3 (July 1883): 411–15.

Santino, Jack. *Miles of Smiles, Years of Struggle: Stories of Black Pullman Porters*. Urbana: University of Illinois Press, 1989.

Schueller, Malini Johar. *The Politics of Voice: Liberalism and Social Criticism from Franklin to Kingston*. Albany: State University of New York Press, 1992.

Sedgwick, Eve Kosofsky. *Epistemology of the Closet*. Berkeley and Los Angeles: University of California Press, 1990.

See, Fred G. "Henry James and the Art of Perception." In Sundquist, 119–37.

Sekula, Allan. "The Body and the Archive." *October* 39 (Winter 1986): 3–64.

Seltzer, Mark. *Henry James and the Art of Power.* Ithaca, N.Y.: Cornell University Press, 1984.

"Physical Capital: The American and The Realist Body." In Banta, 131–67.

Sharkey, Terence. *Jack the Ripper: One Hundred Years of Investigation.* New York: Dorset Press, 1987.

Showalter, Elaine. *Sexual Anarchy: Literature and Culture in the Fin de Siècle.* New York: Viking, 1990.

Simmons, Clare. *Reversing the Conquest: History and Myth in British Literature.* New Brunswick, N.J.: Rutgers University Press, 1990.

Simpson, David. "Destiny Made Manifest: The Styles of Whitman's Poetry." In Bhabha, 171–96.

Spero, Sterling D., and Abram L. Harns. *The Black Worker: The Negro and the Labor Movement.* New York: Columbia University Press, 1931.

Spurr, David. *The Rhetoric of Empire: Colonial Discourse in Journalism, Travel Writing, and Imperial Administration.* Durham, N.C.: Duke University Press, 1993.

Stallybrass, Peter, and Allon White. *The Politics and Poetics of Transgression.* Ithaca, N.Y.: Cornell University Press, 1986.

Stanton, William R. *The Leopard's Spots: Scientific Attitudes Toward Race in America, 1815–1859.* Chicago: University of Chicago Press, 1960.

Steiner, Edward A. *On the Trail of the Immigrant.* Philadelphia: George W. Jacobs, 1906.

Stange, Maren. *Symbols of Ideal Life: Social Documentary Photography in America 1890–1950.* Cambridge University Press, 1989.

Stocking, George W., Jr. *Victorian Anthropology.* New York: The Free Press, 1987.

Story, William Wetmore. *Roba di Roma.* New York: Houghton Mifflin, 1887.

Stowe, William W. *Balzac, James, and the Realistic Novel.* Princeton, N.J.: Princeton University Press, 1983.

Street, Brian. "British Popular Anthropology: Exhibiting and Photographing the Other." In Edwards, 122–31.

Strychacz, Thomas. *Modernism, Mass Culture, and Professionalism.* Cambridge University Press, 1993.

Sundahl, Daniel James. "The High Altar of Henry James's The Tragic Muse and 'The art of figuring synthetically.' " *Colby Literary Quarterly* 24 (December 1988) 4: 212–24.

Sundquist, Eric, ed. *American Realism: New Essays.* Baltimore: Johns Hopkins University Press, 1982.

"The Country of the Blue." In Sundquist, 3–24.

To Wake the Nations: Race in the Making of American Literature. Cambridge, Mass.: The Belknap Press of Harvard University Press, 1993.

Taney, Roger B. *Dred Scott v. John A. Sandford.* 19 U.S. Howard (1857).

Tanner, Tony. *Venice Desired.* Cambridge, Mass.: Harvard University Press, 1992.

Tebbel, John, and Mary Ellen Waller-Zuckerman. *The Magazine in America 1741–1990.* New York: Oxford University Press, 1991.

Thompson, E. P. "The Long Revolution." Review of *The Long Revolution,* by Raymond Williams. *New Left Review* 9–10 (1961): 24–39.

Tintner, Adeline. *The Cosmopolitan World of Henry James.* Baton Rouge: Louisiana State University Press, 1991.

Tomaselli, Sylvia, and Roy Porter, eds. *Rape.* London: Basil Blackwell, 1986.

Torgovnick, Marianna. *Gone Primitive: Savage Intellects, Modern Lives.* Chicago: University of Chicago Press, 1990.

Trachtenberg, Alan. *Reading American Photographs: Images as History: Mathew Brady to Walker Evans.* New York: Hill and Wang, 1989.

The Incorporation of America: Culture and Society in the Gilded Age. New York: Hill and Wang, 1982.

"Ever – the Human Document." Afterword in Rosenblum, 118–37.

Turner, Victor. "Comments and Conclusions." In Babcock, 279–96.

Van Evrie, John H. *White Supremacy and Negro Subordination.* New York: Van Evrie, Horton and Company, 1868.

Veeder, William. *Henry James: The Lessons of the Master: Popular Fiction and Personal Style in the Nineteenth Century.* Chicago: University of Chicago Press, 1975.

Verner, Samuel P. *Pioneering in Central Africa.* Richmond: Presbyterian Committee of Publication, 1903.

Wardley, Lynn. "Reassembling *Daisy Miller.*" *American Literary History* 3 (Fall 1991) 2: 232–54.

Walkowitz, Judith. *City of Dreadful Delight: Narratives of Sexual Danger in Late-Victorian London.* Chicago: University of Chicago Press, 1992.

Waller, Horace, ed. *The Last Journals of David Livingstone in Central Africa from Eighteen Hundred and Sixty-Five to his Death.* New York: Harper and Brothers, 1875.

Walston, Charles. *The English-Speaking Brotherhood and the League of Nations.* New York: Cambridge at the Columbia University Press, 1919.

Warren, Kenneth W. *Black and White Strangers: Race and American Literary Realism.* Chicago: University of Chicago Press, 1993.

Weeks, Jeffrey. *Sex, Politics, and Society: The Regulation of Sexuality Since 1800.* 2nd ed. New York: Longman, 1989.

Weimann, Robert. "Text, Author-Function, and Appropriation in Modern Narrative: Toward a Sociology of Representation." *Critical Inquiry* 14 (Spring 1988): 430–47.

White, Arnold. *Problems of a Great City.* London: Remington, 1886.

White, John H., Jr. *The American Railroad Passenger Car.* Baltimore: Johns Hopkins University Press, 1978.

Wicke, Jennifer. *Advertising Fictions: Literature, Advertisement and Social Reading.* New York: Columbia University Press, 1988.

Williams, Jesse Lynch. "The Walk Up-Town in New York." *Scribner's* 27:1 (January 1900): 44–59.

Williams, Raymond. *Keywords: A Vocabulary of Culture and Society.* New York: Oxford University Press, 1983.

Wilson, Christopher. *The Labor of Words: Literary Professionalization in the Progressive Era.* Athens: University of Georgia Press, 1985.

"The Rhetoric of Consumption: Mass-Market Magazines and the Demise of the Gentle Reader, 1880–1920." In Fox and Lears, 39–64.

Winner, Viola Hopkins. *Henry James and the Visual Arts.* Charlottesville: University Press of Virginia, 1970.

Yeazell, Ruth Bernard, ed. *Sex, Politics and Science in the Nineteenth-Century Novel.* Baltimore: Johns Hopkins University Press, 1986.

Youmans, Edward Livingston, ed. *Herbert Spencer on the Americans and the Americans on Herbert Spencer.* New York: D. Appleton and Co., 1883.

Ziff, Larzer. *The American 1890s: Life and Times of a Lost Generation.* New York: The Viking Press, 1966.

INDEX